THE BIBLE AND AMERICAN ARTS AND LETTERS

SOCIETY OF BIBLICAL LITERATURE

The Bible in American Culture

General Editors:

Edwin S. Gaustad
Professor of History
University of California, Riverside

Walter Harrelson
Distinguished Professor of Old Testament
Vanderbilt University

THE BIBLE AND AMERICAN ARTS AND LETTERS

edited by

GILES GUNN

FORTRESS PRESS
Philadelphia, Pennsylvania

SCHOLARS PRESS
Chico, California

SOCIETY OF BIBLICAL LITERATURE

CENTENNIAL PUBLICATIONS

Editorial Board

Copyright © 1983
Society of Biblical Literature

Library of Congress Cataloging in Publication Data
Main entry under title:

The Bible and American arts and letters.

(The Bible in American culture ; 3) (Centennial publications / Society of Biblical literature)
  1. Bible—Influence—Addresses, essays, lectures.
2. United States—Civilization—Addresses, essays, lectures.
I. Gunn, Giles B. II. Series. III. Series: Centennial publications (Society of Biblical literature)
BS538.7.B53 1983   220.6'0973   83-5634
ISBN 0-89130-625-0 (Scholars Press)
ISBN 0-8006-0613-2 (Fortress Press)

360J83   Printed in the United States of America   1–613

To
Charles H. Long
and
Nathan A. Scott, Jr.

CONTENTS

Editor and Contributors

SACVAN BERCOVITCH is Old Dominion Foundation Professor of the Humanities at Columbia University. He is the author of *Puritan Origins of the American Self, The American Jeremiad*, and many other studies in English and American literature and culture.

EDWIN CADY is Andrew W. Mellon Professor in the Humanities at Duke University and Chairman of the Board of Editors of the journal *American Literature*. He is the author of numerous books on American writing, from a critical study of John Woolman to a two-volume biography of William Dean Howells. He is particularly interested in points at which American literary history intersects with cultural history.

CLIFFORD E. CLARK, JR., is Professor of History and Director of the American Studies program at Carleton College. He is the author of *Henry Ward Beecher: Spokesman for a Middle-Class America* and of several studies on the relations among cultural attitudes, social institutions, and architectural style.

JOHN W. DIXON is Professor of Religion and of Art at the University of North Carolina at Chapel Hill. He is the author of *Nature and Grace in Art, Art and the Theological Imagination*, and *The Physiology of Faith*, as well as of numerous essays on religion and the arts.

EDWIN M. GOOD is Professor of Religious Studies and (by courtesy) of Classics at Stanford University. He is the author of *Irony in the Old Testament* and *Giraffes, Black Dragons, and Other Pianos: A Technological History from Cristofori to the Modern Concert Grand*.

GILES GUNN is Professor of Religion and of American Studies and Chairman of the Curriculum on American Studies at the University of North Carolina at Chapel Hill. He is the author of *F. O. Matthiessen: The Critical Achievement, The Interpretation of Otherness*, and, most recently, *New World Metaphysics: Readings on the Religious Meaning of the American Experience*.

DANIEL W. PATTERSON is Professor of English and Chairman of the Curriculum in Folklore at the University of North Carolina at Chapel Hill. He is the author of *The Shaker Spiritual* and other studies, and he has edited documentary recordings and films about American religious folk art and music.

HERBERT SCHNEIDAU is Professor of English at the University of Arizona at Tucson. He is the author of *Ezra Pound: The Image of the Real* and *Sacred Discontent: The Bible and the Western Tradition.*

ROWLAND A. SHERRILL is Associate Professor and Chairman of Religious Studies at Indiana University, Indianapolis. He is the author of *The Prophetic Melville: Experience, Transcendence, and Tragedy,* and is particularly interested in the relations among literature, culture, and religion in America.

WILLIAM H. SHURR is Professor of English at the University of Tennessee at Knoxville. He is the author of *The Mystery of Iniquity: Melville as Poet* and *Rappaccini's Children: American Writers in a Calvinist World* and other studies on the convergence of theology and literature.

Preface to the Series

To what extent are Americans a "people of the book"? To what degree is the history of their nation intermixt with the theology and story and imagery of the Bible? These and other questions are addressed in the several volumes of our series, The Bible in American Culture.

Initially conceived as part of the 1980 centennial celebration of the Society of Biblical Literature, this series explores the biblical influence—for good or ill—in the arts, music, literature, politics, law, education, ethnicity and many other facets of American civilization in general. It is the task of other series to examine biblical scholarship per se; these books, in contrast, search out the way in which the Bible permeates, subtly or powerfully, the very fabric of life within the United States.

The undersigned heartily commend the individual editors of each volume. They have persisted and pursued until all authors finally entered the fold. We also gladly acknowledge the wise counsel of Samuel Sandmel in an earlier stage of our planning, regretting only that he is not with us at the end.

Finally, we express our deep appreciation to the Lilly Endowment for its generous assistance in bringing this entire series to publication and wider dissemination.

EDWIN S. GAUSTAD
WALTER HARRELSON

Acknowledgments

Grateful acknowledgment is here made for permission to quote
(1) from the poetry of Robert Frost: From *The Poetry of Robert Frost*, edited by Edward Connery Lathem. Copyright 1916, 1923, 1928, © 1969 by Holt, Rinehart and Winston. Copyright 1944, 1951, © 1956, 1962 by Robert Frost. Reprinted by permission of Holt, Rinehart and Winston, Publishers.

(2) from the poetry of Emily Dickinson: Reprinted by permission of the publishers and the Trustees of Amherst College from *The Poems of Emily Dickinson*, edited by Thomas H. Johnson (Cambridge, MA: The Belknap Press of Harvard University Press. Copyright 1951, © 1955, 1979 by the President and Fellows of Harvard College).

(3) from the poetry of Wallace Stevens: From *The Collected Poems of Wallace Stevens*. Copyright 1923, 1931, 1935, 1936, 1937, 1942, 1943, 1944, 1945, 1946, 1947, 1948, 1949, 1950, 1951, 1952, and 1954 by Wallace Stevens. Reprinted by permission of Alfred A. Knopf, Inc.

This book is dedicated to two dear friends and valued colleagues who have, each in his own way, made me more sensible of scriptural cultures and cultural scriptures.

G. G.

Introduction

Giles Gunn

In a manner that finds no exact parallel in any other nation, the Bible has become America's book. The Bible has become America's book not only because Americans like to think that they have read it more assiduously than any other people but also because Americans like to think that the Bible is the book that they, more than any other people, have been assiduously read by. It is not surprising that these two beliefs have complemented one another. On the one hand, Americans have long felt, and not without justification, that the Bible has shaped their historical experience in decisive ways. On the other, they became compulsive readers of scripture in order to make certain that their experience not betray scriptural patterns. Either way, Americans have run the risk of hubris, and willingly. They have cleaved to the Bible as though it were a national cultural possession for the sake of reassuring themselves that their own history was unfolding according to biblical prescriptions.

The dangers inherent in America's special claim upon the Bible have been obvious at least since Cotton Mather first attempted in 1702 to fit our own experience into the Bible's epic structure in his *Magnalia Christi Americana*. In the name of a sacred text that purports to define the ultimate design of all history, Mather presumed to find an explanation for the uniqueness of America's own. But in this Mather was only following the practice of contemporary Puritan historiography. Mather's special contribution to the American theory of biblical interpretation was to suggest the possibility, quite without meaning to, of turning the coin on its flip side. If the Bible could be used to determine America's exceptionality, might not America be used to demonstrate the Bible's? It was easy enough, for example, to see how the evolution of American history represented a continuation of God's plan for all history as expressed in the biblical narratives. With only a slight change of perspective, was it not also possible to view the continuity between biblical history and American experience as a kind of confirmation of scripture? America might then be conceived not merely as an instance or exemplification of biblical patterns but also as a legitimation of them.

Mather did not actually go this far, but others would not remain so theologically judicious. And when they did, as Sacvan Bercovitch points out in his contribution to this volume, the relations between America and the Bible would acquire some disturbing dimensions. The Bible would then be seen to belong to America because America, it could be assumed, already belonged to the Bible, because America *was* the Bible or, better, the realization of its promises. The result of this "interpretive turn" was to reduce the Old and New Testaments to a kind of National Testament and to convert the biblical *Heilsgeschichte*, or history of salvation, into the American salvation of history.

America's veneration of the Bible, which was eventually to give way to this biblicistic veneration of America, all began quite innocently. It began during the years of America's earliest settlement among individuals who were keenly aware of the radical difference between divine plan and human purpose. If the Bible was expressive of the Word that commissioned their "errand into the wilderness," the Bible was also a repository of the norms in relation to which that errand was to be judged. The Bible therefore occupied an extremely ambivalent relation to the emergent culture. On the one hand, the Bible was viewed as creative of the culture whose development it authorized. On the other, its cultural creativity was limited to supplying a rationale for the special mission America was to accomplish and a set of guidelines on how to fulfill it.

Yet throughout the centuries of Western history, the Bible's relation to culture had become ambivalent in still other ways, and by nothing so much as the Bible's success in insinuating itself into the rituals, the rhythms, the very fabric of cultural intercourse. Even when people had preserved a sense of the Bible's authority over against culture, they had not been able to resist thinking in its images, speaking in its language, feeling in its forms. And in America the situation has been no different. The Bible has often been able to infuse culture as a form, or set of forms, in almost direct proportion to the distance it has been set apart from culture as a norm. Thus one finds in America the same paradox that exists elsewhere in the West. The Bible has simultaneously furnished many of the most stable forms of consciousness in the West while at the same time serving as a chief source of dissatisfaction with them.

This paradox has supplied the underlying intellectual justification for the creation of this volume. Assuming that the Bible has at once been responsible for certain basic continuities of experience within our culture, which, as Perry Miller once said, "underlie the successive articulation of 'ideas,'" and at the same time has nourished what E. H. Gombrich was the first to call a sense of "sacred discontent" with those experiential continuities, the contributors to this volume were asked to examine the extent to which the Bible has been a significant factor in one or another of the major American arts or artistic traditions. By formulating the topic this generally, it was hoped that the contributors would feel free, wherever possible, to go beyond the determination of biblical influence on individual writers and movements, or the notation of biblical reference in particular works and genres, to consider issues of wider scope. While such more specific inquiries naturally have their place, it was felt that this volume should exhibit a broader and less specialized focus. Therefore each contributor was invited to consider the following question: How has the Bible, less as a text than as a system or repository of meaning, constituted any kind of presence within the history of this particular American art or tradition? In light of the whole history of a particular tradition or art, where and how within it have biblical ideas, motifs, and conventions been, or not been, consequential? The intent of this question was not to deter anyone from adopting a historical perspective but only to induce everyone to produce more than a historical survey. In other words, all of the contributors were encouraged to be historically selective and interpretively speculative.

It is clear, however, that it was easier for some of the contributors to exploit this latitude than for others. In virtually every case, the limits of interpretive freedom were determined by the nature of the art or tradition involved. It is one thing to note biblical meanings in representational forms like fiction and poetry, quite another to find them in nonrepresentational forms like music or the dance. It is also apparent that certain traditions, like folklore, lend themselves more easily to historical treatment than to more philosophical analysis, whereas other traditions, such as nineteenth-century American fiction, as readily generate theoretical investigations as historical ones.

America's relationship to the Bible has been made particularly problematic, as many of these essays attest, by the strain of antinomianism in our cultural experience. We must write our own Bibles, Ralph Waldo Emerson declared, by which he meant that even where Americans acknowledge the authority of scripture as source, model, or curse, they are compelled, to quote Emerson's improbable poetic descendant, Ezra Pound, to "make it new." And this compulsion to "make it new" has become all the more intense because the scriptural authority of the Bible has frequently been associated in the public mind with official versions of the American cultural experiment. Thus whenever the Bible has been self-consciously expropriated within an art or tradition, the Bible has often occasioned some highly unorthodox and often curiously attenuated acts of adaptation, acts in which the boundary between acceptance and rejection of its authority has been dissolved or transcended. Conversely, where the Bible has been dismissed or neglected or simply forgotten, its absence has often registered itself as an odd sort of presence, resembling nothing so much as "the Distance," as Emily Dickinson called it, "on the look of Death."

Herbert Schneidau points out that the effects of this antinomianism are particularly evident in the American poetic tradition, where we disparage any relation to the past for the sake of encouraging new beginnings and fresh starts. Yet for the American poet to begin again, Schneidau notes, the establishment of an alliance with a venerable tradition of new departures is required, whereupon the American poet's problem with the Bible becomes but one variant of his or her own problem with the tradition. The problem, as William Carlos Williams once put it, is "how to begin to begin again?" and the answer lies in usurping some of the powers of creation usually reserved to God alone—by creating as if *de novo* a new tradition whose function is to reflect or incarnate the glory of creating itself. While this has been observed before, as Schneidau indicates, and most memorably by Roy Harvey Pearce in *The Continuity of American Poetry*, no one has fully appreciated the way in which the Bible has contributed indirectly to the resolution of this problem. This contribution has resulted from the Bible's influence on those forms of antinomianism in the American tradition that have had the most pronounced effect on our poets. Schneidau cites two such forms in particular: the Adamic impulse, which accentuates the strain of origination, of new birth, and the prophetic or denunciatory impulse—Perry Miller was to call it the tradition of the jeremiad—which stresses criticism and the need for reformation.

The legacy of antinomianism is equally apparent, as Edwin Cady makes clear, in nineteenth-century American fiction, though the Bible seems to have played a less obvious or constructive role in overcoming the problems antinomianism creates for the American novelist. In the nineteenth century the serious novelist worked against a background of popular fiction and popular culture in which the Bible had large but often specious authority. Just because of its association with the public professions of culture generally, the Bible frequently had to be demythologized and, in some cases, remythologized before it could lend itself to serious literary use. There were, of course, exceptions among the major writers—Harriett Beecher Stowe stands out most clearly—but the rule among novelists who could turn the Bible into any kind of intellectual or literary resource was suggested by Herman Melville, Cady contends, "a great Biblical, unscriptural writer" whose use of the Bible was "as elusive as the Spirit Spout."

Cady is prepared to suggest that the Bible's curious and mostly intermittent influence on nineteenth-century American fiction may well derive from a formal incompatibility between biblical narrative and the American novel. Quoting Reynolds Price's theory that the classic American novels of the nineteenth century were designed to awaken within the human heart, and in terms that it can comprehend, what is most aptly termed an imagination of transcendence, Cady posits that the more human and secular orientation of these novels may not have been able to accommodate the Bible's more classic sacramental vision. Where the Bible's style is epic and heroic, the style of American fiction, Cady maintains, has always tended toward the mock-heroic and the melodramatic.

As one moves toward twentieth-century writing, the potential incompatibility between biblical and fictional vision seems to disappear in Rowland Sherrill's account. Or, rather, American novelists, he argues, develop new ways of adapting biblical modes of perception to their own problems. This is the more surprising because the textual authority of the Bible has been more deeply undermined in the twentieth century than ever before. Despite this fact, Sherrill is able to suggest striking evidence of biblical imagery and reference in twentieth-century American fiction. More important, he is convinced that twentieth-century novelists have found new uses for biblical ways of interpreting experience. Not only has the Bible served the modern novelist as a literary storehouse for themes and values and images and events; it has also furnished the twentieth-century novelist with modes of vision, of seeing, that remain as hermeneutically useful today as they ever were. Sherrill isolates four such modes—the prophetic, the apocalyptic, the episodic, and the parabolic—and argues that each mode of perception has been appropriated by modern novelists to deal with a distinctive existential problem—respectively, the disintegration of the covenant community, the collapse of culture, the incoherence of history, and the diminution of the individual. While the understanding of these biblical modes of perception has changed over the centuries—modern history is no longer experienced, at least by twentieth-century novelists, as *Heilsgeschichte*, or salvation history—their utility in assisting the mind to wrestle with the problems of coherence and meaning in history has not.

The history of American drama presents a rather different spectacle, according to William Shurr. The nineteenth century made abundant use of biblical material in such plays as Royall Tyler's *Joseph and His Brethren* and *The Judgment of Solomon* or the dramatic rendering of *Uncle Tom's Cabin*, but drama as a whole had not yet found an American form, and reliance on biblical settings and motifs often inhibited this effort. Most of the plays of the nineteenth century were either "bombastic recitals of the classics" or "farce and melodrama," both of which frequently proved all too satisfactory to a public which often went to the theater in pursuit of pleasures that were more erotic than aesthetic.

It was not until the twentieth century, and particularly the advent of Eugene O'Neill, that the situation changed. O'Neill, like many subsequent American dramatists and playwrights from Tennessee Williams and Arthur Miller to the screenwriters of such films as *Apocalypse Now* and *Star Wars*, went back to the Bible for some of his ideas, but most often he incorporated biblical material with material drawn from other ancient sources. This resultant blend of the biblical and the classical can be discerned with particular clarity in a play like O'Neill's relatively unknown *Lazarus Laughed*, which William Shurr exposes to extended analysis.

For reasons that are readily obvious, one encounters special problems of conceptualization and interpretation as soon as attention turns to a consideration of biblical presence in nonverbal arts. There are, of course, narrative elements in predominantly spatial forms like music and painting, just as there are ideational and even discursive or rhetorical elements in stationary forms like architecture and active forms like the dance. But the analogies between the forms in which the biblical materials are cast and the forms by which these nonverbal arts are rendered are in any case more difficult to discern and more resistant to definition. Despite these difficulties, Clifford Clark has made an exciting case for the changing influence of the Bible on the development of the built environment in America.

Clark distinguishes two traditions or streams within the history of American architecture, each of which has reflected the impact of biblical ideas, concepts, and motifs. The vernacular tradition, which originated in the colonial period, was initially organized around the implicit values of a biblical commonwealth. Its emphasis on order, hierarchy, homogeneity, and conformity found its way into a variety of folk traditions throughout the developing culture and was epitomized, Clark suggests, in the buildings of the Shakers. During the nineteenth century, however, the vernacular tradition underwent a massive alteration that eventually led to a new way of applying biblical conceptions to the design of buildings created for mass production. If the implicit assumptions of the vernacular tradition in the eighteenth century were hierarchy and authority, in the nineteenth century they became inspiration and social control, a change paralleling the shift from the Christian emphasis on life after death in the colonial period to the Christian emphasis on God's immanence within life in the national period.

The other tradition Clark discusses in American architecture is the prophetic tradition of the great architectural reformers who sought to challenge the vernacular strain in each of its several phases of evolution. The prophetic or revolutionary strain, according to Clark, was critical, moralistic, and messianic. Composed of such figures as Thomas Jefferson, Andrew Jackson Downing, Frank Lloyd Wright, and Philip Johnson, the prophetic tradition continually redefined and reconstituted itself in the act of denouncing contemporary vernacular practice in the name of an architectural ideal felt to be more commensurate with America's historic aims as a culture. For this reason, Clark calls this second tradition or strain the tradition of the American jeremiad in American architecture. In each of its major American representatives, this tradition insisted, as John Wellborn Root put it, that the American spirit is betrayed unless the internal structure of a building determines its external design. What was wanted was an integral, even organic relation between inside and outside, between inspiration and form, really between soul and body, not unlike that integration of self with others that constitutes the ideal image of the American social commonwealth.

When attention moves from the building arts to the arts of music, it is difficult to find evidence of a similar kind of biblical–jeremiadic influence, particularly on the great reformers of American music. Even though the Bible has exerted a massive influence on many American musical forms, it has not inspired any of the individual works, Edwin Good maintains, that are considered the greatest achievements of those forms. There are several possible reasons for this: the potency that has been ascribed to the Bible in the Jewish and Christian religious traditions; dogmatic interpretations of biblical material that, at least within certain ecclesiastical traditions, have limited its artistic use; the long association of biblical material with liturgical contexts within musical culture itself. In any case, for all its influence on religious spheres of musical experience, the Bible has played a fairly marginal role in secular spheres. This is not to say that use of the Bible has been restricted to music written solely for, and performed solely in, ecclesiastical settings; Good believes that the most interesting religious music in the twentieth century has been composed for the concert hall and the opera house. But the fact remains that the traditional distinction between sacred and profane has still been more difficult to overcome in American music than, perhaps, in any of the other American arts. Not only has biblical material been used more restrictively in music than elsewhere; the development of sacred music as compared with secular, while proceeding usually along the same lines, has also been predictably slower in coming and has exhibited less brilliance or daring along the way.

When one turns to the visual arts in America, one finds some interesting parallels as well as contrasts with the musical arts. On the one hand, John Dixon suggests, American painters have revealed a similar ambivalence about, if not indifference to, the Bible as a resource for visual statement. Even when the Bible has furnished the subject for art objects, as it did so often in the colonial period, the style and treatment of those subjects reflected an Enlightenment sensibility, not a biblical one. But if the Bible has resisted visual translation in American art—the one exception Dixon notes is Thomas Eakins's *Crucifixion*—this is not to imply that American art has been antagonistic to religion. On the contrary, American art has often displayed a religious disposition but one which, from Dixon's perspective, is strikingly unbiblical. As expressed in the Luminists and, perhaps, Frederic Church and Thomas Ryder, the most characteristic quality associated with this religious disposition is the quest for the numinous or the sublime, a quality whose achievement represents the closest approach the American visual imagination has made to an adequate response to the American landscape. But the achievement of this quality has been rare in American painting; the tradition has not met the full challenge of its New World environment. Nothing in American painting, Dixon believes, matches the symbolic integrity of the New England meetinghouse or the United States Constitution, works in which, Dixon argues, theory and practice, ideal and actual, really fuse. And the same thing, Dixon believes, would have to be said about folk or native art: in the light of New World opportunities, its achievements, with few notable exceptions, have been minor.

Daniel Patterson, who writes specifically on American folk arts, both verbal and nonverbal, both representational and nonrepresentational, seems to disagree. If the folk arts are extended to include folklife as well as folklore, and if the artistic representations of folklife are assumed to originate in the experience of immigrant groups compelled to accommodate themselves

to a different cultural environment, then the extraordinary achievement of
these arts, Patterson believes, can be more readily discerned and the formative role of the Bible more fully appreciated. It should come as no surprise,
however, that the Bible served a different function in Catholic, and particularly Hispanic Catholic, traditions than it did in Protestant traditions almost
from the very beginning. The folk arts in Catholic traditions tended to reinforce received custom, while those in dissenting Protestant traditions sought
to challenge custom and to encourage change. Furthermore, Catholic traditions were oriented more toward visual and plastic forms such as painting,
sculpture, and dance, while Protestant traditions accentuated verbal forms
such as the song and the sermon. Nonetheless, even within these traditions
there was wide variation. In the case of Protestant revival spirituals, for
example, the Old Testament was used differently by whites and by blacks.
Though both drew upon the same repertory of images about a chosen
people journeying to a promised land, white spirituals, reflecting the experience of a population caught up in large migratory movements in the North,
South, and West between 1750 and 1850, stressed the importance of decid-
ing to embark for a New Canaan of the spirit. Black spirituals, responding to
the very different experience of a people in bondage, used the same imagery
to provide reassurance in the midst of suffering that God would once again
intervene in history to save his chosen ones. In either case, the tradition of
American folksong, like many other American folk arts, displayed a genuine
symbolic integrity in which a fusion occurred not so much between the
actual and the ideal, or between theory and practice, as between crisis and
interpretation, or between historical situations and imaginative strategies for
encompassing them.

This raises a larger question about the role the Bible has played in the
formation of a national myth that allows us to define such traditions as culturally distinctive. What is the relation between the Bible and the notion of
America as a specific mythic entity? In a more general essay that was
intended to provide a kind of overview for the volume, Sacvan Bercovitch
proposes that the answer lies with the Puritans and with the nature of their
legacy, which was essentially rhetorical.

The Puritans defined themselves as a people of the Word. Their goal, as
Bercovitch conceptualizes it, was to turn logos into logocracy, to use the
Bible to create a commonwealth of words or, better, signs or figures in
which they could read their own spiritual errand as a fulfillment of the
proclamations of scripture. The errand involved taking possession of the
American wilderness in the name of the God of Abraham, Isaac, and Jacob
and his plan for the regeneration of the whole of Western Christendom, and
it proceeded rhetorically in two stages. First came the conversion of America into a text about God's unfolding plan of redemption, and then followed
the reading of the text as though it were chiefly about Americans, the interpretation of America as the destiny of God's redemptive design. If this all

started out rather innocently as an attempt to secure biblical authorization for the American spiritual errand, it held out the possibility of becoming something quite different. The disposition to use the Bible to define America initiated a quest to locate America within the Bible, and this quest could, and did, give way to the conviction that the Bible was proleptically American, that indeed America was, or would become, the Bible. And when, in the nineteenth century, the Bible was displaced by nature as the new source of divine disclosure, the myth of America simply accommodated itself. The New World landscape took the place of the New World errand as the revelatory template, and the engine of mythic consensus steamed on.

But the engine of American mythic consensus has always been threatened with derailment, Bercovitch argues, and by nothing so much as its biblical basis. It has been threatened in part because the Jewish and Christian understandings of the biblical material on which it has drawn are essentially incompatible. From the point of view of the Hebrew material, the biblical myth is communal, historical, nationalistic, incomplete, and prospective. From the point of view of the Christian material, the biblical myth is individual (and institutional), suprahistorical, universal, completed, and retrospective. But national mythic consensus has always been more seriously threatened, Bercovitch maintains, by the possibility that, far from representing a culmination of the biblical promises, America may not even be in the Bible. To comprehend this possibility, Bercovitch insists, would require admitting that the symbolic meaning of America does not exist in scriptural terms and that the American present and future cannot be read as a sacred text. But to acknowledge this, as Bercovitch well knows, would be to acknowledge the need for creating a new history for ourselves as Americans. And so we return to the question our poets have always asked, a question that has acquired fresh urgency in light of the biblical heritage of our culture. The question remains as William Carlos Williams posed it and Herbert Schneidau has repeated it: "how to begin to begin again?"

I

The Antinomian Strain:
The Bible and American Poetry

Herbert Schneidau

The Generic Problem

Having a wheel and four legs of its own
Has never availed the cumbersome grindstone
To get it anywhere that I can see.
These hands have helped it go, and even race;
Not all the motion, though, they ever lent,
Not all the miles it may have thought it went,
Have got it one step from the starting place.
It stands beside the same old apple tree.

Robert Frost, "The Grindstone"

Like Robert Frost's grindstone, American poetry may imagine that it has strayed far afield, but all its labors have not removed it very far from those biblical roots symbolized by that "same old apple tree." Frost was perfectly conscious of his arch allusion to Genesis here; it is typical both of his laconic invocations of important meanings in general and of his attitude toward the Bible, and what is connected with it, in particular. Frost is among the many American poets who feel the Bible to be an inescapable heritage, for better but also for worse. Some of his best known poems are wry protests against the prevalence of old forms of thought, and there is a resentful sigh as well as a sly chuckle in his notation that the apple tree is the "same old" one that has haunted American imaginations from the days of the Puritans. Later in the poem he calls that tree "ruinous." Of course Frost was not writing about American poetry in "The Grindstone." Though the poem is overtly allegorical (one of the laborers is "a Father-Time-like man," "armed with a scythe and spectacles that glowed"), there is no obvious further scheme of meanings to which the allegory appeals, no Christian or even ethical doctrine. The poem is one of that Frostian type I call "allegories of nothingness." This type seems to ask, what if our lives are full of symbols that do indeed point beyond themselves, and ourselves, but lead only to a vast universe whose empty "desert places" are reflected even more terrifyingly within us? In any case, Frost seems in the opening lines to be having some New England fun with various notions and doctrines of progress.

The grindstone like any machine invites us to be presumptuous about how far we can go with it and its fellows. "I wondered what machine of ages gone / This represented an improvement on," Frost grumbles later in the poem. Whatever appearances may suggest, the machine is not a good vehicle. Its legs and wheel will not get us anywhere—least of all away from our preoccupations with earlier ages, no matter how much we bustle and scurry. The poem is ultimately about being satisfied with what one has, but this includes an acceptance of a biblical heritage that Frost sees as both source and burden.

Frost's attitude toward the Bible and its God is not his alone but recurs throughout American literature; and although his particular brand of grudging acceptance is not universal, it does typify the complicated relationship that American writers share to this most provocative and most onerous part of their cultural inheritance. Of American poets there have been only a few, and those not of primary importance, who have had an orthodox or untroubled attitude toward biblical matters. Nor is simple apostasy a solution. Even those undeniably major poets who like Wallace Stevens were frank atheists usually acknowledged their debts to the Bible in a multitude of backhanded or unconscious ways, some of which will be discussed later. Stevens's biblical knowledge was not deep, but when he invoked Susanna and the elders in "Peter Quince at the Clavier" it was not a decorative touch but rather a major theme—and he expected his readers to know the story. Stevens preached against revealed religion with the fervor of one for whom agnosticism is a revelation; yet his rebellion was only one form of the generic American literary problem: how "to begin to begin again," in the words of William Carlos Williams, or how to make an always-fresh and unencumbered start while necessarily repeating the repetitious efforts of progenitors to engender just such a start. The American tradition in poetry as elsewhere is a revolutionary tradition, which to some extent is a contradiction in terms. How does one acknowledge one's forebears without becoming "traditional" in the sense of *derivative*? For some, like Williams, the problem is a source of creative tension, one of those "quarrels with ourselves" out of which we make poetry, as William Butler Yeats said ("out of the quarrels with others we make rhetoric"). For others, the dilemma becomes a morass of bad faith; they become literal minded and orthodox in their nihilism and eventually sink into such sloughs as programmatic spontaneity. It takes real strength to acknowledge a cultural heritage that casts disparagements on cultural heritages, but that is what the American burden amounts to—if it contradicts itself, then it contradicts itself. On the one hand, it demands revolutionary new departures and in its shallowest form becomes antihistorical nativism, Know-Nothingism, "history is the bunk" and "don't trust anyone over thirty." On the other hand, it demands reverence for the fruits of that same tradition of new departure: frontier spirits lead to homesteading, exiles in the wilderness and brave new worlds become old home towns. Declarations of independence lead to constitutions. The theme of several major works of our literature, and of count-less movies, is the need to "light out for the territory ahead of the rest," to keep the exploratory urge alive, unappeasable and peregrine, while "Sivilization" is treading on our heels. This is an active form of facing the contradictions involved in seeking ever to "make it new."

To throw oneself to the winds of chance and change is a perennial temptation and appears as well in Ishmael's need to go to sea as in aleatory art; but a requirement of rule breaking becomes itself a rule and may make us yearn for the old ones, and so finally one cannot even imitate "dada" without acknowledging some kind of father, in a most infantile manner. It is fitting in this Oedipal context that the true progenitor here is Pater, he who proclaimed that "not the fruit of experience but experience itself is the end." This so-called aestheticism conceals a heady nihilism: burn baby burn with a hard gemlike flame. But, as J. Hillis Miller tells us, "nihilism is the nothing-ness of consciousness when consciousness becomes the foundation of every-thing" (4). He means that when we have reduced all values to those we can pick and choose among, then we have implied, knowingly or not, that those values are our creations; and when they lose their footing in anything exter-nal to us, they inevitably slip away into nothingness—including God. As Miller continues, "Many people have forgotten that they have forgotten the death of God, the living God of Abraham and Isaac, Dante and Pascal. Many who believe that they believe in God believe in him only as the high-est value, that is, as a creation of man, the inventor of values." Miller's sharp diagnosis, which is not blunted even if one attempts to shift the burden from "consciousness" to "unconsciousness," points to that generic problem I spoke of that seems to be more perplexing in America than anywhere else—and I shall maintain that the problem of American poets' relations to the Bible is one form of it.

For American poets the Bible is a particularly problematic book, not only because our religious traditions have made the book's symbolism into a form of national tradition or tribal lore but also because of the primary function and importance accorded to poetry within the book. The prohibi-tion against graven images turned Hebrew creative energies into the channel of poetry, with music as an integral but secondary part: to praise Yahweh in psalms was fitting, but any attempt to capture his image in the plastic arts was idolatry. Moreover, the mention of the "Book of the Wars of the Lord" in Num 21:14 (together with the "Book of Jashar" in Josh 10:13 and 2 Sam 1:18) suggests the existence of primitive collections of Hebrew battle songs. These might well have served as cores or armatures around which later prose narratives accreted and on which they expanded. The process is visible enough in the way in which Exodus 14 and Judges 4 are expansions and commentaries on the Song of Miriam and the Song of Deborah contained in Exodus 15 and Judges 5 respectively. In each case the prose narratives add elaborative and sometimes rationalizing detail; e.g., in the Song of Deborah

(Judg 5:27) Jael slays Sisera, with mallet and tentpeg, as he stands ("he sank, he fell, he lay still at her feet"), whereas in the prose version (4:21) he is lying asleep on the ground. The emendation adds credibility; in Exodus 14 the added detail of the parting of the waters, etc., expands the laconic phrase in the Song (15:1), "the horse and his rider he has thrown into the sea," into a dramatic scenario of mythological dimensions. Students of ancient literatures agree that such patterns are typical: the poems come first, in an era of oral performance and preservation, and prose comes in later to fill out and augment, often aided by writing (Freedman, 1972, 1975). It is possible, perhaps likely, that the "Book of the Wars of Yahweh" (in English translations "The LORD" was subsituted for "Yahweh" to accord with the later Judaic practice of never pronouncing the divine name) was a determinative collection for early Israel, firmly establishing the leadership and nature of Yahweh whose "mighty acts" and "outstretched arms and mighty hand" were specifically those of the warrior king, *Yahweh Sebaoth* or Lord Ĝod of Hosts. Miriam sings that "Yahweh is a warrior, Yahweh is his name" in Exod 15:3; this may have been the poetic refrain that implicitly supports such old cultic confessions or credos as Deut 26:5–9, from which I have taken the "arm" and "hand" phrases. In early Hebrew usage "king" meant a war leader rather than an executive or a law giver: to "go out before us and fight our battles" is the phrase used by the people in sinfully asking for a human king, "like all the nations" in 1 Sam 8:20. As I have suggested elsewhere, this text must have expressed the great identity crisis of ancient Israel (see Schneidau: 184–211). I mention all this to whet appetites for the idea that the old poems were not decorative additions to the Bible but crucial texts in the formation of its ancient beliefs. These evidences were not so visible in the era before modern scholarship, but in an earlier America in which almost everyone was a Bible reader and sermon listener, the texts were far more familiar than they are today, and anyone looking for support for the notion of poetry's primacy in the Bible could easily find it. It has long been general knowledge that battle songs, victory hymns, war cries, and taunt songs (of which Judg 5:28–31 is a good example) are part of the cultural foundation of all ancient peoples, from the native Americans to the classical Greeks. Compare the Homeric poems, in which the war cry is often a more formidable weapon than the spear, and in which taunts, boasts, insults, challenges, and laments occur regularly. Some may have been cores around which the more expansive narratives may have been built, as with the Bible. I would speculate therefore that poets in reading the Bible may well have sensed such primacy, especially when given Shelleyan and Emersonian hints that all language is "fossil poetry." From the important place held by the psalms themselves, the songs embedded in the prose narratives, and such closely allied forms as parable and prophetic visions and oracles, it would have been relatively plain that the Bible placed a high value on poetry and on the kinds of insights and dramatic embodiments of which poetry is capable.

We know from the writing of the Puritans and their successors that poetry in early America was held to be so fascinating an art as to be dangerously tempting to literate minds. The preface to the *Bay Psalm Book* (1640) and other early statements make it clear that the good Puritan would curb poetic tendencies if they ran toward excess, but this was not an aversion such as was felt for the theater, which was judged to be a breeding place of harlotry, political propaganda, plague, pestilence, and a host of moral evils. This aversion caused the theaters of London to be closed in 1642 and brought to an end the great period of Elizabethan–Jacobean drama. But it is poetry that Roy Harvey Pearce has chiefly in mind when he writes: "The Puritan had never hated literature—or, for that matter, the arts in general. Rather, he feared that he might like them too much" (18). The forbidden-fruit motif was strong, but with such a host of biblical precedents poetry presented a more complex case than did the other arts. The Puritans were told that they must avoid the entanglements of secular poetry, which might seduce them away from their spiritual tasks into unfruitful idleness. At the same time they received an image of poetry as a hallowed and venerated art, given honor and authority by the example of David and other biblical singers.

The fruits of Puritan practice of poetry in America were abundant but limited in scope, tending to be versified scripture. Obviously the ambivalence toward art held back such native talent as wasted its sweetness in the American "desart." The major poet of the period, Edward Taylor, wrote solely for himself, mindful of various dangers and strictures, and his works were not published until 1939. He had no influence on what followed, but those who were known had only a little more. Anne Bradstreet, honored in her day as the "tenth muse lately sprung up in America," has been drawn to our attention mostly by modern admirers, and not even these can be found to celebrate Michael Wigglesworth, although his *Day of Doom* was once so popular that one copy was sold for every twenty persons in Massachusetts. The true Puritan heritage consists not of poetic achievements as such but rather of a strenuous wrestling with the problems of language and symbolism, a profound investigation of the techniques by which God's will was made manifest in words and related labors, which served to carry forward the Puritan veneration of the Bible's imaginative writing while allowing later generations to abandon cautious scruples about the dangers of worldly art. The most important of these labors was the Puritan adaptation of typology. Originally typology had been a mode of exegesis that allowed Christians to read Old Testament texts as symbolically relevant to themselves. Paul in Galatians, for instance, interprets the children of Hagar and of Sarah as Jews and Christians, one under bond (of the law) and the other free (4:22–31); the Epistle to the Hebrews (not by Paul) presents a Hellenized rationale for seeing the New in the Old Testament. Typology allowed the

Christian to preserve the Old Testament and swallow it at the same time. In contradistinction to allegory per se, which would have explained away the Old Testament texts as a series of symbolic messages with no literal or historical basis, typology insisted that all the events in scripture had actually occurred but that they had been symbolic as well as historical, true prophecies as well as literal happenings. Thus Adam foreshadowed Christ (see 1 Cor 15:47) and Eve, the church (the mother of all living). Harrowing events had creative as well as destructive purpose: the flood was a "type" (in the old sense, an image or adumbration) of baptism, a cleansing of earth's souls. The metaphorical ingenuities that arose from typological interpretation were some of the most remarkable ever seen: Rahab the harlot (Joshua 2 and 6) was a "type" of the church, because the red cord she let down to identify and preserve her house (2:18) foreshadowed the sacramental blood flowing from Christ's side—out of which the church was born. For the Puritans, such ingenuities became the very breath of spiritual life. The American colony was obviously a "type" of Israel in the wilderness, a snake in the meeting house signaled the presence of Satan among them, etc. The world became a potential treasure house of "radical metaphors made by God," to use Charles Feidelson's phrase (78). Feidelson persuasively relates Puritan typological habits to the development of the symbolistic imagination in America. Obviously this inducement to metaphor was vital to the growth of all American literature, and especially to poetry. Given such influence by the Puritans on American thought and imagination, Feidelson concludes that American artists have been exploiting their opportunities and working out their problems ever since. Roy Harvey Pearce agrees: "In form, substance, and method, American poetry from the seventeenth century to the present is on the whole a development of the Puritan imagination" (57). However, Pearce has in mind not only typology and symbolism but also an even larger matrix in which Puritanism foreshadows the American self. He calls it the "compulsion to relate, even to make identical, man's sense of his inwardness and his sense of his role in the world at large." Borrowing Puritan terminology, Pearce surveys all of American poetry in terms of its relation to and reaction toward the "antinomian" impulse—the effort to set up the self against the demands and constraints of culture. In Puritan times, antinomians were heretics and seducers (e.g., Anne Hutchinson) who dared to use the Reformation principles of liberty of conscience and individuality of interpretation—"every man his own priest"—against the Puritan divines themselves: they asserted that they had an inner light, if they were Quakers, or some comparable form of inward revelation that had an equal validity with the community's teachings, or a greater one. Antinomianism is obviously a generic problem within Puritanism, and in Pearce's analysis it is closely related to the generic problem for poets as I formulated it earlier: how to mediate the relation between the individual's untrammeled creativeness and the culture's heritages. Pearce's analysis deserves exposition.

The Strain of Antinomianism

For Pearce, feelings of self-assertion, self-vindication, and even resentment against one's culture are inseparably bound up with the creativity of American poets. "In short, the power of American poetry from the beginning has derived from the poet's inability, or refusal, at some depth of consciousness wholly to accept his culture's system of values" (5). This thesis is best tested by observing the prevalence of an antinomian, culture-questioning thrust in the work of those figures who are emerging as the major poets of their times. In the nineteenth century, for example, the quartet of Edgar Allan Poe, Ralph Waldo Emerson, Walt Whitman, and Emily Dickinson has slowly but surely come to dominate, replacing such earlier favorites as Henry Wadsworth Longfellow, William Cullen Bryant, John Greenleaf Whittier, and James Russell Lowell; and of this quartet Whitman and Dickinson are the salient figures, the true poets of the "American Renaissance." A measure of the validity of Pearce's statement is that these latter two are arguably the most antinomian of the century, although there is a sense in which Poe's alienation is surely antinomian and in which Emerson is very much of the lineage of Hutchinson. As to the twentieth century, the triumph of the antinomian attitude is so complete that it characterizes not only American poets but all of modern writing. Lionel Trilling put it most sweepingly:

> In its essence literature is concerned with the self; and the particular concern of the literature of the last two centuries has been with the self in its standing quarrel with culture. We cannot mention the name of any great writer of the modern period whose work has not in some way, and usually in a passionate and explicit way, insisted on this quarrel, who has not expressed the bitterness of his discontent with civilization, who has not said that the self made greater legitimate demands than any culture could hope to satisfy. (118)

Trilling writes, of course, partly as an apologist for that very modernism he describes; and though some would quarrel with his advocacy, as with his insistence on reading the nineteenth century as a foreshadowing of the twentieth, still we must admit the persuasiveness of his negative test. What writers could we name who do not manifest this attitude in some way? The very concept of the "self" which by Trilling's reading dominates all of literature is a modern invention, conflating for the moment Romanticism with modernism—although as Bercovitch has lately shown, it has its roots in American Puritanism, which looms ever larger and larger in our intellectual history.

This is not to assume that poetry is necessarily equivalent to the creation, invention, or assertion of the self, though it may be very fruitful to read our literature in just that way. The point here is to argue that the specific forms of antinomian impulse that have proved most liberating and productive for American poets are derived largely from powerful biblical patterns. On the one hand, there is what Pearce calls the "Adamic" impulse, following Emerson: "Here's for the plain old Adam, the simple genuine self against the whole world" (quoted in Pearce: 153). Pearce goes on to say that for Emerson the opposition "is especially sharp in the poems, where it becomes a means of transmutation of the world into something freshly seen, fully found, and so a manifestation of the Adamic principle itself." The extension of this mode of vision is apparent in Whitman. The Adamic mode is an attempt to restore unfallen vision, the innocent and harmonic state of one who in seeing and naming all things afresh goes against the divisive and hierarchical tendencies in the culture in order to be wholly at one with the world. In Whitman, the self asserts its camaraderie with all things high and low; the poet is fellow to the humblest creatures, to the grass itself, and he "incorporates gneiss"; he interpenetrates all human moods and acts, celebrating even the suicide, and salutes as an equal even the highest placed. There can be no negation, no shame, no drawing back: the poet's imaginative vision penetrates even to the operating room (though "what is removed drops horribly in a pail"). *Leaves of Grass* begins "One's-self I sing, a simple separate person, / Yet utter the word Democratic, the word En-Masse." The poet merges with his world, against all pretension and preference; when Whitman says the "word Democratic" (and Whitman here uses "word" in a biblical sense, as in "word of the Lord") he means to articulate all of creation, not simply a political system. Creation is an ark, and its "Kelson" is love.

Whitman's most revealing and typical line is "I am the man, I suffer'd, I was there," from the climactic thirty-third section of *Song of Myself*, by far the longest and most complex section of the poem. The section contains some of his worst lines ("Where the alligator in his tough pimples sleeps by the bayou") but also his most exalted and all-inclusive visions, and a key to the latter is his imaginative finding of himself "Walking the old hills of Judaea with the beautiful gentle God by my side." At the same time he sees himself "Hot toward one I hate, ready in my madness to knife him"; the self-contradiction is deliberate, for he is large, he contains multitudes. Hence the climactic line quoted above conflates the creative "I Am" of Exodus (Samuel Taylor Coleridge had already said: "The primary IMAGINATION I hold to be the living Power and prime Agent of all human Perception, and as a repetition in the finite mind of the eternal act of creation in the infinite I AM") with such Gospel phrases as the answers of Christ under persecution and the soaring, almost Gnostic rhetoric that recurs in the Gospel of John: "I am the Way. . . . I am the Light. . . . I am the Bread. . . . I am the Good Shepherd. . . . Before Abraham was, I am." Thus "I suffer'd" incarnates the poet in the Christ who suffered for all, and "I was there" modulates into the voice of the disciples and those who spread the faith by kerygmatic proclamation, bearing their witness to the uttermost ends of the earth. D. H. Lawrence, who hated this empathetic element in Christianity, knew well enough what Whitman's model was, in his *Studies in Classic American*

Literature: "This was not *sympathy*. It was merging and self-sacrifice. 'Bear ye one another's burdens.'—'Love thy neighbour as thyself.'—'Whatsoever ye do unto him, ye do unto me.'" Without such precedents and backgrounds Whitman's poem would have far less force than it does.

We know that the Bible was a primary and poetic source for Whitman, not only because the evidence is scattered through the poems but also because he tells us plainly, in "A Backward Glance O'er Traveled Roads," just what he read in preparation for launching his great life's work, *Leaves of Grass*. "I went over thoroughly the Old and New Testaments," he says, mixing them with Scott, Shakespeare, Ossian, Homer, Dante, the Nibelungenlied, "ancient Hindoo poems" and a few others. We can see why Pearce, mentioning the opinion that *Leaves* should be read as one continuous epic, remarks: "But the evidence from Whitman's later prefaces would urge us to read it as a set of holy scriptures" (72 n.). The Bible was his guide to form; none of the other works on Whitman's reading list would have given him so clear a precedent for a work so various and yet so unified. Moreover, the reverential rhapsodic voice in which his poems ask to be read derives from the Bible as a whole and from ecstatic passages of the prophets and Gospels in particular.

If the Christ who suffered for all was the typological paradigm for Whitman's imaginative projection of himself into the sufferings and feelings of his fellow beings, the example of the Hebrew prophets was ultimately no less powerful. Indeed, Whitman regularly and recurrently thought of the poet as a prophet, and though this concept included that of the classical *vates* or seer, Whitman's natural point of reference was the Bible:

> The word prophecy is much misused: it seems narrow'd to prediction merely. That is not the main sense of the Hebrew word translated "prophet"; it means one whose mind bubbles up and pours forth as a fountain, from inner, divine spontaneities revealing God. Prediction is a very minor part of prophecy. The great matter is to reveal and outpour the God-like suggestions pressing for birth in the soul.

This passage from the late prose is quoted and expanded upon in Albert Gelpi's discussion of pre-twentieth-century American poetry, *The Tenth Muse* (1975:164–65), in which the importance of the seer or prophet as exemplar for poets' self-conceptions is studied at length. For Whitman, manifestly, the prophet is the type of the visionary, the "God-intoxicated man" (as Coleridge called himself), whose eye may see all things with an exalted, truly Adamic, power in those moments in which he is infused with God. Whitman's image of himself and of the visionary innocence out of which his poetic project unfolds owes something to the famous "Peaceable Kingdom" passage in Isaiah 11 ("The wolf shall dwell with the lamb, and the leopard shall lie down with the kid" [v. 6]). Whitman must have seen himself as the "little child [who] shall lead them," all of creation following as a flock. The prophet in this sense proclaims a new universal innocence (*in-nocens*, "not harmful"; "they shall not hurt or destroy in all my holy mountain" [Isa 11:9]), just as the poet proclaims the "word Democratic" that embraces all human beings and creatures.

In all of this, as Pearce notes, Whitman enlarges upon Emerson's Adamic proclamation: the self does not submit to culture by incorporating the world; rather it becomes an infinite self in and through that act, and transcends its culture. Whitman follows the line of universalizing the self into a "transparent eyeball" which produced many revisions of old religious principles as it issued in the Transcendentalism associated with Emerson, among others. But the continuity between the old principles, or at least certain potentialities within them, and the new forms of thought must be stressed; this is emphatically done in Perry Miller's widely honored essay, "From Edwards to Emerson." The mystical and pantheistic strains in Emerson, which point of course directly to Whitman, are traced back by Miller to tendencies in Jonathan Edwards and others who count as visionary revisionists of Puritanism. As a consequence of the realigning of forces in New England society that involved Unitarianism superceding Calvinism, and then the new Transcendentalism attacking "the corpse-cold Unitarianism of Harvard College and Brattle Street," ground was prepared for a new revelation that inevitably reechoed biblical sources, though sometimes distantly: "The ecstasy and the vision which Calvinists knew only in the moment of vocation, the passing of which left them agonizingly aware of depravity and sin, could become the permanent joy of those who had put aside the conception of depravity, and the moments between could be filled no longer with self-accusation but with praise and wonder" (Miller: 130). Whitman had little interest in the philosophic idealism of the Transcendentalists, but he was delighted to appropriate that "ecstasy and vision" that led to "praise and wonder." And he was aware of the relevant passages in the Bible; insofar as Transcendentalism revived the visionary side of Puritanism, it incarnated a considerable amount of biblical inspiration. In support of this observation, some later writers imply that Miller (and Feidelson and Pearce) did not go far enough: "It is safe to assume that the effects of Puritan beliefs upon the American mind habituated it to the symbolic mode of vision, with the result that eventually, in Emerson and other men of his time, the revolt against the jejune rationalism into which the formal theology had developed expressed a sensibility more fundamentally Puritan than the theoretical position it rejects" (Lynen: 44). If John F. Lynen is right, the saturation in the texts of the Testaments that was habitual for Puritans must be seen as an immensely productive source of "ecstasy and vision" and of the symbolistic and poetic imagination as a whole.

Miller's essay is also useful for illuminating the way in which the repressive and conformist sides of Puritanism split off from the visionary tendencies and led eventually to the commercialism and social conservatism that dominated New England when it became a center for shipping and banking (and Unitarianism, which could ingest worldly success with less ambivalence than more literalistic religions). This point is important for Whitman and for the whole of the antinomianism which by Pearce's analysis is central to American poetic creativity. For if one aspect of antinomianism was Adamic and accepting, another entailed denunciatory rejection of culture's self-deifying tendencies, especially as these were manifested in social conformism and exploitative greed. Just as Emerson attacked the crass materialistic commercialism of his day in a way that recalls the force though not the language of the Hebrew prophets, so Whitman also reproached his compatriots for habits that to him were blockages against the revelation of the divine in every person. Lines of social class and concern with money kept people apart and devalued their individuality, turning them into instrumentalities for worldly success and preference; thus Whitman called for their erasure. Though neither he nor Emerson used language as fulminating as that of the prophets against economic injustice and the arrogance of the rich and urbane, their critique is clearly implicit in their works and in the essential solitude they embraced. In the process of denouncing greed, exploitation, envy, self-indulgence, and mammonism, the prophets turned themselves into lonely and alien figures, "troublers of Israel" (see the epithets applied to Elijah by King Ahab and to Amos by the priest at Bethel). They were gadflies, to the king and court as well as to the rich and privileged merchants and landholders. Whitman rejoiced in having a very similar effect on his society. In "As I Lay with My Head in Your Lap Camerado" he confessed:

> I know I am restless and make others so,
> I know my words are weapons full of danger, full of death,
> For I confront peace, security, and all the settled laws, to unsettle
> them,
> I am more resolute because all have denied me than I could ever
> have been had all accepted me,
> I heed not and have never heeded either experience,
> cautions, majorities, nor ridicule. . . .

Thus Whitman embraces not only the alienation and gadfly role of the prophets but also some key Gospel motifs that extend them—Christ's saying that he came to bring "not peace but a sword," the denial by Peter and the desertion of the other followers, Christ's many sayings about being rejected, and so on. A good antinomian must unsettle the settled laws; some extreme antinomians proclaimed that no law was binding on them, a logical enough position if faith is all and works are nothing. Paul's wrestling in Romans with the concepts of law and grace sets forth paradoxes and problems that rise up continually throughout the history of Christianity. If Christ has died to save all, and no one can save oneself with works however good, and if the law, even though it prescribe good works, is at bottom an occasion for sin ("I should not have known what it is to covet if the law had not said 'You shall not covet'" [Rom 7:7]), then how is the Christian to regard the commandments and other moral laws? If God rejoices in showing his power by extending grace even to the blackest sinner, "What shall we say then? Are we to continue in sin that grace may abound?" (Rom 6:1). These tangles are full of latent antinomianism, even where Paul, the church, and the Puritans devised ways out (the Puritans preached that works, i.e., obedience to the law, were a sign of grace though not a means to it). Paul's persuasion that Christians were freed from the law was a crucial factor in the universalization of the church, since it allowed believers to become Christians without first becoming Jews. But it planted antinomian seeds that from time to time both enriched and embarrassed the Christian community. And in all the quarrels that arose, several biblical texts and patterns were repeatedly cited: anti-institutional tendencies, hostility or indifference to social orders, readiness to disturb established views and practices—all these facets of antinomianism found ample support in scripture. Whitman, like William Blake and others who inherited antinomian viewpoints, must have been acutely aware of these. In heeding neither "experience, cautions, majorities, nor ridicule" he does precisely what Hosea and Jeremiah, Jesus and Paul, had to do. Those who are gadflies must be ready to be scapegoats: they must accept scorn, loneliness, isolation, all sorts of ill-treatment. Reviled and persecuted, mocked and derided, the prophets of both Testaments suffered even martyrdom for proclaiming that human institutions and human laws were incapable of enshrining divinity. The abuse and neglect that were Whitman's fate testify to his willingness to suffer for his equally unsettling proclamations.

Whitman would have found much solace in the texts that promote the undermining of social privilege and snobbery that recur throughout the Bible. From the beginning the Old Testament heroes are set against the rich and mighty of their times: Abraham and his descendants are always in tension with the powers of Canaan; Moses defies and defeats Pharaoh; Joshua conquers and humiliates the petty princes of the promised land, as do the judges who succeed him. The earliest kings lead their people against the sophisticated armies of the Philistines, and when the prophets arise they reproach all human self-aggrandizement, even of their own kings and nation. Samuel rebukes Saul, Nathan chastises David, and Elijah's denunciations of Ahab and Jezebel almost cost him his life. Amos, Isaiah, and the rest of the great writing prophets, conduct a running campaign against the kings and the rich who enlarge themselves at the expense of the poor and the needy and who for defense against Assyria rely on armies instead of faith in Yahweh. Except for David, whose lament for Saul and Jonathan furnishes the refrain that can serve as a motto for the Old Testament— "How are the mighty fallen!"—no Hebrew king embodies a heroic Yahwist faith equal to that of these prophets. The equivalent motto in the New

Testament is Jesus' repeated saying, "The last shall be first," and Paul, John the Baptist, the writer of Revelation, and all the New Testament heroes reenact the pattern of hostility to the powers that be and the rulers of this earth. Kings, emperors, the rich, the learned, the mighty of Rome, all serve as targets of wrath and prophecy. Paul insists that they are all as nothing before the grace and power of God, and surely his sublime assurance is indebted to the Yahwistic vision generalized throughout the Old Testament, which sees humanity and all its works and pomps as no better than undifferentiated dust when set before the overpowering fact of God's existence. So, at least, would a determined antinomian read the Bible, and such texts would be the refuges of Whitman or any other antinomians questioning and criticizing the values of their culture. All pride, arrogance, luxury, and complacency can be attacked on a biblical basis, as can all reliance on one's powers or achievements, be they ever so impressive, or all assurances of salvation that come from the law or the temple or from having Abraham as a father. Moreover, these attacks can be transposed to fit any cultural milieu, and determined antinomians must stand to their cultures in exactly that adversary, gadfly role that Trilling and Pearce and others mark out for these great authors. The hostility to culture and all its works is so unremitting in the prophetic traditions of the Bible, so unprecedented in the world of its time, as to furnish zeal and energy for an antinomian strain that runs undiminished through millennia. Imagine with what joy both Puritans and antinomians would have read the Song of Hannah (1 Sam 2:1–10), especially these verses:

> The bows of the mighty men are broken, and they that stumbled are girded with strength. They that were full have hired out themselves for bread, and they that were hungry ceased. . . . The LORD maketh poor and maketh rich: he bringeth low, and lifteth up. He raiseth the poor out of the dust and lifteth up the beggar from the dunghill, to set them among princes, and to make them inherit the throne of glory . . . by strength shall no man prevail. (KJV)

Whitman, inheritor of a tradition that sustained itself on such visionary images, found that he could imaginatively recreate the work of the Lord in raising up the needy from the ash heap and treating him as an equal to the prince. Whitman is significant in American poetry not so much because he celebrates the common person or the democratic ethos, nor even because he dares to confess such improprieties as homoerotic yearnings, as because he achieves a dynamic adaptation of the prophetic and antinomian strains to his own unique visionary mode of art.

If much of the value placed on Whitman today comes from his innovations in form and technique, his liberation of the line and the whole poem from traditional restrictions, we must remember that such freedom is itself part of the visionary mode and owes much to the antinomian attitude. Whitman could no more pour his words into other writers' forms than conform to their polite mores or restrict himself to genteel subject matter. When we compare him and Emily Dickinson with the poets they now seem so easily to surpass, not only Longfellow and the other "Fireside Poets" but even Poe and Emerson, we notice at once their powerful creativity in form: their poetry on the page looks nothing like that of their predecessors. Whitman more obviously and Dickinson more subtly achieve styles and idioms that are completely their own and have as few imitators as precedents. This remarkable independence was their form of dealing with the generic problem of the American tradition as discussed earlier. They follow the precept that new departures, radical innovations, dynamic adaptations are necessary for creative life; if any precedents for poetry are followed, they must be in effect created anew by adaptation and change. For them the tension that inheres in this problem was creative and heuristic; it forced them into experiments in which they forged their styles and in doing so let forth unparalleled floods of artistic energy. Their work and their unforgettable insights are inseparable from their stylistic freedom, as the attempts by well-meaning editors to regularize and domesticate Dickinson's savagely unique style show.

If Whitman is the antinomian as inclusive, accepting visionary, Dickinson is the antinomian as eccentric recluse, and her insight into the nature of her solitary existence shows as clearly in her stylistic practices as in the spare and strange records of her life. A sketch of her stylistic innovations by Albert Gelpi is useful for summing up why she is sui generis as a poet:

> She chose words with stinging freshness; she flavored speech with earthy New England colloquialisms; she often dropped the "s" of the third-person singular of the present tense to suggest the enduring quality of the action; she emphasized nouns by the striking addition or omission of the preceding article; she sometimes used singular nouns where plurals were expected and vice versa; she made parts of speech perform unorthodox functions, used words in startling contexts, coined words when none seemed available or apt. Like Ezra Pound, William Carlos Williams, Marianne Moore, and E. E. Cummings, Emily Dickinson sought to speak the uniqueness of her experience in a personal tongue by reconstituting and revitalizing— at the risk of eccentricity—the basic verbal unit. (1965:147)

Gelpi's comparison of Dickinson with the great experimentalist poets of the early twentieth century is apt enough to make us see just how much she ran counter to the cultivated practices of her day. Even in such a matter as punctuation she refused to use the accepted forms. Like other prophets, especially the biblical ones, Dickinson seems mislocated in time. Mentally she dwelt in a world that her contemporaries could not understand, and she spoke, as she well knew, not to her own generation but to a set of readers who could be assembled only in a visionary context, as it were, outside of time. Only by isolating herself could she reach this ideal audience. Resisting publication in her own lifetime, Dickinson awaited vindication as only the prophet and antinomian can. Not so much from the future: she was concerned with eternity.

The contemporary poet John Ashbery has spoken of the American tradition in poetry as a tradition of eccentricity, citing the "isolatoes" who make up the mainstream while the traditionalist figures, in the European sense, remain on the fringes. While English poetry in some of its greatest periods has triumphed through subtle adaptations to conformity, as in the Renaissance fascination with the sonnet and other forms that require endless variation within relatively tight restrictions of form and theme, this has never been the character of the best in American poetry, simply because of the generic problem inherent in the phrase "American tradition." Emily Dickinson is of course a primary exhibit for Ashbery's thesis. No other poet, probably, has ever worked so essentially alone—not only secluded from her neighbors and townspeople, but starkly isolated even from any literary milieu. Hence her eccentricities in style of life correspond more or less to those in her style of poetry.

In these circumstances, working in effect without a tradition, Dickinson found the Bible all the more important as a source of linguistic inspiration. She presents the extreme case of the familiar paradox: the more antinomian the American poet, the more he or she falls back on the traditional guidebook. Her most authoritative editor and biographer, Thomas H. Johnson, states the paradox in more general terms, but they apply directly to her use of the Bible: "Conformity with received traditions she disdained because she felt it led to moral stagnation, yet her most powerful compulsions derived from her Puritan past" (4). Johnson himself describes most succinctly the role of the Bible in her work:

> It was the primary source, and no other is of comparable importance. Even when she draws her figures of speech from the language of the sea, of trade, of law, or of science, they usually suggest that they have passed through the alembic of the King James version of biblical utterance. . . . There are several score of poems where the biblical metaphor is direct and self-evident. But the shaping of her thought in terms of biblical incident, events, and precept is apparent in almost every poem that she wrote. She transmuted universals into particulars by means of such figures of speech: "location's narrow way," "the smitten rock," "broad possessions," "this accepted breath," "the scarlet way," "the morning stars," "the straight pass of suffering," "the apple on the tree," "the sapphire fellows," "moat of pearl," "the fleshy gate," "this meek apparelled thing," "the primer to a life." All are drawn from the Bible, and require on the part of the reader a like familiarity if the full import is to be rendered. (151–53)

Johnson goes on to analyze several poems in which oblique and often complex but nonetheless fundamental dependence on the Bible is apparent, and he concludes: "It is not too much to say that in almost every poem she wrote, there are echoes of her sensitivity to the idiom of the Bible, and of her dependence upon its imagery for her own striking figures of speech. The great reservoir of classical myth she rarely drew upon. . . . She found the Bible her key to meaning" (153).

And yet Emily Dickinson was most antinomian in her use of the Bible, because she used it wholly against the grain of its accepted interpretations in her time. She had sloughed off the orthodox Calvinism and conventional piety of her region and her family early in life and went on to challenge concepts of "Heaven," "Eden," and "Eternity" with her own bold definitions. In this as in so much else she shocked family and friends more than a little, yet her remarks and observations were so strangely forceful, so wittily uncanny, that no one seems to have felt quite sure of what she was saying. Tell all the truth but tell it slant—that was her motto. Gelpi says: "So irreverently could she take the words of Holy Scripture that her sharp wit regularly turned them to her own humorous ends. . . . From Emily Dickinson's letters and poems we can piece together a kind of Devil's Dictionary" (1965: 49). Since the antinomian is always overtly or covertly hostile to orthodoxy of any kind, we should not be surprised that she often put her impressive knowledge of the Bible to mocking uses. Knowing how this would shock her loved ones, she had to explain that "Much madness is divinest sense / To a discerning eye," an antinomian's credo. As Gelpi remarks, one of the predictable outcomes of a Calvinist heritage passed on to unorthodox minds is a satiric or parodic treatment of its beliefs and precepts, especially those like infant damnation, innate depravity, and so on. Once these are taken out of their serious context in the passionate intensity of Puritan conviction, they seem at best butts of scathing humor. The inverted Calvinist may make mocking remarks about God himself that depend on orthodox doctrine being taken literally but defiantly. Gelpi cites many poems embodying such humor in his two studies. "God preaches, a noted Clergyman," she wrote, and in another poem calls him a jealous God who "cannot bear to see / That we had rather not with Him / But with each other play." She could mock even the Bible itself, in spite of her intimate relationship with it. Another poem begins, "The Bible is an antique Volume / Written by faded men / At the suggestion of the Holy Spectres. . . ." That such an attitude is in some ways more true to the Bible than standard pieties is an easy case to argue and requires only an understanding of the antinomian attitude. The prophets in denouncing the mores of their day were hardest on religious hypocrisy, on those holier-than-thou among the privileged Hebrews who staged elaborate sacrifices or festivals while planning more and more exploitation of the poor and the needy. Isaiah is particularly vivid: he portrays God in heaven being nauseated by the smell of burning sacrifices and revolted by the vain protestations of the people. "Your new moons and your appointed feasts my soul hates. . . . Your hands are full of blood" (1:14–15). Not only sacrifices and offerings but all forms of comfortable religious self-assurance earned the wrath of the prophets; and Jesus is equally hard on those who thank God that they are not like other men, who pray loudly and boast of their observance of the law (Luke 18:11). From many such texts the antinomian can easily find support for hostility to priestly and prelatic authority and to community conviction. The work of Amos, the first of the great "writing" prophets, centered on his harsh inversion of his contemporaries' belief in a "Day of the Lord" that would save them from the Assyrian armies. Amos promised them that the day would be "darkness, not light," a day of wrath and judgment. From this to the New Testament denunciations of "scribes and Pharisees," a pervasive suspicion of communal orthodoxy runs through the Bible. Emily Dickinson's poems, her letters to the world that never wrote to her, sometimes have the reproachful tone of the prophet warning the "majorities" that their most cherished beliefs and assurances might be delusory or even idolatrous. The Bible denounces all forms of idolatry, for nothing earthly can contain the creator; by implication, it denounces even those who would make an idol of the Bible itself. So the irreverence and mockery of inverted Calvinists and other antinomians are not really perverse but have biblical precedents: "Do not walk in the statutes of your fathers, nor observe their ordinances, nor defile yourselves with their idols" (Ezek 20:18).

Twentieth-Century Versions

Robert Frost

Frost is the poet who in one sense breaks off the American tradition of eccentricity but in another sense seems to inherit an antinomian attitude almost as if directly from Emily Dickinson, and perhaps from Melville too. For all Frost's apparent satisfaction with traditional verse forms and standard themes, there is a rebellious streak in him that shows up most clearly in his grudging acceptance of the Bible as source and burden, as argued earlier. Could not Dickinson herself have written his little couplet: "Forgive, O Lord, my little jokes on Thee / And I'll forgive Thy great big one on me"? Frost's ambivalence toward the Bible is readily apparent, as is his familiarity with it, and the compound can easily be seen to produce the metaphysical resentment that lies underneath the grim humor of the couplet. Frost treats the painful paradoxes of Job, the most predictably antinomian of texts, in his most explicitly biblical poem, A Masque of Reason (1945); he calls it the "forty-third chapter" of the book. Underneath the bantering tone (Job's wife asks God if she can call him "Lord God of Hostesses") one can see Frost's morbid absorption in the parable of humanity made to suffer unjustly. He is as fascinated by the story of Job as was Melville. The somber witticisms at the expense of hardhearted Calvinism sometimes get boringly sophomoric, but Frost is a strongly representative figure. Even the most glancing of his biblical allusions, such as his naming the faded beauty queen "Abishag" in

"Provide, Provide," marks his obsessive concern with God's problematic justice and humanity's ambiguous rewards in life (see 1 Kings 1–2). Like all Calvinists, inverted or upright, Frost is haunted by what he calls in "The Oven Bird" "that other fall we name the fall": i.e., the manifestation in the human situation in Nature of separation from God through original sin, leaving us to make what we can of a "diminished thing." Very often Frost's poems embody in one form or another a sense of malevolence in the universe that may well mask the so-called wrathful God of the Old Testament. Note the hint made by the clouds above the destructive ocean in "Once by the Pacific" of "locks blown forward in the gleam of eyes." Quite naturally in the last line the destruction hinted at by the apocalyptic ocean is connected to "God's last *Put out the light*," which inverts the *lux fiat* of Genesis into the murderous words of Othello. Frost looks for vindictiveness even in the Gospel (see the reference to "Saint Mark" in "Directive"). In some fashion he consistently affirms his belief in malign agency, "design of darkness," in the universe. Antinomianism in the atomic age seems to bring forth a neo-Byronic sense of radical injustice in the cosmos. No wonder earth's "desert places" scare Frost. He has more than a touch of that "power of blackness" that Melville found in Nathaniel Hawthorne, and he preaches an apocalypse more subtle but no less savage (ice rather than fire, perhaps) than that of John on Patmos.

Wallace Stevens

The Bible does not in fact play a constitutive role in many of Stevens's poems; such familiarity as he had with it did indeed breed contempt. However, the poem in which he dealt most explicitly with a biblical subject is one of the superlative poems of the twentieth century and is sure to be one of the achievements for which Stevens will be best remembered. In "Sunday Morning," Stevens contrasts the world of natural vitality with the static funereal observances of Christianity. A woman dawdles in comfort on a Sunday morning, wondering why she is not in church, and her thoughts stray to "silent Palestine, / Dominion of the blood and sepulchre." But her heart does not go with her thoughts. Instead she instinctively recoils: "Why should she give her bounty to the dead?" Like Chaucer's Wife of Bath, she is sure that life is for the living and that dead men tell no tales. Unlike Yeats, who reproached Christianity because "Odour of blood when Christ was slain / Made all Platonic tolerance vain / And vain all Doric discipline," Stevens chastises the visions of Christianity as if they represented a frozen immobile state of changelessness, out of the flux of life, as the ideal or paradisaical condition. Against this Stevens wants us to believe that natural process, including degeneration and death, is the force to be truly venerated: "Death is the mother of beauty," he proclaims, offering to us an epitome of the fuller version he gives in "Peter Quince at the Clavier": "Beauty is momentary in the mind— / The fitful tracing of a portal; / But in the flesh it is immortal." But the poem is a magnificent backhanded tribute to the Bible precisely because that idealized changelessness of which Stevens complains represents a later Hellenization of New Testament concepts, not the doctrine of the text itself. Indeed, had Stevens wanted to look harder into the Bible he would have found just what he says he wanted. "Is there no change of death in paradise? Does ripe fruit never fall?" What better gloss could be made on this rhetorical question in which Stevens impugns Christianity's sense of the natural world than the famous parabolic utterance by Jesus about the sacrificial nature of his death: "Truly, truly, I say to you, unless a grain of wheat falls into the earth and dies, it remains alone; but if it dies, it bears much fruit" (John 12:24). The magnificent passage that closes "Sunday Morning" ends with the image of flocks of pigeons sinking "Downward to darkness, on extended wings," which obviously is to be set against the descent of the dove in the Baptism story. Yet it is motivated by a feeling not different in certain essentials from that of "Consider the lilies of the field. . . ."

T. S. Eliot

Eliot is a fitting figure with which to close not only because of his deep interest in the Bible as the holy book of his religion but also because he represents a superb example of the force of the antinomian impulse in American poetry. In a modern context which Eliot sees as that of "decent Godless people," orthodoxy itself can be chosen only as an expression of antinomian and prophetic witness, a symbolic protest against an affirmation of self that has come to be self-indulgent and self-important. Eliot's return to the religion and homeland of his forebears figures not only a closing of historic circles but yet another new departure: "In my end is my beginning." Eliot declares that the war against tradition is over, that the repressive potentialities of traditionalism are no longer dangerous, and that antinomianism itself, in its older forms, has become an orthodoxy with a new set of threats. He urges us not to return to the narrow insular forms of tradition against which we have successfully rebelled, but to a tradition far more broadly conceived, reaching back to the art of the "Magdalenian draughtsmen" on the walls of prehistoric caves, which in his view derives its force from a veneration of the eternal Wholly Other, to use Rudolf Otto's memorable phrase. Only by acknowledging this power outside and beyond humanity can we go beyond the perils of humanism and of an etiolated religion that has "forgotten that it has forgotten the death of God," that picks and chooses among beliefs as if in some cafeteria of platitudes, and that slips inevitably toward our peculiar forms of nihilism.

In counseling this recovery of sacramentalism Eliot argues not for a particular brand of religion but for a surrender of the self to something more important. His witness is a form of kerygmatic proclamation that precedes his formal conversion to Anglican Christianity in 1927. In his essay of 1919 on

"Tradition and the Individual Talent," he had argued that this self-surrender and self-extinction is as necessary to the artist as later, he was to find, to the religious man. Eliot thus manages to complete the nineteenth-century project of fusing poetry and religion, not in the genteel didactic form envisioned by Matthew Arnold but in the vatic, prophetic sense embodied in the oracular writers from William Blake to John Ruskin and onwards. What gives life to the artist is self-transcendence, he argues, since self-expression can go only so far and must inevitably be succeeded by some form of escapism. In a series of essays that condemn "Whiggery" and "The Inner Voice" as subtle conformisms to a debilitating modern ethos, he delineates artistic values that issue in strange-looking pronouncements: Baudelaire is his example to demonstrate that "blasphemy is closer to belief than mere indifference," that a sense of sin and of damnation is more vivifying for the artist, as for the common man, than an adherence to contemporary forms of "healthy-mindedness." But his principles are clear enough: we are willfully shutting ourselves off from true creativity by trying to realize the Enlightenment dream of human per-fectibility. He takes dead aim at "the new Humanism," arguing like many other thinkers that this represents merely the idolatrous theologization of humanity itself, in the form of the modern "self."

Eliot's reliance on the Bible for his insights is amply attested in his poems and plays, and the preconversion *Waste Land* is as full of biblical allusions as are the *Four Quartets. The Waste Land* is a kerygmatic poem, so conceived from its chaotic conception to its final form. The visions are gathered together as those of Tiresias but are all those of prophets biblically conceived. If the notes to the poem are "a skit," they at least serve to acknowledge the force of his biblical borrowings, explicitly to Isaiah and Ezekiel and the New Testament, implicitly in the coherence of the visionary experience itself. Tiresias is a convenient name for the blind seer, but the overriding voice of the poem is that of John the Baptist, the voice singing from the well (see also Jeremiah 38) that resounds from the desert a warning of coming sterility and of the need for repentance. "I John saw these things and heard them," a line that appeared in the early drafts, conflates the three Johns of the New Testament, though it was excised as too overtly keryg-matic. The poem approaches its climax in the lines telling us that we have existed and can exist only in "the awful daring of a moment's surrender," a phrase that startlingly combines the religious and the erotic in a synthesis worthy of John Donne, Eliot's true predecessor.

The evidence of the depth of Eliot's biblicism is not only in these cita-tions and in those that could be made from *Four Quartets*, where the descent of the dove and the Pentecostal tongues of flame can be seen even in the annunciatory violence of attacking Stuka bombers. It is best seen by comparing his orthodox yet antinomian recovery of the sense of God with this summation, from the historian Henri Frankfort, of the vision enshrined in the Old Testament:

The God of the Hebrews is pure being, unqualified, ineffable. He is
holy. That means that he is *sui generis*. It does not mean that he is
taboo or that he is power. It means that all values are ultimately
attributes of God alone. . . . "We are all as an unclean thing, and all
our righteousnesses are as filthy rags" (Isaiah 64:6). Even man's righteousness, his highest virtue, is devaluated by comparison with the
absolute. (241–42)

If it is ironic that Eliot brings the antinomian vision back finally to such
an overpowering sense of God, that irony is part of the tensions between the
Bible and American culture that have proved so consequential in our lives.

WORKS CONSULTED

Feidelson, Charles, Jr.
1953   *Symbolism and American Literature*. Chicago: University of
                      Chicago Press.

Frankfort, H., et al.
1959   *Before Philosophy*. Baltimore: Penguin Books.

Freedman, David Noel
1972   "Pottery, Poetry, and Prophecy: An Essay on Biblical
                      Poetry." *Journal of Biblical Literature* 91: 5–26. Reprinted
                      in *The Bible in its Literary Milieu*. Edited by John Maier
                      and Vincent Tollers. Grand Rapids, MI: Eerdmans, 1979.
1975   "Early Israelite History in the Light of Early Israelite
                      Poetry." In *Unity and Diversity: Essays in the History,
                      Literature, and Religion of the Ancient Near East*. Edited
                      by H. Goedicke and J. J. M. Roberts. Baltimore: Johns
                      Hopkins University Press.

Gelpi, Albert
1965   *Emily Dickinson: The Mind of the Poet*. Cambridge:
                      Harvard University Press.
1975   *The Tenth Muse: The Psyche of the American Poet*.
                      Cambridge: Harvard University Press.

Hoffman, Daniel G.
1962   *American Poetry and Poetics: Poems and Critical Docu-
                      ments from the Puritans to Robert Frost*. New York: Anchor
                      Books.

Johnson, Thomas H.
1955   *Emily Dickinson: An Interpretive Biography*. Cambridge:
                      Belknap Press of Harvard University.

Lynen, John F.
1968   *The Design of the Present: Essays on Time and Form in
                      American Literature*. New Haven: Yale University Press.

Miller, J. Hillis
1965   *Poets of Reality*. Cambridge: Belknap Press of Harvard
                      University Press.

Miller, Perry
    1940   "From   Edwards   to   Emerson." In *Interpretations of*
                    American Literature. Edited by Charles Feidelson, Jr., and
                    Paul Brodkorb, Jr. New York: Oxford University Press, 1959.

Pearce, Roy Harvey
    1961   *The Continuity of American Poetry.* Princeton: Princeton
                    University Press.

Schneidau, Herbert N.
    1976   *Sacred Discontent: The Bible and Western Tradition.* Baton
                    Rouge: Louisiana State University Press.

Trilling, Lionel
    1968   *Beyond Culture: Essays on Literature and Learning.* New
                    York: Viking Press.

Waggoner, Hyatt H.
    1968   *American Poets: From the Puritans to the Present.* Boston:
                    Houghton Mifflin.

II

"As Through a Glass Eye, Darkly":
The Bible in the Nineteenth-Century American Novel

Edwin Cady

To gain the advantages of a parsimony of necessity, I rule out Brockden Brown and Hugh Henry Brackenridge as eighteenth-century novelists, say that the otherwise indefinable nineteenth-century novel starts with James Fenimore Cooper, and assert that it ends with Frank Norris. Though Samuel Clemens was busy damning the "literary offenses" of Fenimore Cooper when he charged that "Cooper seldom saw anything correctly. He saw nearly all things as through a glass eye, darkly," there is good reason to suppose that he would, at least in private, have said the same for the religion of Cooper's fiction. Yet the remark illustrates an odd displacement of the Bible in major novels throughout the period. It tended to disappear.°

"As through a glass eye, darkly" may be the best joke in the funniest piece of literary criticism of the century. Yet that is in part because it is a multiple jape, with several wry angles. To catch it all, you have to know Paul's first letter to the Corinthians exactly, along with its prophecy of resurrection and the fulfullment of faith: "For now we see through a glass, darkly; but then face to face: now I know in part; but then shall I know even as also I am known" (1 Cor 13:12 KJV).

In art as in faith, by Clemens's agnostic day matters of vision and knowledge had come to tantalize the writers and readers of "Old Times on the Mississippi," or "The Beast in the Jungle," *The Shadow of a Dream*, or *Maggie, a Girl of the Streets* almost beyond endurance. Out of such novelists' struggles with vision and knowing would emerge the artistic resources of the novel of high modernism.

°Thinking through this assignment, it seemed to me that one must write either a personal essay at the assigned length or a scholarly book not asked for. I think there is good scholarly or critical warrant for everything said here; but it would take the length of a book to moot all the points. Please take it, then, as a scholar's personal essay. The general American literature field, presently in a sort of Alexandrian phase, overflows with bibliographical aids. It seems absurd to pour in another pint.

To see "through a glass, darkly" is dubious; "through a glass eye" becomes darkling altogether. The phrase bespeaks a writer who knows the Pauline text precisely; expects his reader to know it as well; knows that the reader is used to a now almost lost humor of joking with well-loved but too familiar words of scripture; feels that perhaps fiction and scripture make an unevenly yoked team; has, though reared to biblical knowledge, come to doubt or disbelieve it; at least knows very well that one does not wish to be preached at from the novel.

Behind Clemens's joke lies Henry David Thoreau's archness of familiar quotation from an ostensibly unnameable "old book." All the variations on ignorant rant and cant related to "The Harp of a Thousand Strings" and "Where the Lion Roareth and the Wang-Doodle Mourneth" are there. William Dean Howells's having Bartley Hubbard fail to outrun the bullet in Whited Sepulchre, Arizona, required an exact sense of Matthew 23:27 together with a sophisticated reaction against the Tombstone, Arizona, myth of *The Police Gazette* and a penetrating grasp of Hubbard's moral nature. All through the novel of that century ran the same mix of conflicting emotions: yearning, rebellion, and the tendency to distance one's art from the actual Bible that informs Emily Dickinson's "The Bible is an Antique Volume—"

I

With the conspicuous exceptions of Harriet Beecher Stowe and George Washington Cable, who among the major novelists of the period was even firmly churched? Cooper, a believer obviously trending ever closer in his late romances, was not even confirmed as an Episcopalian until the very last. Is there another?

As Howells remarked in reviewing *The Adventures of Tom Sawyer*, Tom, like any boy of his time and place, was brought up "to fear God and dread the Sunday School." Largely understood, that would seem to cover Melville's case as well as Clemens's. There was that same tendency in the novelists which Henry Adams noticed with a mild surmise in his own generation of the family: the religious sentiment seemed to have died out of it— the active sentiment, not at last the yearning. The Jameses, like Howells, were brought up within an intellectually esoteric sect, Swedenborgianism. Serious argument is advanced to show that Hawthorne, after his fashion, was a Christian. But if he was, he had a dramatic imagination anything but biblical. Hawthorne the serious historian knew that as conversationalists, diarists, correspondents, and preachers, Puritan men and women habitually quoted and cited scripture. But in what Henry James called "scenes," Hawthorne's Puritans never talk so, not even in extremis. Goodman Brown, in agony at the Witches' Sabbath, cries out in the language of Sir Walter Scott, not Gospel, to exorcise "the wicked one." What was ever Arthur Dimmesdale's text from a pulpit? With what bit of sacred text was he wont to sweeten his mouth? Do Hawthorne's people ever speak biblically—or had he an inner ear that censored out the Bible more rigidly than the ears of unbelieving Melville or Clemens or Howells?

Even from the scenes of believing novelists, biblical speech sounds surprisingly seldom. Something like a pair of archetypes appears as early as the climaxes that end Cooper's *The Prairie*. It is a romance in which dramatic propriety, integrity of characterization, and total intellectual implication might demand biblical immediacy. Cooper gave us a darkling distance. The first resolution is that of a violent, illegitimate patriarch, Ishmael Bush. Without a covenant, indeed a fugitive from justice and presently a kidnapper, Bush arrives at the end at a perplexity neither violence nor craft can solve. Within his clan, his brother-in-law has treacherously murdered his son. What shall he do? Illiterate, he turns for light to his termagant wife, more doubly torn than he. Will her Bible not guide them? Somehow the scene foreshadows the typical relation of the American novel to Holy Writ throughout the century to come.

The sole true remnant of a civilization that their atavistic regression to the patriarchal had eroded away from the Bushes was Esther's "fragment of a Bible which had been thumbed and smoke-dried until the print was nearly illegible." In it, says the narrator, she fumbled, saying, "There are many awful passages in these pages, Ishmael, . . . and some there ar' that teach the rules of punishment." When she had found what suited him, he determined on retribution. Never, though, does the narrator reveal what "awful passage" it was that settled Ishmael on cold revenge. Why not? Why should we be told only that in pronouncing sentence he said, "You have slain my first-born, and according to the laws of God and man you must die"?

From the introduction of his charactonym—"Ishmael Bush," the guerilla of the outback—to his sullen retreat toward the east, the intellectual argument of the book had pointed to its truth that such anachronism, a regressive thwarting of God's plan, was a false patriarch's sin within the largest historical frame of things. Cooper's melodramatic imagination contented itself with a climax of pure, powerful Gothicism—as intellectually empty as Poe said it ought to be. If that begged the intellectual question, it somehow suited Cooper's structural imagination. For the purposes of this essay, the striking fact is the insufficient existence of that "fragment" of a Bible—stained, soiled, largely illegible, a shard in the matriarch's hand. It has degenerated into something all too like a half-decipherable Dead Sea scroll of the Great American Desert—to be seen, as through a glass eye, darkly.

But what of the opposite, far higher, brighter climax, the calm triumphant Christian death among adoring Indians and civilized whites—only a few among the latter of whom know that "the trapper," however perfectly nature's nobleman, is also Natty Bumppo, the mythological Leatherstocking himself? On the throne of honorable death where the pious Pawnees have placed him, at peace with God and humankind, with savagism and civilization, his historic mission accomplished, his long race finished, waiting for the call home, the Leatherstocking's thoughts wander to his father's tomb and the biblical inscription he had caused to be carved on it back near the shore of the far distant Atlantic. He turns to the present representative of that family which symbolized Cooper's ideal for civilization in America with burial wishes. "Anything!" is the earnest response.

He would like a Christian headstone, presumably much like his father's: "just the name, the age, and the time of the death, with something from the holy book; no more, no more." Presumably the Bible verse was that also on his father's stone. The novel ends: "In due time the stone was placed . . . with the simple inscription which the trapper had himself requested. The only liberty taken by Middleton was to add—'*May no wanton hand ever disturb his remains!*'"

As a climax, that to *The Prairie* stands as perhaps the best Cooper wrote, perhaps the most successful holy dying in American fiction. But it leaves a nagging mystery: just what *was* the little inscription "from the holy book"? Why don't we know? Perhaps more to the point, did Cooper know? If the answer to either or both questions were no, would that be one of Cooper's "literary offenses"? Or does it tell us from very early on that the Bible stood in a peculiar relation, not explained and not easy to explain well, with the nineteenth-century American novel?

II

Some keep the sabbath going to Church—
I keep it, staying at Home—

So began Dickinson in perhaps the most Concordian of her poems. When Thoreau and Hawthorne were both in town, a large fraction of the whole number of the best minds in America, including its greatest living novelist, was on any given "Sabbath" faithfully "keeping" the day holy by staying away from church. Out in nature, or safe in their alabaster studies, they may have thought of matters religious, probably did. But they seem much more likely to have been thinking in language and figures taken from Edmund Spenser or John Milton, John Bunyan or the Gitas, than in the terms or tropes of the Old and New Testaments. Milton somehow spoke to their condition. Even Cooper had taken many and many a chapter head-piece from him.

When you come to think of it, the fact so striking about the Puritans who so obsessively possessed Hawthorne's imagination is how very seldom they think or speak biblically. It would not do to challenge Carlos Baker's insights that "Hawthorne's working knowledge of the Bible, . . . helped him to infuse a continuous lurking sense of the remotely antique, the exotically oriental, and the far distant in time and place into such localized New England novels as *The Scarlet Letter*, *The House of the Seven Gables*, and *The Blithedale Romance*." For it is true. And so is Baker's saying, "The method of Hawthorne is instructive for any reader whose religious commitment is deep rather than loud, and whose taste in fiction has been formed by a study of the masters. For it seems to suggest the important aesthetic law that the use of Biblical materials should always be made with extreme delicacy . . . that a writer who turns to a Biblical episode for any metaphorical or illustrative purpose ought to be content to treat it allusively, to allow it to operate in the realm of suggestion. . . ."

It is easy to see the point. And yet, and again perhaps yet—what about dramatic propriety? What about dramatic intensity? Turning to *The Scarlet Letter* for biblical richness of allusion, of intensity in scriptural matters—to Puritans, at least, of the last intensity—one is met not merely by restraint but something like an embarrassment of parsimony. That attenuation of American life Henry James found in Hawthorne glares from the unbiblical texts of his dramatic scenes. Hawthorne's historic Puritans seem as dimly scriptural as the Yankee generations long gone from the Puritan faith of Howells or of *Ethan Frome*—or Freeman or Jewett, for that matter.

It becomes somehow a matter of moment that the one vital biblical quotation is made by the narrative voice and echoed rather absent-mindedly by the sweet old Reverend Mr. Wilson in his frustrated catechization of Hester's elfin bastard child. Surprisingly late in the book the narrator confides rather lamely that Hester "named the infant 'Pearl,' as being of great price,—purchased with all she had, her mother's only treasure!" Said Wilson, "'Pearl, . . . thou must take heed to instruction, that so, in due season, thou mayest wear in thy bosom the pearl of great price.'" It is not that anything goes wrong here but that it does not artistically go notably well. Dimmesdale's rather scared but successful plea that Pearl shall not be taken from her mother has about it somehow more the ring of Bronson Alcott than the Bible.

The trouble is much the same as that with the iconographical allusion (to which Baker calls attention) plain in the narrator's "picture" (the other side of Henry James's narrative coin) of Dimmesdale's study. Upon its walls were tapestries, reputedly Gobelin, "representing the Scriptural story of David and Bathsheba, and Nathan the Prophet. . . ." Though Baker leaves us in a suggestion of doubt on the point, that is, of course, one story. David the king lustfully coveted the beautiful wife of a faithful captain, arranged to get his good soldier killed in combat, possessed himself of Bathsheba, and Nathan the prophet denounced David, speaking the word of the Lord. To be sure, this iconography Hawthorne so handled as to meet Baker's criteria of delicacy, indirection, and avoidance of the banal. But, doing so, has he made it biblical? Nathan was anything but delicate or indirect. Is it Puritan? They seemed to prefer square, public, tactless confession. In fact, what does it do for Hawthorne's reader? The best I can suggest is that one more time it underscores the fact that no Lord sent Arthur Dimmesdale any Nathan. He had his own darkling way to grope to his dying "confession" on the scaffold:

and that remains so loaded with Hawthornian suspended ambiguities that it is the critic bold indeed who rushes in to tell us all precisely what baldly took place and effect.

This is not, of course, to say that Hawthorne's handling of the biblical or of the Puritan or of both together was "wrong." On the contrary, it was altogether right because it was altogether Hawthornian. As an artist and an ethical visionary Hawthorne was to himself exactly as one of the many readings of the great novel required—in this case in its own words—"Be true! Be true! Be true!" Somehow it seems to come more easily to Hawthorne's imagination to relate Chillingworth to a fiend out of Bunyan than to connect Hester and Pearl with Mary and the child or Dimmesdale with King David.

Hawthorne's problem, as apparently Henry James could not see, was the same one Jonathan Edwards faced and won a stalemate, Emerson and his followers faced and triumphed over. It was of course the American need, always present, to "make it new"—in language, perception, idea, esthetic vision, artistic realization—to renew the old ever-pitiable human realities in an American world. To use the Bible and yet "make it new" one had at once to know its language in the marrow of the bone and yet escape the prison house of worn-out forms. In a new world, without crown and garter, miter and cross, the great matters had to be demythologized, remythologized, and spoken in words that would pierce the vast, callous, distracted public ear— made common, too, yet not vulgar. Perhaps Hawthorne's sense was that with the Bible the artist indeed needed to be oblique, disguising it in other media, be rather distant, make it a memory quickening aroma, not a noise.

Thus, perhaps, his spiritually sensitive, compassionate, profound personal religious vision might find a voice. Did he not once, guard down perhaps, irony so high he thought he could not be taken seriously, confide that he himself was the only Christian he had ever known? Or is that an unreliable remark? At any rate, as even Melville discovered, Hawthorne dove deep, deep, so deep he could not be companioned.

III

On Melville and the Bible one feels so set free by Nathalia Wright's work, at once pioneering and definitive, that one may say with Whitmanian insouciance what one pleases. If Ahab was a grand godlike ungodly man, Melville was a great biblical unscriptural writer. Anything may be, indeed the rule of the reader's road is to expect it, inverted, pulled inside out, torn down, and reconstructed into its mirror opposite. In Melville's hands anything may happen to the biblical—almost certainly will. Yet at last, no matter what Melville did with the Bible, it is certain that he could never have been Melville without it.

In observing all that, perhaps it is best to stick to the Melville who these days seems increasingly to tower over all his other avatars, the author (better yet, his text) of *Moby-Dick*. Only it and the lyrical poems are supremely worth reading.

Considered esthetically, *Moby-Dick*'s massive reference to biblical materials becomes as elusive as the Spirit Spout. Can Melville be playing fast and loose, as Poe recommended, with vague, unresolvable allusions for the mere sake of a riddling, if musical, *"richness"*? The gains for *Moby-Dick* won from Shakespeare and Milton in creating young America's "Big Book" seem evident enough and artistically effective. However bizarre in staging, Father Mapple's sermon presents a drama nothing short of superb.

And what it says, taken singly, moves one deeply:

> But all the things that God would have us to do are hard for us to do—remember that—and hence, he oftener commands us than endeavors to persuade. And if we obey God, we must disobey ourselves; and it is in this disobeying ourselves, wherein the hardness of obeying God consists. . . .
>
> Woe to him whom this world charms from Gospel duty! Woe to him who seeks to pour oil upon the waters when God has brewed them into a gale! Woe to him who seeks to please rather than to appal! Woe to him whose good name is more to him than goodness! Woe to him who, in this world, courts not dishonor! Woe to him who would not be true, even though to be false were salvation! Yea, woe to him who, as the great Pilot Paul has it, while preaching to others is himself a castaway!

Were one exactly a believer either in the Bible or in *Moby-Dick*, those could be words both deeply moving and productive of deep reflection. But will the novel permit one to believe either within its boundaries? Is the good Father on Jonah not sadly undercut by the dry mock of "Jonah Historically Considered"? Where is "the great Pilot Paul" when, concerning ambergris, we are persuaded Rabelaisianly to bethink ourselves "of that saying of St. Paul in Corinthians, about corruption and incorruption . . ."? Are we not "diddled," as Melville liked to say, or "sold," as when in "Stowing Down and Clearing Up" we are insincerely invited to consider how a tried-down whale has passed "like Shadrach, Meshach and Abednego . . . unscathed through the fire"? Do not we and they all, in, sailor-talk, somehow get the Deep Six as obliviatingly as Bulkington? Where are we all by the time the *Rachel*, weeping for her lost children, looms upon the horizon? Asleep, asleep in Davy Jones's Locker where the oozy weeds about us twist?

When all the returns are in, then, there would seem to be a great deal less than first strikes the eye in Nathalia Wright's two mighty topics conjoined: Herman Melville and the Bible.

"'Ego non baptizo te in nomine patris, sed in nomine diaboli!' deliriously howled Ahab, as the malignant iron scorchingly devoured the baptismal blood." Is there something metaphysically profound here or only another bit of good, mid-nineteenth-century literary Gothicism out-Byroning Byron?

"'AND I ONLY AM ESCAPED ALONE TO TELL THEE.'—JOB" Is
there somehow here a penitent turning again of a new Jonah to Father
Mapple's moral: "'. . . it is in this disobeying ourselves, wherein the hardness
of obeying God consists'"? Or is there only another far echo of the Ancient
Mariner, of the Lone Witness device, the technical ploy for establishing a
complex, first-person eye-narrator through whom to secure a reader's willing
suspension of disbelief?

Of course the answers to these questions, which so very much more
easily put than answer themselves, may well be "both" and "neither" and "a
good deal more than you see to ask" and, finally, "but that is not the right
question." Yet somehow the impression that will not be put down is that
after the Bible has been boiled in try-pots heated in all the *Pequod's* hellfire,
what remains is at least as much antic Rabelaisianism as anything. One's
mind goes back and back to that last Melville comment of Hawthorne's
English Notebooks, recording their last good talk: "It is strange how he per-
sists—and has persisted ever since I knew him, and probably long before—
in wandering to-and-fro over these deserts. . . . He can neither believe, nor
be comfortable in his unbelief. . . ." Neither could even the greatest of his
great art.

IV

But if the late Ellen Moers was right in her contention that there were
five, not four, great American writers in the "American Renaissance," surely
her fifth, a woman with one book many people besides Moers have thought
"great," was also greatly biblical in that best book. Harriet Beecher Stowe
was a conscious, committed, churched Christian and minister's wife. The
hero of *Uncle Tom's Cabin* was designedly a black saint. How stands the
Bible there? Much less naively, more complexly and effectively, than any
connoisseur of miscast bloodhounds leaping from one fake ice-cake to
another might ever have supposed. The Beechers reared no boobs. The children were given an acute, intense training in biblical learning. From it
Stowe could and did find exactly the biblical form, not seldom sophisticated,
on which to ground every narrative structure she wished to build. *Uncle
Tom's Cabin* was not merely the one Christian serious novel of the age; it
was fascinatingly biblical.

As the late Howard Mumford Jones said with characteristic shrewdness,
Uncle Tom was rivaled among nineteenth-century fictional heroes only by
Jean Valjean of Victor Hugo's *Les Misérables* in a sort of modern hagiogra-
phy: the life of the saint who achieved total obedience to the Christian com-
mandment, "Love your enemies, bless them that curse you, do good to them
that hate you, and pray for them which despitefully use you, and persecute
you." Like Joan of Arc or John Woolman, Tom saw visions, heard voices,
found himself personally supported by a sense of the presence of Christ.

Like the martyrs of old, he won through exile, grief, abuse, terror, torture, and death by torture to "the Victory" by faith.

Everybody knows that Uncle Tom, Blessed Tom, Saint Tom became a paragon of the nonresistant, nonviolent way of the beatitudes. That knowledge has given him several kinds of bad names in our time. But what I think is not so well noticed is that much of the esthetic tension that lends power to Stowe's apprentice novel takes its rise in thorough dramatic investigations of most, if not all, of the relevant biblicisms. Taking martyred Tom as one pole of a continuum, we must see not only that George Harris—likened to St. George the Warrior at one point—stands at the opposite pole but also that there are a good many linking points on the line between.

One row of these points relates to the Tom phase of the plot and seems to anticipate Leo Tolstoy. It connects to Augustine St. Clare's picture of Jesus' healing by human touch and Augustine's memory of his mother's saying, "If we want to give sight to the blind, we must be willing to do as Christ did,—call them to us, and *put our hands on them.*" To teach this lesson of common true humanity and actual love, wild wicked Topsy is sent to plague and instruct that prismatic self-righteous hypocrite of a Vermont abolitionist and pharisaical "professor" of Christianity, Miss Ophelia. Only when she can learn to douse her pride and learn that neither cleanliness nor moralism but love *is* godliness, may Ophelia "save" Topsy—and herself.

Farther down the continuum (and of course we are skipping) comes the debate, long prepared by the narrator, between Augustine St. Clare and his planter brother Alfred about the justice and social safety of slavery. Augustine, attacking, could not have been supposed to know Woolman and does not mention Thomas Jefferson or Nat Turner. The forebodings of Woolman and Jefferson and the fact of Turner are remembered in recurrent mention of Toussaint L'Ouverture. Augustine argues, urging the same sense as Thomas Jefferson's half-reluctant query and confession in *Notes on Virginia*: ". . . can the liberties of a nation be thought secure when we have removed their only firm basis, a conviction in the minds of the people that these liberties are the gift of God? That they are to be violated but with his wrath? Indeed I tremble for my country when I reflect that God is just; that his justice cannot sleep for ever. . . ."

Pooh! pooh! scoffs Alfred. Right and wrong, God and justice have nothing to do with what is merely a matter of power. Only degenerate Frenchmen could have been done in by Toussaint. It can't happen here. To be sure, he admits, not mentioning Jefferson either, that the circumstances of slavery exert evil effects on the education of a gentleman. Perhaps a lad should be sent north to school. But danger? Pooh! Neither he nor Stowe could have guessed how soon Julia Ward Howe would set the world to sing "He is trampling out the vintage. . . ."

At quite another set of points along the continuum, within the balancing plot, stood the Quaker laborers on the underground railroad conducting the

Harrises to freedom in Canada. Yet Stowe was conscious of multiplicities among their views. Nonviolent after John Woolman's way, these Christians, again in Woolman's fashion, were decidedly not nonresistant. God-moved by "a concern," they were prepared to spend and be spent, be fined or imprisoned if caught, to suffer prejudice, injustice, even persecution for conscience' sake. But they did as they must and obeyed God, not any human. They organized, provided, and worked—well and hard—to move escapees toward the north star and freedom.

At the breakfast table of Ohio Quaker Simeon Halliday, never mind the two pistols and Bowie knife at George's belt, George Harris felt a new sensation. Reunited, among friends, with his wife and child:

> It was the first time that ever George had sat down on equal terms at any white man's table. . . . This, indeed, was a home—home,—a word that George had never known a meaning for; and a belief in God, and trust in his providence, began to circle his heart . . . the light of a living Gospel, preached by a thousand acts of love and good will. . . .

Amid such perfection, no boy, of course could be at rest:

> "Father, what if thee should get found out again?" said Simeon second, as he buttered his cake.
>
> "I should pay my fine," said Simeon, quietly.
>
> "But what if they put thee in prison?"
>
> "Couldn't thee and the mother manage the farm?" said Simeon, smiling.

By the next scene, however, the whole party finds itself in danger of ring-tailed roaring frontier-tough slave-catchers:

> "Is God on their side?" said George. . . .
>
> "Friend George," said Simeon, from the kitchen, "listen to this Psalm; it may do thee good."

It is Psalm 73 (KJV), both minatory and consoling. Simeon reads verses 2–6, concerning "the prosperity of the wicked . . . pride compasseth them about as a chain; violence covereth them as a garment. . . . They are corrupt, and speak wickedly concerning oppression. . . ."

> "Is not that the way thee feels, George?"
>
> "It is so indeed," said George. . . .
>
> "Then, hear," said Simeon.

And he reads verses 17–18, 20, 24: "Then understood I their end . . . thou castedest them down to destruction. . . . Thou shalt guide me by thy counsel, and afterwards receive me to glory. . . ." Much, very much of the Bible is agonic: good struggling, warring, oft defeated, always finally triumphant over evil. *Uncle Tom's Cabin* registers those agonies in many tonalities; and the Quaker sense of resistance, nonviolently, to the evils of human bondage is far from the most minor key.

Yet the context sets us another point yet toward the final polarity of warring George. In the community lives a "convinced" not "birthright" Friend, Phineas Fletcher, a frontiersman. Not unimaginably of the Leatherstocking, he has married into meeting, been accepted as "convinced," a convert. Yet at heart he represents the phenomenon that would, not long after Stowe's novel, turn the Philadelphia Meeting on its ear—a fighting Quaker. Whatever the elder and orthodox might say, why should one not, in all biblical tradition, be seized by a concern to take arms against Satan and all his minions and fight for what one, like Stowe, even Simeon, saw as altogether the ultimate right—freedom for the slave? If read out of meeting for flouting of the Testimony of Peace, they would (and did) form rival schismatic meetings. The Fighting Quakers even turned Hicksite, following the lead of one of Walt Whitman's personal heroes.

As matters stand on the George Harris side of *Uncle Tom's Cabin*, Phineas Fletcher has spied out the plans of slave-catchers and planned well to thwart them. It is he who finds the Harris party a refuge not unlike the Leatherstocking's hideaway at Glens Falls in *The Last of the Mohicans*. When Tom Loker, the one true "ring-tailed roarer" among the slave-catchers, has been wounded by George Harris but leaps the gap into their refuge anyway, it will be Phineas Fletcher who calmly remarks, "'Friend, thee isn't wanted here,'" and pushes him off into the "chasm" of dead trees below, where he will be impaled though not killed. For the rest of the dreadful slave-catchers, *exeunt omnes.*

Loker will be saved and nursed back to health by Quakers. The Harrises will reach Lake Erie and, in disguise, win through to Canada. Meanwhile, taken all together, George Harris's attitudes will grow from natural desperation to understanding of how the social contract principles of the American Revolution have been denied him as a slave (compare Jefferson and Augustine St. Clare). He will grasp his "inalienable rights to liberty" and reject the nugatory slave laws that would deny them to him, seize upon his rights to escape and defend himself and his God-given rights to justice by necessary force, and at last perceive not only the right but also the duty to wage a just war, even a divinely sanctioned war against evil. He will become something like a Reinhold Niebuhr neoorthodox liberal. Recognizing that warfare is a sin yet that no one can avoid sin, he will oppose righteously his lesser sin of personal violence to fight the great unforgivable sin of human enslavement to still other sinners. Who would have thought Stowe's popular book capable of such sophisticated varieties of biblical understanding?

Against slavery she was no naif, not a sentimentalist, not a crude artist (though on other grounds she was indeed sometimes all those things). Nor was she a mere lucky miniaturist of unforgettable characters (though she was sometimes that). She was a well-prepared student of the possibilities of American response to the Bible; and she had seen exactly how to make her understandings hit home. In that exact judgment she has had no parallel in fiction before or since. She was not (and knew it, whether it was patronizing or not) "the little lady who started this great big war." She was really, however, a unique American literary artist, vitally biblical.

V

Nothing comparable happened in fiction, as we know, during the war or even, in consequence of it, after the war. As Henri Peyre thought, wars as such do not make literature in their own times. Perhaps it is reactions to postwar cultural conditions that make things happen in fiction. Further, of course, the one thing we may be sure of about a war is that its outcomes will be different from any anticipated by its participants at the outset. How could the authors of "Voluntaries" or "Little Giffen" or "The Battle Hymn of the Republic" or "Charleston" have dreamed that the postwar novelists would be antiromantic scoffers at the sublime, mockers of ideality, agnostics, Darwinians, and realists—of this world, worldly? But they were, and perhaps the greatest and most typical was the infidel who could not let the Bible rest in his imagination, Samuel L. Clemens, inventor of a multiple literary instrument called Mark Twain.

Mark Twain and the Bible—nothing but a superb modesty could have led a scholar of Alison Ensor's learning to make a slim laconic volume from so rich and boundless a topic. There are no places really to start or stop except to cover the Clemens canon with a tome. But the indispensable books at which to glance are *The Innocents Abroad, Adventures of Huckleberry Finn*, and *A Connecticut Yankee in King Arthur's Court*.

Amidst our fashionable frenzy to strike through every mask, turning the reading of literature into an antiliterary game of Biographical Fallacy, Clemens presents a baffling, patently infuriating case to critics who do not care for literature. As frontispiece, the new California–Iowa first volume of juvenilia supplies a most informative portrait. From it a hard-eyed tight-mouthed ruffianly youth stares out defiantly, his right hand tilting toward the lens a huge presumably brass belt-buckle cut into huge letters proclaiming "SAM."

It is "Sam" who remains and always was the enigma. Said Howells, the most psychologically acute and intelligent of all Clemens's intimates, "He was apt to smile into your face, with a subtle but amiable perception, and yet with a sort of remote absence; you were all there for him, but he was not all there for you."

One of the major sources of Sam Clemens's success in evading comprehension was the genius with which he invented protean masks and alter egos. Though Howells signed hundreds of personal letters to him, "W. D. Howells," addressing them to "Clemens," the replies came addressed to "Howells" but signed "Mark." The reason it is too simple to say that "Mark Twain" was the invention of the literary convenience of Samuel Clemens is that there were so many markedly various Mark Twains: they were narrators, authors, thespian creations, and characters within narrations who told stories and jokes, played jokes, were fools and buffoons easily "sold." Some were sharp practitioners of the "sell" and practical joke, victims of bad luck, grief, tragedy—one could go far before exhausting the list, in part because not all of them were called "Mark Twain." But they were all personae, creations, disguises, shape-shifters. In defiance of foolish consistency they outnumbered Emerson's or Whitman's shifts of identity by a numerical landslide.

Almost all had religious sentiments and interests and knew a great deal about the Bible—often "incorrectly." Much of the "error" aimed at (and hit) comic qualms about the truth or usefulness of such matters. Though Howells, reared in a domestic Swedenborgianism, understood the issues by observation more than by experience, there was a hidden third term behind his joking equation of the American boy who was reared "to fear God and dread the Sunday School"—because that boy might turn out to be the sort of militant atheist who does not just quietly believe there is no God. He passionately hates, defies, and wars upon God. Though Clemens of course made sincere efforts to achieve peace, believe, and be reconciled, the bulk of his mockery of things biblical and religious, properly assembled, would constitute a small library. For mockery alone, he filled a late page of *Life on the Mississippi* with the following:

> How solemn and beautiful is the thought that the earliest pioneer of civilization, the van-leader of civilization, is never the steamboat, never the railroad, never the newspaper, never the Sabbath-school, never the missionary—but always whisky! Such is the case. Look history over; you will see. The missionary comes after the whisky—I mean he arrives after the whisky has arrived; next comes the poor immigrant, with axe and hoe and rifle; next the trader; next, the miscellaneous rush; next, the gambler, the desperado, the highwayman, and all their kindred in sin of both sexes; and next, the smart chap who has bought up an old grant that covers all the land; this brings the lawyer tribe; the vigilance committee brings the undertaker. All these interests bring the newspaper; the newspaper starts up politics and a railroad; all hands turn to and build a church and a jail—and behold! civilization is established forever in the land. But whisky, you see, was the van-leader in this beneficent work. It always is. It was like a foreigner—and excusable in a foreigner—to be ignorant of this great truth, and wander off into astronomy to borrow a symbol. But if he had been conversant with the facts, he would have said: Westward the Jug of Empire takes its way.

In character as *Omoo*, for instance, Melville had been verbally lynched in the religious press for far, far less a generation earlier. The times were "a-changing."

Because he was at once fundamentally developing the Mark Twain personae, because he was still not settled in the necessity of belief, because he
reported an avowed pilgrimage to a Holy Land for which, in his way, Clemens was as little prepared as any "Pilgrim," *The Innocents Abroad* may be
the most revealingly biblical of all the books he wrote. Supposing "Sam" to
have had even so little of actual experience as would (theoretically) have
sufficed for Henry James, Clemens had imagination enough to store up in
memory the artistic autobiography, or at least the highlights, of "Old Times
on the Mississippi," "The Campaign that Failed," and *Roughing It* before he
ever signed up for the *Quaker City* voyage.

Of course it matters that he actually wrote the "Sandwich Island" travel
letters before he took his pierhead jump for the Holy Land, and that the
literary experience of *The Innocents Abroad* and his part of *The Gilded
Age* had sophisticated his artistic eye before he wrote *Roughing It* and "Old
Times." How green my personae—no matter how many times he said it or
dramatized it, his American Innocent would esthetically become more artistic until it peaked out at Master Huckleberry Finn. And yet, Mr. Samuel L.
Clemens, "Sam" several times grown up, recultivated, and refined, was a
subtle, river-smart, wilderness-wise, newspaper paragrapher when he con-
tracted to go on pilgrimage. He may have been the toughest proposition
outside the stokehole.

In various shapes, the narrating "I" of the book was always one or
another "Mark Twain." His creator had wandered through certain towns as
a jour-printer, had learned to "read the river" and its folk, had seen all he
needed of war, had spent months "at the mines" with men who customarily
gave scant consideration to "what comes next." He was seasoned and had
seen the Elephant; he was no common respecter of persons; and he knew a
surprising lot about the Bible. Concentrated study, if only for "copy," during
the trip would teach him much about the book and about its professed
American believers, his compatriots. Clemens had already mastered, as
Howells said paraphrasing Hamlet, the stops of that simple instrument, man.

Really three lines of narrative perception govern the use of the Bible
in *The Innocents Abroad*: the representative pious pilgrim was a faithful
chucklehead—a fatheaded egotist, braggart, self-romancer, vandal and
brute, a religious swindle. To keep his balance, "Mark Twain" had to adapt
two familiar antiromantic techniques to keep from drowning amid the patent
evidences of hypocrisy that kept rolling toward him in waves of disillusion. It
was requisite "to begin a system of reduction." He had to learn that only the
false lights of night, reverie, and memory could preserve either romance or
religious faith. Testing their material reality against the falsehoods of tradition,
like perceiving them by the light of common day, destroyed both.

It was the same as with Venice or Leonardo's *Last Supper*. Moonlight
saved Venice. Only make-believe could save Leonardo's masterpiece. "Night,"
he found, "is the time to see Galilee." The sight of Gennesaret "under these

lustrous stars" *almost* "makes me regret that I ever saw the rude glare of the day upon it. . . . But when the day is done, . . . the old traditions of the place" steal upon one's "memory and haunt his reveries, and then his fancy clothes all sights and sounds with the supernatural":

> In the starlight, Galilee has no boundaries but the broad compass of the heavens, and is a theater meet for great events: meet for the stately Figure appointed to stand upon its stage and proclaim its high decrees. But in the sunlight, one says: Is it for the deeds which were done and the words which were spoken in this little acre of rocks and sands eighteen centuries gone, that the bells are ringing today in the remote isles of the sea and far and wide over continents that clasp the circumference of the globe?

At Esdraelon, "the magic of the Moonlight is a vanity and a fraud; and whoso putteth his trust in it shall suffer sorrow and disappointment."

Almost resistlessly, the Mark Twain reader's imagination is first thrown back upon the imagined autobiography and the pages on learning "to read the river" in "Old Times on the Mississippi." To the eye of the "uneducated passenger," who cannot read its book but only gaze ignorantly at the illustrations, one marvelously painted "certain wonderful sunset" presented nothing "but all manner of pretty pictures." To the eye trained to read the text, read the river, however, "these were not pictures at all but the grimmest and most dead-earnest of readin; matter." Not only were "all the romance and beauty . . . all gone from the river," all the loveliest features of the sunset picture bespoke menace. A right reading of the river became tragic.

In a fascinating turn, the features Hawthorne fixed upon as the peculiar privileges of the romancer inverted themselves for Clemens. If by the manipulation of "the atmospherical medium" Hawthorne achieved romance and ideality, the truth of the human heart, Clemens saw truth the other way around. In "romance and beauty" lay fatal falsehood. "The magic of moonlight" was not the ground of faith in ideality for the artist of the beautiful. It was "vanity and a fraud," the *ignis fatuus* lighting a path to "sorrow and disappointment."

So matters surely turn out among the *Adventures of Huckleberry Finn.* Miss Watson's hellfire Presbyterianism is "a vanity and a fraud." Christian "sivilization" turns out murderous chuckleheads among the feuding Christian gentry, camp-meeting suckers for the king, sensation-hungry softheads, lynch mobs, yearning for "soul-butter and hogwash" around Mary Jane Wilks and intellectually feeble nearly up to the level of Sancho Panza in Uncle Silas Phelps. Such is the self-proclaimed core of a "sivilization" that would apply to Miss Watson's Jim, a true man, the consequences of what had been Stowe's original subtitle: "The Man Who Was A Thing." Blessed are the poor in heart . . .

Though it is really clear enough in the text, the effect in *A Connecticut Yankee in King Arthur's Court* of Dan Beard's wonderful illustrations has such power of impact it is not really the same book without them. Now at last we get the whole point of Huck Finn's little reflection, "Sometimes I wish we could hear of a country that's out of kings." We remember with a start that it was against cross and crown—established church and hereditary monarchy—that Americans revolted. The one hand washes the other; but they are institutional, not biblical. Certain ironies militating against callousness, cruelty, deprivation, exploitation, terror, real and manipulative superstition contrast with Christian charity. But after the interdiction and after the triumph of technology in surrounding the boss and his boys with a ring of putrid death, what is left? Only, a while later, the superb brilliant ironies of "To the Person Sitting in Darkness." In Christian—in *American, democratic, Christian*—civilization, the peoples sitting in darkness have seen a great light of fraud. After that, what? Only the great dark.

VI

To cure part of his series of adolescent neurotic breakdowns, Howells was deliberately set by his father to reading George Eliot's translation of Strauss's *Leben Jesu* in order to liberate him from an oppressive supersition. Though the boy had, in the isolated family Swedenborgianism, certainly not learned to "dread the Sunday School," that same father had instructed him at the hearth in religion. Howells's subsequent lifelong religious equations shifted through many phases. Though they have never been carefully studied, there would always be at one pole a yearning will to believe balanced at the opposite by a necessary agnosticism.

Nevertheless, as a creative artist Howells commanded the Bible subtly and exactly and used it for fine effects. As I long ago pointed out, the imagery and allusiveness of the realist tend to point inward, intensifying the organic effect, not outward toward truths of the human heart or humanity's place among ultimate verities.

Sharing something of the James family's denominational alienation from the mainstream of the religious culture, having experienced his father's therapy of doubt, Howells also was to meet the force of the "Victorian Dilemma" more directly than Clemens or James. Cambridge associates like James Russell Lowell, Charles Eliot Norton, John Fiske, and "The Club" of local intellectuals held him in constant contact with "the newness." Reviewing for the *Atlantic Monthly* had him handling tens and dozens of the great current controversial books. He became so to take nonbelief for granted that, just after he had resigned from the *Atlantic* and was out walking near Florence one afternoon with a group of writers and other artists, it would "strike him like a blow," he said, to realize that there were literate men of his own generation who were serene, firm believers.

Nevertheless, with a memory perhaps at least as retentive as Clemens's, Howells knew much of the Bible, as he did the poets, by heart. And whatever the relevance, to the end of his life he kept the agnostic yearning to believe. Tolstoy almost converted him—but not quite. Howells wished to join the Episcopalian Church of the Carpenter, begun for the working poor in the slums of Boston, but he was compelled to leave in irrevocable revulsion the first time the rector celebrated the Eucharist.

Though he wrote striking religious poems, perhaps the finest moment of his biblicism came at the climax of his best-known novel, *The Rise of Silas Lapham*. His theme was the story of Jacob. Unless one has powerful faculties of recall, a reader will have to rework Howells's text at least a second time to see how subtly the novel has handled its Jacob theme. Like Jacob with Esau, Silas Lapham fell into the trap of the usurper, the supplanter. Before the presented action of the novel, Silas, needing capital to develop Lapham's Mineral Paint, had taken an inept financier as a partner. Just as the business began to go well, he had forced Rogers out—an ancient trick.

Technically, that is, Rogers had not been swindled; he got his money back, with some profit. But the ancient business sarcasm had been fulfilled: when my partner and I began together, I had the money and he the experience; when we broke up, he had the money and I had the experience. In a real, and therefore moral, sense, Silas had become a millionaire by "using" his partner. He usurped Rogers's part of the chance to make a million.

Though we are told that Mrs. Lapham has not a live religion but a genetic habit of Puritan conscience instead, Persis can give Silas no rest about Rogers. Early in the novel she nags at him, using language too specifically allusive to be (for the novel) inadvertent. "You had made that paint your god," she scolds Silas, "and you couldn't bear to let anybody else share in its blessings." It was, of course the paternal "blessing" of blind, dying Isaac, the right of the firstborn son, which Jacob had usurped from Esau by fraud.

Persis's trick of language would have little significance were it not that later, at the moral climax of the novel, her mind would suddenly clear to tell itself (and the novel) what lay at the next level down in her preconscious mind. Now we see that the text has played a game almost worthy of a Brahms—who will, apparently inadvertently, quote once and again in the middle of quite another symphonic development a theme around which at last he will build a climax.

Toward the end of the novel, Silas Lapham, solid man, fighting soldier, captain of industry, and patron of his people, has fallen low. Bad judgment, gambling on stocks, economic depression, the rise of a dangerous competition, the loss of fiscal fluidity—a mass of business hard luck and poor judgment— have brought him down. Personally he is isolated, his wife alienated by a moment of stupid baseless jealousy, his daughters bewildered in a maze of feminine romanticism, and Rogers at him to save himself and Rogers from ruin by palming off at a price that would save him a parcel of worthless western land to a team of cheap confidence men looking for an ideal setup with which to swindle an immensely wealthy English philanthropy. Shall Silas fall forever into mere scoundrelism or can he rise from the pit, recovering his soul at the price of his fortune?

All night he walks the floor, brooding, fighting the world and the self. As he paces, Persis, self-isolated, lies awake and listens and suffers doubly. At last, the narrator tells us:

> But when the first light whitened the window, the words of the Scripture came into her mind: "And there wrestled a man with him until the breaking of the day. . . . And he said, Let me go, for the day breaketh. And he said, I will not let thee go, except thou bless me."

One needs to know more scripture and be alert to its implications and reflections to get the full force of the allusion, however. There is a great deal more than wrestling till daybreak in the Genesis narrative. It is the story of Peniel, of the reconciliation of Jacob with God as well as Esau, and the reverberations of what the narrator does not relate about the scripture dominate, indeed unify, the climax of the novel.

The sound reader needed to be able to move both backward and forward in the Bible story to get the point. Justly frightened, Jacob was advancing toward the reconciliation with Esau that the Lord had commanded. What he found was, in Old Testament history, a reconciliation with God that preserved the line of the heavenly promise to Abraham and his seed. Just before the lines Persis's inner monologue supplied, the verse says, "And Jacob was left alone." In the novel's ellipsis, Gen 33:25 says, "And when he saw that he prevailed not against him, he touched the hollow of his thigh, and the hollow of Jacob's thigh was out of joint, as he wrestled with him."

After the demand for the blessing to break off the match, the text goes on:

> And he said unto him, what is thy name?
>
> And he said, Jacob.
>
> And he said, Thy name shall be called no more Jacob, but Israel: for as a prince has thou power with God and men, and hast prevailed. . . .
>
> And Jacob called the place Peniel: for I have seen God face to face, and my life is preserved.
>
> And as he passed over Peniel the sun rose upon him, and he halted upon his thigh.

Saved, crippled, restored to himself, reconciled to God and his brother, Jacob becomes a complex type-model for Silas. For not letting go into "rascality," Silas's reward is to "feel" guilty but *be* himself again. Then he can squarely resist the temptation to let an incautious would-be purchaser of the business buy without knowing its true condition. Then he can return to the common order of simple, real men. Deliverance from the pit is the rise of Silas Lapham.

There is, however, another perhaps even more important order of moral insight in *Lapham* with which Silas as a type of Jacob connects. The unavoidable "love interest" of the novel takes place between Silas's daughters and Tom Corey, a fine Boston gentleman. With a revolutionary feminism, the novel has Tom in love with brunette, bookish, witty, saucy, defiant, intelligent Penelope, who thinks for herself—in fiction a traditional, conventional feminine menace. Everybody but Tom thinks convention must reign and Tom love ravishing blonde Irene, who knows nothing and wouldn't like it if her mind found two ideas to rub against each other. When the truth outs, Penelope, true to the conventions of the romances she, like everybody, reads, feels that she must "sacrifice" herself for Irene, making everybody miserable.

When the parents go to the Reverend Mr. Sewell for pastoral advice, Sewell says what an embattled realist would have him say, ". . . we are all blinded, we are all weakened by a false ideal of self-sacrifice," which must come "from the novels that befool and debauch almost every intelligence in some degree." But he concludes in words that express, in one of Howells's most memorable phrases, one of Howells's important ideas. Among the three young people, he suggests, it is mere good sense that "one suffer instead of three, if none is to blame. . . . It's the economy of pain which naturally suggests itself, and which would insist upon itself . . ." were we not all "perverted" with "sentimentality."

At bottom it is for "the economy of pain" that Silas wrestles with his angel, sacrificing his idolatry of "that paint," his pride in success. He will not see the English philanthropists or the poor they seek to rescue hurt. He will not join in "that easy-going, not evilly intentioned, immorality which regards common property as common prey, and gives us the most corrupt municipal governments under the sun—which makes the poorest voter, when he has tricked into place, as unscrupulous in regard to others' money as an hereditary prince." But of course he would thereafter limp, no "prince" but a common true man recovered of his true self, forever crippled by his fight to rise again to himself.

Though Howells, if less strikingly, would to the end work in his own realistic mode biblically, I cannot seem to see that Henry James ever even unconsciously did so. Surely the ideas of, for instance, "The Beast in the Jungle" and *The Wings of the Dove* can be taken to be Christian. They seem to be "father's ideas," for instance the ideas of Henry James, Sr.'s *Society the Redeemed Form of Man*, humanized by agnosticism. As such they, like other Jamesian ideas, are profoundly instructive. But they seem somehow utterly "postbiblical." If Henry James himself knew the Bible, it seems seldom to appear that his art knew it. Neither his imagining eye nor composing ear seems biblical. To them "religion" seems as alien as it was to Gibbon. It might be argued that, among other things, it was from biblicism that Henry James had disciplined himself to be liberated, modernized.

The imaginably "biblical" in James seems absent-minded, accidental, perhaps even designed as a false scent. A typical case might be his title *The*

Golden Bowl. It has, of course, a good biblical source, possibly. The difficulty, as Conrad remarked about another matter, is "to see the relevance."
The biblical source could be Eccl 12:6. The governing context is "Remember
now thy Creator in the days of thy youth, while the evil days come not. . . ."
Thereafter "evil days" are poetically characterized:

> . . . and desire shall fail: because man goeth to his long home, and
> the mourners go about the streets: Or ever the silver cord be loosed,
> or the golden bowl be broken, or the pitcher be broken at the
> fountain, or the wheel be broken at the cistern. Then shall the dust
> return to the earth as it was. . . .

It is profoundly poetic, this dirge; but to the actual James novel, if Ecclesias-
tes supplied the title, one can see no relevance. Neither does any suggestion
in James's *Notebooks* hint at its biblical relevance.

VII

Significant literary periods go by historical accident—a war, a reign, a
political revolution. Or they go by decades or moments, or by generations or
by schools—by whatever serves to lend significant shape to sets of relationships. In terms of the significant events, hardly any decade appears more
chaotic than the American 1890s, though valiant efforts to shape these years
into form have been made by able scholars.

Perhaps as significant an anomaly as any in the serious work of the "new"
novelists of the decade—Hamlin Garland, Abraham Cahan, Kate Chopin,
Stephen Crane, Harold Frederic, Frank Norris—is the displacement of the
Bible from the serious novel by the romance of reform or the utopia or by
"pop" religion like that of *In His Steps*. But what does it signify? Offhand, one
could expect *The Damnation of Theron Ware* to be a happy hunting ground
for significant biblical reference. It is nothing of the kind. What stands out is
that the novel will use anything that comes to hand—scraps of Catholic liturgy,
the Methodist Discipline, tags of theological controversy, scientism, bits and
pieces of old hymns—anything to suggest the inapplicability of such
flummeries to the novel's reality principle. The latter is political, power-
minded, business-minded, concerned with the mystiques of institutional force
and the petty cynicism of minding the main chance. Heuristically, the mind of
the novel could be said to have been reading Herbert Spencer, William
Graham Sumner, Edward Tylor and James Frazer, Robertson Smith and
Andrew Lang, eventually Thorstein Veblen.

The Damnation of Theron Ware is rooted in Theron's simplicity and
gullibility. He is a sort of 1890s Candide. He is not of this present world—
with the usual results. But the novel had its eye on "religion," on "institutions," a world of vast menacing currents of force in which only the cynic
swims long or well. Religion, says "savvy" Sister Soulsby, the evangelist, is
only "emotion." She and Brother Soulsby "get saved" again every time.

Otherwise, their act would flop.

Among all their totally different worlds, much the same would seem true of Cahan's *Yekl*, who is a survivor, and the heroine of Kate Chopin's *The Awakening* or the hero of Frank Norris's *McTeague*, who are not. We feel the altogether inhuman might, the mainly inscrutable mystery of the forces, the tears of things in the helplessness of persons. But among the many forces God is absent, and nobody really thinks of or by the Book. I do not think I am talking of "naturalism" or pegging a time after which the biblical would not be heard again in the American novel. We know better. But for the moment, at least, there is a strange hiatus. It would be especially strange if Frank Norris had been right in his contention that just then the novel had displaced the pulpit, the press, and all other competitors and become "the Great Bow of Ulysses," to string and wield which was irresistibly to control American public opinion. When very young, Norris permitted himself a number of such large fancy generalizations.

Perhaps the situation of the Bible in the novel of the nineties becomes most interesting in the fiction of the one meteor whose passage was wholly confined to the decade—the preacher's kid, Stephen Crane. He wrote in overtly biblical rhythm and diction when engaged (or lapsed) in what he himself thought the tomfoolery of his "clever Rudyard Kipling" style, early renounced. Otherwise the texture of his prose, with colorations all its own, is perhaps deliberately nonbiblical.

Beyond that, the major fiction reveals perspectives of thought and feeling which one can hardly suppose not to have roots in the preacher's kid's perception that the unassailable position of revolt against his family, with all its yearnings for Christianity and gentility, condemned itself by contrast with the simple love, humility, self-sacrifice, self-abnegation, and trust of a pure primitive Christianity. Though he could not presume to claim such things for himself, it was all too plain that "Christianity as it may be seen about town" could claim no more; and it bore the onus of hyprocrisy to boot. One was entitled to have "no opinion of it." Crane felt "obliged" to preserve the "blasphemy" of *The Black Riders*. You could feel the power of Crane's demurral by seeing that in effect it required the adoption of the primitive Christianity of Uncle Tom by the world of Augustine St. Clare. The irony was radical, liberating, altogether tragic.

There is no denying Daniel Hoffman's contention in *The Poetry of Stephen Crane* that one finds the artist's own religious insights. From the realists he had learned that it was never the business of a novelist to preach. The business of a novel was to provide its reader a true use of the eyes; the aim at last was a revelation achieved by the reader's newly aligned vision. The revelation toward which his novels typically direct us is that a life run counter to pure Christian principle—a life like his own—exposes itself to withering tragic irony because it is selfish and cowardly.

Though the terrible ironies of *Maggie* center on everyone's directing the innocent, "Ah, go teh hell," and condemning her when she has done as they made her, nothing overt is made even of that climax in which the fearful dragon of a mother, bearing the common sacred name "Mary," screams, "I'll fergive her." It is only there for us to see. Likewise, nothing undramatic is made of the reductive contrast between the implied Christian pacifism of Fleming's mother and the endless follies of Private Fleming, his several battles. In *The Red Badge of Courage* as in *Maggie*, little or nothing of the textures is overtly biblical. If there is a revelation in either or both that might lead a triumphant reader to reflect curiously back to implications biblical (among other things) at several removes, perhaps the artist has won his game.

VIII

The trouble with a truism is commonly not that it is false so much as that there is nothing much you can do with it. Such is the case with the truism that American speechways and prose, and therefore the writing, of the nineteenth century tended to be saturated with rhythms, locutions, and imagery from the King James Version of the Bible. The like held for given names, significant or not, allusions to parables and biblical narratives, quotations, misquotations, comic variations, even travesties—great and small—of scripture. The homelier the author, the likelier and more various the fiction's biblicisms. The condition could be more radical than that which disappointed the mythical sophomore: Shakespeare, he found, was "just a collection of old clichés."

There comes, therefore, a point of diminishing returns beyond which panning for diffused, golden biblicisms in the novels ceases to find enough "color" to pay for the day's work. One needs to look for those veins or pockets where the real paydirt lies. And that will be only in the serious novel. Otherwise, there glitters fool's gold enough in the mountains of bygone best sellers, many of which were to the nineteenth century as *The Day of Doom* was to the seventeenth century or *The Robe* to ours. When you do find real gold in the serious novel, however, you have a treasure of wisdom.

And yet there is really in the serious novel of the nineteenth century shockingly little of the real thing. Was the Bible a major living force and presence in that novel? I am not sure the affirmative could be proved (a surprise to me). And that leads to the question whether one should have expected to find so very much. Are the novel and the Bible quite compatible? It can be argued that in fact they are not.

It seems to me almost self-evidently true (after he has argued the point), as Reynolds Price says in *A Palpable God*, that narrative like biblical narrative is a means to bring home to the human heart through the imagination the sense of the transcendent, the ineffable. A brilliant insight for certain kinds of narrative, perhaps, on the other hand, it does not quite apply to the imagination that wrote the nineteenth-century American novel, or even romance. American art came late and obliquely to the Atlantic community phases of Western culture. To change focus for an instant, it may be true that the American imagination works better with human and secular than with heroic and sacramental dimensions of life. The possibility distressed Tocqueville. As I have argued elsewhere, not the *Iliad*, the epic and its major phase, but the mock-heroic and its reductive phase, as in the *Batrachomyomachia*, suited American fiction. The Bible, with its vision of supernal warfare in history and the divine victory when time shall have a stop and humanity enter upon eternity, is nothing if not heroic, transcendent. Perhaps the fiction of the American nineteenth century fitted most readily the nongenteel, as in Natty Bumppo, or the rebellious, as in Hester Prynne or Ishmael. Perhaps it felt most at home with "ornery" folks like Silas Lapham, Huck Finn, Hank Morgan, Maggie Johnson, Theron Ware, Henry Fleming, or McTeague. That novel smacks of democratic, secular ages. It brings "oneself, . . . a simple separate person," home to the human heart, alone. Having done that, it gives the heart to think that it is human, common, not alone. Then it may "utter the word . . . Democratic": the word? Community.

III

The Bible and Twentieth-Century American Fiction

Rowland A. Sherrill

In the course of a tirelessly bitter indictment of modern Western life, only apparently aimed at the rise of Nazism, Katherine Anne Porter's *Ship of Fools* (1962) occasionally relents in its fierce misanthropic abstractions to touch briefly on a character in whom the reader can see some human dimension. For one such moment, the narrative enters the decent consciousness of Schumann, the doctor of the ship, but finds even in him Porter's sense of the toll of modern experience:

> a confusion so dark he could no longer tell the difference between the invader and the invaded, the violator and the violated, the betrayer and the betrayed, and the one who hated or who jeered or was indifferent. The whole great structure built upon the twin pillars of justice and love, which reached from the earth into eternity, by which the human soul rose step by step from the most rudimentary concepts of good and evil . . . this tower was now crumbling and falling around him. . . .

Schumann's abrupt transformation of his personal confusion into an abstract cultural crisis, itself in turn enlarged to range metaphysically "from the earth into eternity," might jar the twentieth-century reader no longer accustomed to talk in any but chimerical ways about the groping of "the human soul," but for all its possibly histrionic character the doctor's confusion has the effect of forcing a recollection of the great modernist era—the generation of Yeats, Pound, Eliot, Joyce—and its sense of immediacy about the moral and spiritual dissolution of Western civilization into a "waste-land" of empty values, dessicated or vicious sensibilities, fragmented or fascist social and political orders, and truncated or vacuous traditions. Yeats's anarchic "Horses of Disaster" seemed stampeding through contemporary history, and the grip of futility had seized the heart.

And no matter how forced and contrived Dr. Schumann's emotional reaching might appear, his metaphor for the foundation of the crumbling tower of civilization—"the twin pillars"—also calls particular attention to the modern sensation that the old biblical truths, the stories in the Hebrew Bible and the New Testament of "justice and love," could no longer support the vast and frequently distorted architecture that the history of Judeo-Christian culture had piled upon them. Indeed, by the time of the arrival of the twentieth century, that history itself seemed to have rendered obsolete the substance of the experience of ancient Israel and early Christianity. The force and impact of nineteenth-century science, founded on evolving rational and empirical modes, had deeply eroded faith in the supernatural events that finally made the sacred text coherent, and the philosophies and religions of secularism, albeit under other names, had marched forward to replace such superstition with more tangible and durable meanings and explanations. For those in whom even the *crisis* of faith persisted, the horrors of World War I seemed the final and conclusive evidence: if there were a God, his provident hand had been withdrawn to permit human history to play out its chaotic and destructive course. The God of the Bible—and the book itself—belonged to an antique moment in history during which humanity could find solace in such "primitive" answers. Indeed, the very way of the "new" culture of approaching its own history—the aim of historicism to see the past "as it really was" (*wie es eigentlich gewesen ist*)—stripped the Bible even of the relevance of its mythic and metaphorical hold on the truth by promoting a sense of the sheer pastness of the past and its radical discontinuity with the present.

Whether a lamented victim of or a conscious sacrifice to the flow of history, then, the Bible, the book at the sources of the Western tradition, had taken on deeply problematical status in early twentieth-century culture, even in the United States which, as Alexis de Tocqueville had seen so clearly in his *Democracy in America* (1835), had cut the fabric of its cultural, social, and political cloth on a decisively biblical pattern of values. As early as the first decade of the century, one who had come of age in the central warp and woof of the culture was worried in *The Education of Henry Adams* (1907) that the Dynamo, with all its thermodynamic potential, had replaced the Virgin at the symbolic center of cultural history and that cultural change, with all its inchoate rapidity, was somehow out of control or was, at least, beyond anyone's capacity to keep pace.

Given this cultural vista in the early part of the century, which would seem largely unrelieved in its general senses of loss and confusion by the following decades of wars, depression, and social unrest—indeed, given the fact that a "voice" of the public culture like *Time* magazine could muse about "the death of God" in the middle 1960s—readers might have been at least mildly surprised as late as 1971 to encounter the set of questions that opens Walker Percy's *Love in the Ruins*:

> Now in these dread latter days of the old violent beloved U.S.A. and of the Christ-forgetting Christ-haunted death-dealing Western world I came to myself in a grove of young pines and the question came to me: has it happened at last?
>
> Is it that God has at last removed his blessing from the U.S.A. and what we feel now is just the clank of the old historical machinery, the sudden jerking ahead of the roller-coaster cars as the

chain catches hold and . . . carries us out and up toward the brink from that felicitous and privileged siding where even unbelievers admitted that if it was not God who blessed the U.S.A., then at least some great good luck had befallen us . . . ?

The fear of impending catastrophe in Thomas More, Percy's protagonist, is finally drafted into the service of other designs in the novel, of course, but its expression testifies vividly to a trait of persistence in the American mind in construing American experience in extraordinary terms even after the tides of modernity have washed over it. More's reference to the "God who blessed the U.S.A." quickly retrieves the mythic and symbolic vocabulary of an earlier American conception of the country as an elected nation, a chosen people, built on the biblical narratives of ancient Israel and the metaphors of "the new convenant." Even for "unbelievers," the bright promises of American life, though largely unfulfilled, could frequently be retained in the face of that modern experience which seemed only to interrupt and not to nullify an immense divine and ameliorative "plan" for the nation. Twentieth-century novels like *Love in the Ruins* and F. Scott Fitzgerald's *The Great Gatsby* (1925), Robert Penn Warren's *All the King's Men* (1946), John Steinbeck's *Grapes of Wrath* (1939), Norman Mailer's *An American Dream* (1964), and Thomas Pynchon's *The Crying of Lot-49* (1966) possess what are surely more covert or circuitous reflections on the religious meaning of America than their great nineteenth-century predecessors like *The Scarlet Letter* and *Moby-Dick*, and, in their indirect and perhaps grimmer meditations on the symbols of covenant, destiny, and redemption, their authors might be thought to have suffered something of that loss of "the immediacy of belief" in symbols in general which Paul Ricoeur identifies at the heart of "the distress of modernity" (351–52). Possibly only a "haunting" of American culture by its earlier monomythic version of itself, its biblically anchored "myth" and "symbol" so decisive in those earlier centuries studied by Sacvan Bercovitch (1975, 1978), this continuity of concern in twentieth-century American fiction has nonetheless barely been disguised in many works.

But even in those fictions that are less intent on deciphering the religious meaning of America in terms of their particular drives, the presence of the Bible has frequently proved a force. The titles alone of many works— Steinbeck's *East of Eden* (1952), Porter's *Pale Horse, Pale Rider* (1939), Fitzgerald's *This Side of Paradise* (1920), William Faulkner's *Go Down, Moses* (1942), Nathanael West's *The Day of the Locust* (1939), James Agee's "documentary," *Let Us Now Praise Famous Men* (1941), James Baldwin's "letters," *The Fire Next Time* (1963), Ernest J. Gaines's *In My Father's House* (1978), Shirley Ann Grau's *The Keepers of the House* (1964)—begin to convey something of the extent to which American authors have continued in this century to imagine the forms and substances of the experience represented in their fictions in terms of figures, ideas, and images, even phrases, derived from the Bible and the apocryphal literature.

Thus, without any cataloguing of the biblical models on which a large number of recent fictional characters are constructed or without any pointing toward the biblical sources of the epigraphical materials with which many novels "open," the point seems nonetheless clear that the Bible remains a sizable reservoir of images and stories for the contemporary American writer. American books, fictions, often urge the reader backward to what still seems *the* Book and cast their imaginative renditions of experience in terms of what seem yet regarded as the paradigmatic models the Book contains. If the results of such a tendency reveal in general only the painful discrepancy between the perceptions of life in the "Biblical *Epos* and [those in the] Modern Narrative," as Amos Niven Wilder has argued, the point remains that the Bible stands even in the twentieth century as a discernible element in the American literary tradition.

Literary study performs a real service, of course, when it delineates the ways in which this or that literary character is presented as a "Christ figure" (for instance, Ziolkowski) or the ways in which literary themes—creation, sinfulness, redemption, and so on—have their roots in the ideas of biblical theology (for instance, Hoffman, Killinger, Brooks) and when, with these accounts, it is able to trace out those lines of literary continuity and change between ancient text and contemporary narrative. For critics to size up the necessities of modern storytelling of coherent and meaningful patterns of articulation and to demonstrate how, in the inchoate welter of modern experience, such patterns in fiction are sometimes hinged in a vital way on biblical narratives counts as an important matter as well. Or, again, it has been significant for criticism to follow out the literary artist's search for a "world" held in common with his or her auditors—a crucially important matter for the purposes of communication, but made more crucial still by the withering effect of modern epistemologies on any such notion of a "shared world"—and to find how, for twentieth-century American writers, this "world" of mutual perception, when it can be located at all, is informed frequently by biblical material and imagery. In these and other ways, then, literary criticism benefits an understanding of the literary role and significance of the Bible for the novelist in our time.

It would be a mistake, however, to think that the continuing forceful life of the Bible for the twentieth-century American writer has been or is now exclusively, or even most importantly, a matter of its strictly literary properties or a matter of the ways, as a literary document, it aids novelists in answering only to the technical requirements of their craft. Although it would be quite wrong to underestimate these matters, the great modern temptation of criticism has been to calculate the presence of the Bible—when indeed it has even been interested in that matter—only in this way. That is, it has most ordinarily been viewed only as a literary work that stands as a literary storehouse of profound themes, colorful and dramatic figures, and serious events, serving something like the same function for the modern writer in these respects as, for instance, Plutarch's *Lives* and Holingshed's *Chronicles* served for Shakespeare's dramatic art.

Such approaches and the understanding they can yield need to be completed by a fuller comprehension of the deeper decisiveness of the Bible in framing those modes of perception and the forms of consciousness and articulation stemming from them, with which the writer meets and imagines the terms for establishing coherence and meaning in the modern world of experience. No one would want to make the vast claim that the perceptions, beliefs, and values of all modern American writers have been determined by biblical theology or by any subsequent formulations deriving from it. Any such claim would flatly repudiate that complex entangled modern history which in so many respects distances the ancient text from the modern moment especially for those, the writers, whose vocation by its very nature charges them to practice the keenest alertness to the shape and tenor of contemporary experience. Nor would one be inclined to suggest that, whatever the fate of the Bible as a "sacred text," the derivative myths and symbols of the American public imagination keep the writers of the country steadfast and unwavering in a simplistic patriotism on these national items of belief. Any such suggestion would refuse the necessary distinction between the "world" of public perception and the "worlds" of imaginative literature—the former socially constructed as "reality," the latter individually expressed as "possibility."

Still, averting these erroneous claims and suggestions, it can be said that the Bible has figured as an influential and effectual presence for twentieth-century American writers in fulfilling the modern requirements facing narrative art and that its deepest influence for our writers has been much less in its character as a reservoir of timeless religious truths, as a storehouse of literary figures and allusions, or as the cloth out of which the pattern of American culture was cut than in its giving examples of some stable ways of understanding and representing experience even in the midst of the bewildering complexities of the modern situation. The Bible supplies the modern writer in a great many instances with modes—prophetic, apocalyptic, parabolic, and so on—for understanding life in history which surely have a different character when that history is no longer viewed as *Heilsgeschichte* but which, nonetheless, answer formally at least to the challenges our modernity presents both to our ways of understanding reality and, thus, to our senses of what is possible for the art of the novel. What follows in the discussion here, then, is an exploration—necessarily in general terms—of the ways in which twentieth-century American novels represent the terms, conditions, and possibilities of their imaginative worlds continuously with some biblical modes in narrative and to suggest how the perceptions and valuations resident in those modes, now used in narrative reflection on contemporary experience, begin to sustain the novelist in wrestling with problems of coherence and meaning in the modern legacy.

The Diminution of the Individual and the Form of Parable

The rise of mass and totalitarian societies in the twentieth century has been one of its most distinctive characteristics, as Hannah Arendt and others have demonstrated, and the corollary erosion of the uniqueness and significance of the individual man or woman has entered the scene as a decided malaise of modernity. Whether the singular man or woman has ever possessed a full sense of his or her importance and meaning is much less to the point here than the prevalent sensation in the twentieth century that the general, corporate, mass, or state life has diminished the individual in favor of the group, the personal effort in favor of the team, the unique action in favor of conformity, the private in favor of the public. And the whelming odds against the "self" experienced by modern people have not only cost a loss of personal esteem, not only sapped a sense of effectual personal decision and action in the single man or woman, but also have resulted in both a lack of commitment to ideas of personal involvement and accountability in the public realm and a general attitude of what Rollo May terms "affectlessness," the feeling that one cannot affect others, cannot make a difference, cannot matter. The distinctiveness of each person is buried by bureaucracy or blurred in the computer; the effort of a personal decision is obliterated in the anonymity of the row house or the subdivision; the sphere of individual importance is annihilated in the swirl of the urban throng; the movement, meaning, and implication of a single life are lost in the long dance of history. Disconnected from the larger patterns of life, at least at the level of feeling, the modern man or woman suffers anxiety, loneliness, and emptiness—the most severe diminution of personal, individual life—in the midst of the crowd.

One form of biblical discourse, the parable, brims over with notions of the importance of individual life. In the kinds of figures, situations, objects, and styles the New Testament parables draw on, there is the implication that, abundant as life is with interpretive possibilities, each aspect of it is valuable and significant not only for didactic purposes but also in and of itself in relation to more encompassing patterns of meaning in moral and eschatological terms. The attitudes toward experience conveyed in the parables of Jesus, quite apart from the heuristic and allegorical uses the narratives are finally able to render, disclose senses of certain convictions resident in or assumed by the form: the distinctiveness of individual lives, however usually ordinary; the significance of personal and daily situations, however normally mundane; the value, range, and effect of single motives and actions, however apparently isolated. Although the gospel writers' conceptions of the parables tend to differ slightly, what seems consistent for the most part among them as literary forms of teaching are the ideas that an experience, isolated in narrative form, contains metaphorical meaning even when the "truth" of it needs to be puzzled out and that the truth of an individual experience is ranged, as it were, on a larger truth about the kingdom of God which encompasses all experience. In this regard, the New Testament parables open outward in their briefer formal thrusts toward longer narratives of the Hebrew Bible like the stories of Job and of Abraham and Isaac, stories that stand in literary conception as self-contained dramas whose concerns are with individuals in their situations but whose meanings can only finally be settled in the larger context of the Yahwistic vision. But if the particular figure or object or situation at the center of attention of the parable achieves importance mainly in terms of larger lessons to be taught and learned, the importance of that figure or situation remains, nonetheless, without diminution because the story of his life, his situation, somehow embodies the lesson, pushes him forward out of anonymity, no matter how temporarily, and seizes on his significance to place him in touch with the general scheme of existence.

Although the overtly didactic impulse of the ancient parable would not hold up under the confusions of modernity, which place great pressures on narrative art, and although the larger circumscribing visions for the parables of the New Testament and the unitary dramas of the Hebrew Bible do not now prove sustaining in general for modern writers, the broad commitments with respect to the nature and dynamics of experience, which are implicit in these biblical literary modes, nonetheless make a guarded reappearance in twentieth-century American fictions, frequently submerged just beneath the surface of their reflections on contemporary secular experience. The persistence of these commitments in twentieth-century fiction no doubt involves a complex symbiosis of cultural factors—including the rise of the middle class, the democratic celebration of common humanity, the appearance of modern psychological science—but what is important here is that these factors have been absorbed into the evolution of the fictional genres in a way that makes one stripe of those genres insistently resonant with ancient parabolic discourse, especially in its efforts to discern the metaphorical shape and significance of the ordinary life of the individual man or woman and to measure that life on some larger scale of meaning.

The various forms of these modern parables have the effect finally of emphasizing or proposing different thrusts that belong to the parabolic mode, but twentieth-century American fictions of this type consistently suggest—in both selection of subject and adoption of style—that the stories of ordinary people in their secular circumstances might contain pattern and meaning and that their stories "matter" in the midst of the general contours of experience since their lives and situations, conceived in brief or extended metaphorical narratives, are potentially everyone's. John Updike's *The Centaur* (1963) pushes the life of George Caldwell, an ordinary schoolteacher, into the reaches of mythology and explores the complex dynamics of guilt and atonement in the son, Peter, who grapples with the meaning of his father's life. From *Rabbit, Run* (1960) to *Rabbit Redux* (1971), Updike's Harry Angstrom moves from the row house to the suburb in a small Pennsylvania town, but the world of "facts" through which the old basketball player runs turns out, under Updike's hand, to be a world of metaphor and fable for Harry's seeking. Saul Bellow's *The Victim* (1947) raises insistent questions about the meaning of human goodness by isolating his Asa Leventhal to face the problem of the extent to which he is or is not "his brother's keeper" and, at the same time, by presenting to Asa and to the reader the stuff out of which an enlarged definition of the "brother" might be formed. Following the course of griev- ing for a father in a middle-aged woman, Eudora Welty's *The Optimist's Daughter* (1972) measures out broader forms of forgiving in the protagonist's recognition of the continuity of love, and, in the scenes of a reunited family in a poverty-stricken rural area, her *Losing Battles* (1970) discovers sources and reserves of sustenance in the midst of suffering. Bernard Malamud's *The Fixer* (1966) forces an obscure Russian peasant, Yakov Bok, into extraordinary trials in order to gauge the mode and meaning of his heroism. Stripping her stories virtually to the level of allegorical action, Flannery O'Connor over and over again returns to the reader the intensities of sin and guilt and rage in the modern shapes these take in her fallen Southern world, in the amazement and frustration of sim- ple and "lost" country people. Less brilliantly, Larry McMurtry's *Horseman, Pass By* (1961) and *The Last Picture Show* (1967) recover out of the ano- nymity of small-town Texas what O'Connor calls "the world of guilt and sorrow," retrieving it with sheer attentiveness to its otherwise trivial and obscure characters. In Carson McCullers's work, the small and apparently unimportant lives in *The Heart Is a Lonely Hunter* (1940), the ordinarily insignificant longings of a child in *The Member of the Wedding* (1946), and the ostensibly peripheral and grotesque behaviors in *The Ballad of the Sad Café* (1951) are invested with lyrical moment and bearing that redeem the characters in their dingy environments by transforming their situations and gestures into larger fables of human need and longing. If the substance of these twentieth-century American parables seems in general to confirm the modern testimony about the reduction of the individual—if, that is, the characters appear generally as hapless, ineffectual, drained-out creatures— their significance in embodying parabolic patterns and meanings, to be extended in metaphorical fashion by the work of imagination, has not been lost on those writers committed to the idea that individual experience can still matter in this way.

These parabolic forms in modern literature, of course, are not finally put in general into the service of some controlling religious vision, but they have the effect, if not the intention, of their biblical predecessors of proposing how even confusing experience yields to narrative formation and interpretation and how even habitual incidents can be infused suddenly with a significance that transposes them out of the particularities of the moment to a connected larger realm of meaning. As fable, as heuristic narrative, the twentieth-century literary parable operates under just that tightly controlled effort of clarification and connection that animated the New Testament form—the smallest metaphor struggling toward metaphysics, frequently by way of allegorical interpretation. Bent too strenuously toward abstraction—in, say, the disarrayed tale of prodigality in Robert Penn Warren's *A Place To Come To* (1977), or in the contrived and uninspired philosophical groping of Thomas Wolfe's *The Web and the Rock* (1939)—the form consumes itself: the "metaphysics" gobbles up too quickly the metaphor on which its sustained life depends. At its best—in, say, Hemingway's *The Old Man and the Sea* (1952)—the manifest stuff of the metaphor is not annihilated in favor of the headier stuff of metaphysical connection. The juxtapositions in the narrative of the old man's loneliness and suffering and of his dreaming might ultimately lead to the vision of the closing paragraphs of the lions made lambs, but nothing in that closure asks the reader to forget or dismiss the ways the vision grows out of its original metaphors of the old man's rope-burned hands and fatigue, which are emblematical finally for the anguished conditions of life that make him earn the peace of his hopeful dreaming.

But even a "failed" modern parable perhaps indicates something important about the presence of the parabolic conception of experience in the twentieth-century American novel. In a novel like Joseph Heller's *Something Happened* (1974), for instance, the potential heuristic and metaphysical thrusts are stymied at the same time that the narrative extends the reader's sense of the Job-like intensity of the puzzlement and suffering of the protagonist. Heller's story is finally opaque, dissolving in paradox because its meaning and connection will not render somehow. Like some of the biblical parables, whose interpretations are clouded or whose meanings depend on designs beyond human ken, Heller's novel touches on the heuristic limits of the parable while exploring its subject in the ways, or at least with the attitudes toward experience, of the parabolist. In this, with full attentiveness to its focal subject in his more or less ordinary character, the novel alludes not only backward toward the precedent of the Job story but also outward toward the modern pressures that confront the form. If Hemingway's *The Old Man and the Sea* never loses sight of its animating metaphors in its quest for the larger vision, *Something Happened*, which adopts a parabolic perspective, cannot manage to find in its subject the answers to the questions of pattern and meaning, cannot locate the configuring metaphor, much less the larger vision, but, failing as parable in formal ways, it nonetheless sustains the parabolic imagination of experience in its restoration of the significance and value of the individual as a focus of respect and attention and as a source of possible meanings.

If formal echoes of biblical parables persist in twentieth-century American novels and if these forms have the effect of conveying at least similar valuations of experience in certain respects, the differences must also be allowed. The ancient parabolist sought to tell the universal truth about experience as that truth was resident in the microcosmic experience of his attention, there to be discerned and interpreted in the narrative form experience itself possessed. The modern literary parabolist works under no such assured convictions. In his or her work, although attempting to express a kind of personal truth about experience, the writer of fiction proceeds with a full sense of its fictive and hypothetical character, less convinced that meaning inheres in experience than brought to think that it must be created or devised by imposing on experience the narrative character it does not itself contain. Even with these and other distinctions secured, however, there remains in modern American fiction a frequent flash of the parabolic imagination, committed to seeing the value of the unique stories of individual lives, in their ordinary operations and in their extraordinary moments, as potential bearers of larger meanings. Whether discerning meaning in or devising it out of experience, the literary recovery of these stories after the manner of the parable also serves to retrieve the weight, bearing, and value of obscure personal and individual life, to restore a sense of its significance at least in fiction, and to remind us that there are "selves" who uniquely mean and matter, though they are now threatened with diminution.

The Incoherence of History and the Form of Saga

One of the signal characteristics of those who would call themselves "modern," according to Carl Jung, appears in their refusal to participate in the collective humanity of traditional life. Modern individuals live by a full consciousness of the present which repudiates the past, breaks with tradition, and thus claims simultaneously to be "unhistorical," in the sense that they are not formed by the past, and to be "radically historical" in the sense that their existence is deeply embedded in the temporal present. Conceiving of the past as a mire of irrelevant superstitious life, they think of themselves less as the human culmination of the past than as the answer to its shortcomings. But within the horizon of time, which is full of transient flux and contingency, they are everywhere presented with what Whitehead referred to as "perpetual perishing," the constant reminder of the flow of life toward fatality. Although some processive views of experience and history can find positive resources in this conception of time, an all-too-frequent response of modern men and women is to sense themselves caught between a dead past, which they spurn, and an oblique and threatening future, which is to be, and to be suffered, as the consequence of their own making. And now, having refused as so much archaic nonsense any faith in a transhistorical principle that directs the flow of time toward some hoped-for end, moderns experience what Mircea Eliade calls "the terror of history," the sensation that everything fades with time, that the dance of time is random, and that history itself is unintelligible, without presiding pattern and meaning. When modern people, braced with secular ideas of history, turn to accounts of the past, they are confronted with a dead thing, unrelated to them, by which, in a turn of temperament, they now see themselves abandoned, shipwrecked in the clutches of a time uninformed and unaided by the past. Tempted to a nihilistic interpretation of history by their positivist approaches to the past, they have lost the Greek notion of *paideia*, the idea of the powerfully formative grasp of the social and cultural tradition on personal identity and existence. Time in the present lacks meaning because the meaning of the past is lost or spurned, and contemporary life falls victim to the inclination to regard its own inheritance as anachronistic and its own history as discontinuous and meaningless.

The presence of the saga in the Hebrew Bible stands as a testimony to an understanding of history that answered in the life of ancient Israel to the need for a sense of a past that flowed vitally into the present and the need for a way to conceive history coherently. For the writers of the Old Testament saga, the blending of the historical and the legendary in constructing a usable past issued in mythic–poetic accounts (in the stories of Abraham and Jacob, for instance) of the historical past which began in a conception of the world in terms of the family and which wanted to see salvation history in the continuous unfolding of familial lineage. As Klaus Koch has noted in his observations on biblical saga, "there is hardly a story where God does not play a positive part, whether in a foreign country, as in the case of the ancestress of Israel, or in the internal conflicts in Israel, such as those between Saul and David" (150). Founded on the conception that pattern in history was to be discerned in the drama of generations, each crucially affected by the preceding ones, the saga created the past with an intensity of fictional technique, incorporating the facts into the overriding mythological vision, but for all of that what was erected and maintained as a past had no unreality about it because the poetic and mythic truth was, for these writers, the essential truth for which mere descriptive chronicles could not account. In its formal character, then, the saga delineates the course of events within the generations in terms of a concentration on a relatively few characters, who are emblematically pulled to a vivid foreground in a scenic duality that has only two main characters or groups "on stage" at a time. The stark contrast of these characters in their emblematic meanings enables the past to be recounted in terms of these meanings within the larger drama of salvation history. And the thrust of the form is not only to legitimate the present by actualizing a continuous past but also to include the present in the unfolding history as a dramatic moment whose shape and character are deeply informed by its relation to that meaningful past. The concern of the saga, as Koch points out (154), is finally to include the auditor in history by giving him a past which allows him both to understand the pattern and significance of historical experience and to find, in the molding influence of lineage, his own place in the temporal world.

Although modern writers cannot very well rely fully on the assumption of "corporate personality," which is foundational in the Hebrew Bible for the conception of history as implicating and determining the contemporary man or woman in the terms of his or her geneaology, there is a discernible trace of the saga in those examples of twentieth-century American fiction which create a familial past leading to an effort of contemporary self-understanding. Without recourse to the circumferential mythology of salvation history, which supplied the context for the coherence of the Israelite sagas, modern writers have in some instances seized on the potential of the saga as a form to evoke the ways in which the substantive life of a generation might have its coherence and in which the contours of that life might follow either a culminating or a tragic design. Our writers have sometimes picked up the deeply embedded idea of experience resident in the operations of the saga as a biblical literary form that an individual life central to the familial or tribal drama reaches its full denouement in relation to the potentials for glory and for tragedy which belong to the lineage—in the ways and in the measure, that is, that that life emblematically incorporates or plunges away from the redemptive possibilities open to it in its generation.

Like the forms of the saga in the Hebrew Bible, the vestiges of it in twentieth-century American fiction display a variety of focal subjects and present several thrusts. Traces and elements of the patriarchal saga, like that of the story of Abraham in the Old Testament, appear in the fundamental drives of works as different as William Faulkner's "The Bear," John Updike's *The Centaur*, Harold Robbins's *The Carpetbaggers* (1961), and Thomas Berger's *Little Big Man* (1964), as authors or narrators dive back into the past in a search for, or a mythopoetic creation of, the paternity and originating sources of a familial lineage that has become a commanding, even decisive, factor in understanding the nature and possibility of the present. The central characters within the generation stand prominently in a foreground that emphasizes their commanding and often emblematic presence, and, in varying degrees from work to work, the presentation of these paternal figures measures them on a mythic scale. Alex Haley's *Roots* (1976) calls attention with its subtitle, *The Saga of an American Family*, to the fact that the past he recovers merges the fictive with the historical in an effort to discern the patterns of coherence and meaning in the generational experiences of his family and recognizes in mythic styles at many moments the struggle for freedom and the capacity for endurance which are ascribed to the lineage of Kunta Kinte and which reach forward to inform the present with a necessary truth in legitimation of its own striving. In another set of instances in twentieth-century American fiction, the primary thrust of the saga is etiological and topographical—like the narrative of Sodom and Gomorrah in the Hebrew Bible—in its concern to locate the causal shapes and circumstances for the passing of generations in a particular setting. Works as various as Grace Metalious's *Peyton Place* (1956), Faulkner's various Yoknapatawpha-novels, A. B. Guthrie, Jr.'s *The Big Sky* (1947), and Edna Ferber's *Giant* (1950) each recreate a locale whose boundaries figure positively or negatively, but in all cases influentially, in the lives of the linked generations that inhabit its landscape, and the fusion of spatial and temporal dimensions, scene and history, charges the atmosphere of the story with special significance.

One of the most heightened twentieth-century American novels in the form of the saga is Ross Lockridge, Jr.'s *Raintree County* (1948), a prodigious evocation of an Indiana county that lives by its dreams for itself and out of which dreams the people "built a fiction . . . with the gigantic labor by which the earth is rescued . . . from chaos and old night." Lockridge's novel not only resonates with the ancient form of the saga but also catches the poet-historians in the act of creating a mythic past that retrieves the pattern and significance of history on behalf of the contemporary moment. Beyond the etiological and topographical thrusts of the work, *Raintree County* points toward another version of the saga, the heroic, which wants to isolate in the foreground of the dramatically rendered past the mighty pageant creatures who stand for the nation or the region or the tribe. As Lockridge's narrator hints at the matter, the self-conscious character of saga in bulwarking the present with a meaningful and necessary past begins to be revealed: "And slowly he discovered . . . he had been making the legend of a hero. This hero was Humanity, and the place in which the hero strove for beauty and the good was the Republic. Both Hero and Republic were immense fictions. They could never have existed without their poet, but neither could he have existed without them." The past is no less real for being mythical, the narrator suggests; it lives more vibrantly for the present by virtue of its endowment of that meaning and significance mere chronicle cannot locate: "only myths can be eternal."

But, if the twentieth-century American novel borrows from the form and conception of history and experience characteristic of the several versions of the biblical saga, it does so under special pressures in our time. Frequently it appears to be undertaken less with a sense of the reality of the past it proposes than with a frustrated realization of the obscurity of what it seeks to restore. John O'Hara's prolific class sagas, which celebrate the capitalist hero, and Margaret Mitchell's *Gone With the Wind* (1936), which seems bent on satisfying the etiological, topographical, and heroic craving of a region, might ring with authorial convictions about the reality of the history each creates, but they reveal at the same time the urgency of their respective authors' needs to depict and to seize strenuously on a past each fears lost to the throes of time, to the march of modern life. In other cases, the shape of the modern saga reveals itself bereft of the redemptive direction that circumscribed and sustained the generational dramas of ancient Israel. The lineage of the Loftis family in William Styron's *Lie Down in Darkness* (1951) plays out a tragic course as the characters debate whose is really "the lost generation" and as they find themselves stranded in time without resource or prospect for any culmination of a historical meaning. In the recovery of the history of Cass McMastern and in the discovery of his own geneaology, Jack Burden, in Robert Penn Warren's *All the King's Men*, finds himself fully implicated in a past and a present whose courses, though continuous, leave him only with "the awful burden of time" and without faith in its salvific movement. In search of the familial, etiological, and topographical evidence that will help him find his own place in the world of the South, Quentin Compson hears the three versions of the saga of Thomas Sutpen in William Faulkner's *Absalom! Absalom!* (1936) which he recounts for his Harvard roommate, but in the confusion of pasts, each created out of the self-need of the teller, Quentin can only locate a saga-sized history of betrayal and repudiation, suffered in amazement and outrage, which undermines an effectual past and which, *The Sound and the Fury* (1929) suggests, leads to his suicide. Still, if the efforts of the saga in these instances lead to a discovery of a past that seems to betray, or a past that implies a tragic denouement for the present, the significance of the effort is not lost, for the saga even in its modern shape depends on a conception that experience remains significant enough in the twentieth century to contain tragic potential, that it has pattern and meaning at least in fiction. If the design of history follows a tragic pattern, as the past is interpreted to lead to and to shape the present, the presence of such a pattern redeems history at least from triviality and meaninglessness, averts the nihilistic alternative, and raises the insistent question of generational accountability to the formative past which lies behind and the future which stretches ahead.

The Disintegration of the Covenant Community and the Form of Jeremiad

Whether conceiving it as the breakup first of the Puritan synthesis and then of what intellectual historian Henry F. May called "the Victorian compromise," as the shift from a natural to a rational community described by sociologists, as the inevitable movement to mass bureaucratic society posited by political theorists, or as the consequence of unfettered capitalism argued by Marxist economists, thoughtful observers of the modern scene generally agree that our time has suffered in sometimes painful ways the failure of community in America. The causes of this failure are complex, but the evidence of it seems clearest and perhaps most poignant in the general loss felt by twentieth-century men and women of the special promise of America—the loss of bonds of solidarity achieved and maintained under a controlling vision of the community—as a moral community acting in the name of a higher vision. On the personal pulses, men and women experience this loss, it seems, as a break with a simpler, more coherent, and somehow purer past in which the promises of national fulfillment were radiant in their clarity and in which one could feel a deep sense of identity and belonging. In the more fluid and more complex modern world, the nature of personal and communal responsibility in political, social, and moral realms—not to mention any controlling religious vision—suffers confusions that not only erode the bonds within community but also cloud the higher purposes so decisive for the community in its self-conception. The covenant, the world of the fathers, the continuity with the promises of the past and, thus, the deepest fulfillments possible in the life of the present, all seem to be disintegrating under the pressures of modern circumstances that conspire against the American "covenant" to be a certain kind of moral community in history, or else the community itself has lost both its own originating vision and with this the terms of its solidarity and coherence.

When the community of ancient Israel either bent to the forces of the cultural environment or for any reason seemed in danger of losing or compromising the terms of its covenant with Yahweh, the Hebrew Bible presents in the record of the experience the appearance of a particular form of prophetic discourse, the jeremiad, which served the function of calling the people back to the central vision giving the community its substance and significance. The prophet, willingly or not, took his commission from God and found it his irresistible responsibility to give his highest loyalty to the message he was charged to address to the community. In order to fulfill this responsibility, he had first to be isolated from the corruptions of the community and, in this, to be confirmed or authorized, as it were, as the bearer of Yahweh's message. The remove achieved in this accreditation process enabled the prophet both to discover his vocation on behalf of the community and to gain a historical perspective on the present experience of the community. In its formal design, then, the prophet's discourse presents an indictment of Israel for its apostasy and ingratitude, a reminder that present pains and sorrows flowed from unfaithfulness to the covenant, a dramatic threat of the kind of punishment to come, an evocation of a golden age of true religious faith, a plea for lamentation for what had been lost, and a call for a return to the vision of life which alone gave the community its saving meaning. As a mode of discourse, the jeremiad relies on certain convictions about the nature of experience which it wants to recover in or instill in its auditors. It argues that present experience needs to be interpenetrated by past promises of the community; it issues out of the belief that meaningfulness in temporal experience in general depends absolutely on seeing the present in terms of the afterglow of the past covenant tradition; and it contains the notion that present experience has within its own keeping the bright visage of a salvific principle. Regardless of the apparent forlornness of Isaiah or the scathing critique of Jeremiah in their challenges to the current life of the people, the jeremiad is fundamentally hopeful, insisting in both form and content, as it does, that the community can yet repair its life, can still find in its tradition and experience the images and motives for its meaningful continuity.

Although achieving prophetic credentials in a somewhat different manner than Isaiah and although ordinarily finding senses of vocation under different rubrics than a Yahwistic vision of life, twentieth-century American writers have frequently practiced fictional modes of discourse reminiscent at least of the jeremiad. In the unique imaginative transactions with experience at the heart of narrative fiction, they have in many works adopted just that remove from and perspective on the life of the community which allows a jeremiadic posture, and the various thrusts issuing out of such a stance on the part of the writers often seemed aimed at calls to the community to recognize its flawed responses to life and to embrace the deeper terms and commitments of its experience.

The particular forms of such calls are various, but in each case the present failure of the moral community comes in for critique on the basis of its past promises to itself. In some instances, the form is discernible in those narratives which contrast the times—with a nostalgia for a purer, simpler, and brighter world of innocence, now lost or battered in a more complex and corrupt present. F. Scott Fitzgerald's *The Great Gatsby* challenges the tawdry life of careless wealth and foul grime of "the valley of ashes" and issues in its closing paragraphs a dirge for the end of a special imagination of experience which the "Dutch sailors" must have possessed when they first beheld the American continent. Ernest Hemingway's *The Sun Also Rises* (1926) depicts in a hauntingly biblical style the senses of emptiness of characters who have lost tradition and community and explores their experience in search of the grounds on which some communion can yet be forged. In John Knowles's *A Separate Peace* (1959), the tacit promises made to the school boys are broken by and in the ampler world of adult warfare but for a narrator who can learn gradually, painfully, to critique the actions and attitudes of the community with his own recovered sensibility and with his reimagination of what must necessarily constitute the "facts" of life. Echoes of the jeremiad in other instances—as various as Norman Mailer's *An American Dream* (1965), Ken Kesey's *One Flew Over the Cuckoo's Nest* (1962), Sherwood Anderson's *Winesburg, Ohio* (1919), Katherine Anne Porter's *Pale Horse, Pale Rider*, and even J. D. Salinger's *The Catcher in the Rye* (1951) among a great many others—expose the insanity, corruption, viciousness, or emptiness symptomatic of the failure of community in modern life in relation to or in contrast with at least hints of a vision of community in the past, the loss of which now requires lamentation. Excoriation of the society by these modern prophets, charged with testing the community with images of its own past possibilities, does not arrive unaccompanied by the measurement in imaginative terms of the experience that contains the substance for the renewal of the community.

Perhaps the most directly discernible instances of the likeness of the jeremiad in modern American prose fiction are those in which the prophetic challenge arrives in terms of the moral and religious promises the community made but failed to keep. John Steinbeck's *The Grapes of Wrath* and *East of Eden* appeal explicitly to the biblical sources of the American promise to figure in history as an inclusive, accepting community—doing so at a time when recourses to Marx were decidedly more fashionable—and sustain their appeals, at least at the level of ideal reminiscence, in the face of systems of power, wealth, and realty that violate the promise by building their glory on the fatiguing labors of the impoverished. Lillian Smith's *Strange Fruits* (1944) presents the failures on the racial question of the Christian and American commitment to "the brotherhood of man" by representing the ways in which those Christians, those Americans, straying from the vision, have become in the words of another of her titles, "killers of the dream." Although pressed finally into other services, Faulkner's *Intruder in the Dust* (1948), his *The Sound and the Fury*, and William Styron's *Lie Down in Darkness*, along with others, also contain elements of jeremiadic criticism of white Christianity for its failure to enlarge its sense of possible community and for its failure to recognize some of its own deepest, if now only latent, substance in the examples of the black Christian community living on its peripheries. In these and other examples, the nostalgia and the cause for lamentation refer not so much to a simpler time past as to an imagery and a dream unrealized.

Something of the same effort to restore or to reify at last the vision of the fathers animates James Agee's *Let Us Now Praise Famous Men*, a "documentary" accompanied by the photographs of Walker Evans, which draws on all of Agee's powers as a narrative artist to transcend mere documentation in its meditations on and challenges to the American sense of community. The central substance and bonds of the legacy Agee wants to recover lie in America's "covenant" with itself to give a life of dignity and meaning not only to the famous and affluent but also to the obscure and impoverished. For Agee, the terms of this covenant are to be found in the apocryphal *Ecclesiasticus, the Book of the Son of Sirach*, which calls for an encomium, a memorial, for those whom time forgets, for those "who are perished as though they had not been born" (44:9) and a remembrance that "their children are within the covenants" (44:12). The particular subjects of Agee's attention are three tenant-farming families in Alabama during the Depression whose lives of misery and ignorance and poverty have put them outside the covenant in the eyes of the culture by stripping them of the essential dignity that would make them human. Plying every novelistic technique he can, Agee attempts to revise, to see anew, both the beauty and the bearing of the tenant farmers' lives, redeeming them for the covenant, and the social and cultural causes and conditions in American life, leaving them unredeemed. His scathing indictment of modern liberal culture, carried out in the name of an older moral vision, combines with an intense and complex reimagination of contemporary experience in order to seize the ways the covenant can still be fulfilled. Like other examples of the modern jeremiad in twentieth-century fiction, *Let Us Now Praise Famous Men* wants what it understands as the sounder vision of the past to penetrate into the present moment and to challenge the community with its own past sense of itself.

If these modern prophets do not take their commissions as messengers of Yahweh, their vocation as imaginative writers nonetheless places them, as Lionel Trilling put it, "beyond culture," from which remove they seek to retrieve for the community a sense of deeper possibility if not higher destiny than its present state seems to afford. In this seeking, like the old jeremiahs, they depend on a particular understanding of experience—that the present achieves its glory by consummating the brightest visions of the past and that the present moment has in it the latent possibility of such fulfillment— which is enlivening, if not restorative, for the modern community threat- ened with disintegration. As Gerhard von Rad has pointed out (100–102), the "message" of this form of prophetic discourse is not a general one: it presents particular messages, exhibiting particular concerns with deft liter- ary talent, to the community in its ever-changing specific cultural situations, as it runs the danger of altogether losing the terms of its coherence. Thus, again like the ancient prophets, the modern literary jeremiahs are charged with securing a surer hold on the visions of the past and a keener sense of the meaning of the present just on behalf of a community largely to be known for its forgetfulness. In a time when the terms of the community's coherence are in disarray, it might well be that our writers have fewer resources in past visions than in their own imaginative capacities for creat- ing new terms for fulfillment, forged out of the situation of the culture in its particular moment.

The Collapse of Culture and the Form of Apocalyptic

When Jules Michelet concluded in the nineteenth century that, however much the religious world was a divine creation, the social world was a human creation, thus extending the course of rationalist philosophy to include reflections on society and history, the doors opened wide to new secular interpretations about human nature and human responsibility in making the world a fit habitation. The assumption was that humanity had achieved a historical maturity freeing it from dependence on divine inter- ventions and guidances in its history and allowing it to develop political, social, and cultural courses of redemptive activity that stood as appropriate alternatives for modern men and women. Although the representatives of these alternatives have ordinarily used a vocabulary cast in terms of "progress"—or, in flightier moods, of "perfection"—more than they have referred to "redemption," the nature of their confidence in the realms of social management, economic systems, technological advancement, and so on, has largely had the effect of eroding faith in any supernatural direction of history along a course of salvation, indeed of replacing such a faith with a modern secular reasoning, frequently under the rubric of a philosophy of emergent evolution. The project of the present and of the future, for the new secular imagination of the culture, is the work of men and women. From time to time, however, economic depression, political turmoil, clashing interest groups, indifferent bureaucracy, all generate intermittent sensations that the capacity of the society to solve its problems has fallen away and that the toll on the culture by historical circumstances is too great somehow for it to survive. And when attention is returned to an estimate of the nature and capability of men and women to maintain the world they have created, but which seems disheveled and deteriorating, they seem far from being up to the enormity of the task. They seem all too frail and vulnerable, powerless in the face of the enormity of it all, or else they have an appearance of greed, corruption, vicious self-interest, even malice, and thus seem not only to thrive on but also to be the sources of the ills and evils of the culture. In sum, these perceptions create an urgency about the course of experience and a despair about what seem the shrinking possibilities within the ambit of the culture to right itself. Long having lost or refused the idea of any providential ordering of historical experience, modern men and women, in the moments that portend the imminent collapse of the culture, live with an anxiety about a disastrous ending of the history for which now they alone are responsible but continue to look, as they must, to human resources, with no other apparent alternatives for ways to shore up the future.

From those writers of the Hebrew Bible and the New Testament who suffered senses of cultural disintegration and historical crisis with such urgency and intensity that remaining human possibilities evaporated, a visionary rhetoric of apocalyptic appeared. Unlike the jeremiad, which could identify for the community the modes and resources in its contemporary experience for the fulfillment of the covenant, the message of apocalyptic contained a deep pessimism about the character of the present, and the form of its presentation derived from a view of world history that involved the idea of the predestined destruction of all human achievements in a cataclysmic future ending of history and the idea that this ending would issue in a renewed time, the eternal time of the kingdom of God. The scenario developed in apocalyptic through the presentation of dreams and visions—in, for example, the Old Testament book of Daniel and the New Testament book of Revelation—projects a future, vividly informed by a symbolic interpretation of history that depicts the presence of the beast and the increase of evil in the world. The staple of apocalyptic is the stuff of wild supernatural beasts, fire, war, pestilence, unremitting violence and death, the ultimate confrontation between the forces of goodness and evil in the universe. The saving event, for the apocalyptic writer, is not in history but at the end of history, in the ultimate victory of righteousness, of God, over the rampaging evil that is symbolically to be discerned, as von Rad observes, "in the nature of man and the kingdoms which he establishes" (273). Full of dubiety about the power of human kingdoms to save themselves, the apocalyptic writer creates an eschatological hope in the effort to remythologize the end of history, to endow it with cosmic scope, and to pose the necessity of a divine solution to the unending record of human failure. In this sense, as Paul D. Hanson has pointed out, apocalyptic is at least continuous with the prophetic tradition of Jeremiah and Isaiah (12). If its frantic scenario for the end stems from a more desperate sense of the state of the cultural present and seems to embody an ahistorical and otherworldly longing, it can stir the critical imagination of the culture to search out its ills, to identify what in it should be brought to judgment and remedy, to acknowledge the limitations on its own life, to recognize the essential absurdity of its pretensions within the shadow of a longer vision, a larger plan. In its rhetorical response to experience, apocalyptic reveals both a sense of emergency about the times and a hope for the emergence out of cultural chaos of a new order of life. Its creation of a visionary future generates a sense of the critical present, now invested with ultimate meanings that provide the grounds for its self-critique.

Although modern writers, owning up to the radically secular character of contemporary life, are not often able to propose the suprahistorical forces which, for the ancient apocalypticists, would redeem time in the creation of a new heaven and a new earth, they have frequently produced works which ring with the urgency of apocalyptic about the frailty or absurdity of cultural illusions and which present, in their secular and historical scenarios, both the imagery of evil and the tone of impending catastrophe and judgment in the drama of social and cultural experience. If these writers have lacked recourse to a universal world view that called the temporal into the judgment of the eternal, they have nonetheless expressed themselves in their imagination of contemporary experience in discernibly apocalyptic moods of despair about human nature and secular kingdoms. Without access to an understanding of the divinely providential course that grounds eschatological hope, some twentieth-century American writers have found at least derivatively apocalyptic forms to be an appropriate way to present to the culture those damning images of itself which supply the terms for its self-criticism. Above all, the writers who have practiced in this mode seem to sense that the tone and character of apocalyptic can serve the present by investing it with that full dramatic sense of crisis which arrives in the expectation of catastrophe. Such an investment, in heightening the critical character of the moment, might evoke the stirrings of an awakening to the deeper meanings the culture can locate for itself, the only form of hope left when psychic repose is to be found in meaning and not in a supernatural saving event.

One of the shapes of apocalyptic in the twentieth-century American novel is cast around topical events and situations in cultural experience whose dynamics themselves suggest the presence of insidious forces or the onslaught of terrific violence or the riot of insane malice in the human heart. In Thomas Pynchon's *The Crying of Lot-49*, the bizarre twists of Oedipa Maas's search for the legacy of America, undertaken with trepidation and paranoia, lead her into a complex and furtive network of wealth and power, a conspiracy of evil influences, whose full appearance she cannot locate but whose final significant and imminent revelation she awaits in the closing pages, now completely alarmed and close to insanity after the chaotic course of her experience. Or, again, the violent impulses of Rojack, at a moment when he seems close to having grasped the golden ring of the culture in Norman Mailer's *An American Dream*, combine with the overt corruption and the hidden underworld, hinted at as the central matrix of the social world, to throw a nightmarish light on a "kingdom" suspended before a disaster. The so-called war novels, like Mailer's *The Naked and the Dead* (1948) and James Jones's *From Here to Eternity* (1951), gauge the nature and capacity of human beings in the violence and madness of the conflicts stemming from cultural and political and personal bravado, and, at the same time, expose human frailty and vulnerability in the face of conflicts that individuals can no longer control. The chaos, conflagration, and fatality of war amply provide the imagery of cataclysmic ending which is a central facet of the apocalyptic form, though in those war novels committed to literary realism this imagery of an ending arrives not in surreal and dreamlike configurations but in the actual horrifying machinery and activity of warfare. Truman Capote's nonfiction novel *In Cold Blood* (1965), in developing its narrative out of the brutal murders of the members of a Kansas family, proposes that the presence of the beast and the hint of an impending ending are to be found in those discernibly human shapes running viciously through the society which created them, or at least contains them, and cannot redeem them.

Other traces of apocalyptic in the twentieth-century American novel appear in some of those works which build their imageries and cast their scenarios with less emphasis on the identifiable evils in the culture and with more attention to the fantastic worlds apocalypse proposes. In some cases, like the Pynchon novel mentioned above and like his *Gravity's Rainbow* (1973) and Joseph Heller's *Catch-22* (1961), the narrative works suddenly or gradually to transform the recognizable world. In constructing an intensified depiction of a bizarre tumultuous world by exaggerating those facets of the "normal" world which are themselves chaotic, enigmatic, and sometimes dangerous, the comforting world indeed seems to give rise to a presaging, critical, even catastrophic world in which evil and innocence contend. John Barth's *Giles Goat-Boy* (1966) alludes outward toward the ordinary world, seen as a universe-ity, but within the framework of the narrative itself the "world" is in a state of unmingled craziness, full of wild promiscuity, demonic forces, secret passages into arcane life. It is completely out of control, and it hovers at the edges of utter explosion at the hands of the insane people who run it. In other cases, the stuff of apocalyptic vision arrives in the ways critical moments in waking life are magnified, twisted, and rendered portentously threatening and revelatory in dream life. Kurt Vonnegut,

Jr.'s *Slaughterhouse Five* (1969), exposing the effects of the saturation
bombing of Dresden by the Allied forces on an American prisoner of war
who was held there, presents the fantastic dreamlike voyage of Billy Pilgrim, who seeks the psychically necessary world of peace which he can only
hope will follow the apocalypse. The waking world of Miranda's life in the
title story of Porter's *Pale Horse, Pale Rider* presents her with the anguish,
confusion, and sense of fleeting time on the homefront in World War I
which are transformed into the hallucinatory nightmare of apocalypse when
she falls into the delirium of illness and confronts the fact of death.
Reversing this order, Ira Levin's *Rosemary's Baby* (1967) presents to the
reader a juxtaposition of Rosemary's wild dream of demonic impregnation
with an ordinary "real" world that slowly for her becomes the nightmare. In
a slightly different way, Norman Mailer's *Of a Fire on the Moon* (1969),
taking its bearings in the complex machinery of space voyaging, extends the
scene and action into a dream state in which the pride of astronautical
achievement gives way to reflections on the death-seeking character of earth
and to questions about the presence of the devil.

     Still another trace of apocalyptic seems to have its sources in the oppres-
sive experience of life of those for whom the social and cultural world has
frequently failed to hold out any positive meaning and possibility. For black
writers in the twentieth century, the progressivist and perfectionist imagination, even in its best-intentioned moments, has all too often ignored or dismissed the blocks to progress explicit in truncations of social justice, and the
writers have located the polemical potentials of apocalyptic, the ways the
mode can be opened by the disenfranchised to attack the systems of the
powerful. The turbulent course of Bigger Thomas's life in Richard Wright's
Native Son (1940) involves a deep critique of the failing culture which
stands at the source of Bigger's mental chaos and which finally, having
pushed him into violence, pursues him in violent mob. In James Baldwin's
Another Country (1962), the confused entanglements of race and sex,
embitterment about the white world, and violence and brutality in human
relationships create the scene of a tortured world on the edge of collapse,
and Rufus Scott's wanderings in New York City, depicted with powerful
apocalyptic touches, lead him to a personal ending in suicide. Unlike much
of Baldwin's work, in which a smoldering rage keeps the narratives on the
edges of violence, Ralph Ellison's *Invisible Man* (1952) follows its young
protagonist in his clash with and betrayal by a society nearly lunatic in its
irrational hatreds as he moves out of innocence—through stages of incredu-
lity, concession, anger, and evasion—into a recognition about the futility of
it all. Along the way, he successively attempts the apparent alternatives held
out to him by the society, each of which turns out to be a deception, and the
record of his efforts and their betrayal also portrays a society whose
hypocrisy, corruption, and madness put it on the brink of the abyss. If the
young man finally resigns himself to isolation and goes underground in his

despair to find peace, or at least quiet, his story reminds the reader that there is another figure in the streets, Ras, who is bent on destruction in a world whose apocalyptic moment seems upon it.

Now, of course, these novels are not coextensive in every way with the forms of apocalyptic in the Hebrew Bible and in the New Testament, even if they reveal traces, facets, and thrusts of the ancient form. While these and other twentieth-century American novels can express themselves in the tones of panic and despair that marked the biblical rhetoric of apocalyptic, they have quite lost the possibility, within the secular framework, to sustain anything similar to the eschatological hope that nurtured the ancient apocalyptic imagination. The novels can identify hints of an ending, with apocalyptic overtones, in the wounded thrashings of society, but the twentieth-century American writer cannot appeal credibly, in the face of cultural convictions, to a transhistorical intervention and an arrival of a new order of life. The impending or projected catastrophe is all the more fearful for this in some respects because its inevitability instills a sense of fatality about the course of experience, in the death march of that history of humanity's own making and because it rings with a tone of finality about the cataclysm out of which there will be no new world. If the fearfulness increases in the scenarios of modern apocalypse, now without hope, a major thrust in the form of apocalyptic, however, is strained by the absence of the longer view of time. Without the visionary perspective on history in its totality, the effort of apocalyptic to renew the present with meanings derived from the projected future begins to fall away, and the question remains of how to redeem the time. Still, even missing some of the vital ingredients of the apocalyptic mode, the twentieth-century writers who practice their art in this vein have nonetheless frequently seized on the yet unspent potential of apocalyptic to heighten the intensity of present experience, to invest it with urgency and crisis, and thus to expose it for self-criticism. If modern secular life, so full of concentration on its own moment, cannot afford the vision of a historical ending on the basis of which to locate the deeper meaning of its temporal life, the modern American novel, in creating an apocalyptic characterization of the cultural moment, poses the necessity of an imagination of the future—which is to say that it insists on asking the culture to evaluate the potential for disaster along the course it charts in the present for its entrance into the territory of the future.

Beyond these four major and distinctive biblical modes—parable, saga, jeremiad, apocalyptic—which reassert themselves at least in the vestiges and traces of their formal conceptions of experience to be detected in twentieth-century American fiction, there are other biblical dispositions of mind which continue to be powerfully influential in modern life without the full formal nature of the modes discussed above. For instance, there is a decided disinclination in the Hebrew Bible to warrant those forms of organized religiosity practiced by the community which bent toward corrupt and corrupting images of this world at the level of worship, and the revulsion toward such practices sometimes prompted the writers to bitterly pointed attacks on such flawed responses. But these intermittent expressive passages were not presented in the forms of narrative and lacked the stable techniques and conventions that characterized, say, parabolic or jeremiadic presentations. Nonetheless, the twentieth-century American novel has sometimes involved a similarly concentrated critique of contemporary religiosity which, in its antiauthoritarian distrust of the "leaders" of this world, seems continuous with the biblical writers' attitudes. Peter DeVries's *The Mackerel Plaza* (1958), J. F. Powers's *Morte d'Urban* (1962), and Sinclair Lewis's earlier *Elmer Gantry* (1927), as examples of this thrust and attitude, work in their various ways to expose the muddleheadedness, the limitations, the sham and hypocrisy of contemporary religiosity. Like the more carefully delineated and controlled forms, these discursive motives are largely heuristic, as they were for the biblical writers, given to the intention in the forms of parable, apocalyptic, and so on, to clarify life in its essential coherence and meaning. As Herbert N. Schneidau has argued persuasively, a major effect of this drive to teach, to clarify, to call into question, was to present to the community that the writers served the continuous and decisive means for self-criticism, and the place and power of such prophetic discourse, which the culture senses is necessary even in its most obtuse moments, has been built as an ineluctable element into the Western tradition of self-conscious life.

But the point of the preceding discussion has been to suggest that the biblical inheritance is more than a general one, deep in the cultural marrow by way of the traditions of Judaism and Christianity. If the forms of fiction in some measure always present and test the possible terms and modes of contemporary self-understanding, then the reappearance in the twentieth-century American novel of saga, jeremiad, apocalyptic, and parable suggests that these narrative forms contain particular terms for achieving coherence, for locating the illuminating pattern, and for understanding experience in certain valuable ways, which are still possible at least in imaginative renditions. And if these biblical modes suffer truncations of religious vision and reveal some attenuations of full formal efficacy in the transformed configurations they take in the altered circumstances and pressures of twentieth-century reflection, it is surely more important that their particular substantive attitudes and assumptions about the nature of secular experience can be transposed from ancient to modern life than that the formal characteristics and historically particular religious beliefs have not been transposed whole-cloth. Even in the new shapes that parable and saga and jeremiad and apocalyptic must now take, the novels tell us, their essential dispositions toward the significance of individual and ordinary life, toward the formative power of past time and lineage, toward a committed present, and toward an informing future, all yet remain available—indeed present themselves as necessary—in the throes of our own late, bad time. Finally, then, while it might be the case that Western novelists' perceptions of historical experience since the eighteenth-century rise of the genre have been essentially shaped by a general biblical inheritance in the kinds of obvious or subtle ways traditions reach forward to affect even those who would spurn them, it is surely an indication of something more particular about the persistent influence of the Bible that even in the twentieth century—even, that is, when Porter's Doctor Schumann, along with many others, thinks "the whole great structure" of the Judeo-Christian civilization "now crumbling and falling"—many novelists have carried on what Stephen Spender calls "the struggle of the modern" in forms continuous with those in biblical narratives. Consciously or not, novelists have had recourse to biblical modes, to their particular conventions for understanding and articulating experience, and have found in those modes the formal ways to render patterns of coherence and meaning in the fictive "worlds" their works seek to explore and illumine. And, perhaps what is most significant, they have with such recourse, perhaps without recognition, frequently discovered or managed to propose how the biblical conventions—at least in our fictions—might prove bracing or even restorative in our grappling with some of the various "distresses" of our modernity.

WORKS CONSULTED

Arendt, Hannah
    1968   *Origins of Totalitarianism*. New York: Harcourt, Brace, and World.

Bercovitch, Sacvan
    1975   *The Puritan Origins of the American Self*. New Haven: Yale University Press.
    1978   *The American Jeremiad*. Madison: University of Wisconsin Press.

Brooks, Cleanth
    1963   *The Hidden God: Studies in Hemingway, Faulkner, Yeats, Eliot, and Warren*. New Haven: Yale University Press.

Eliade, Mircea
    1959   *Cosmos and History*. Translated by Willard R. Trask. New York: Harper and Row.

Hanson, Paul D.
    1975   *The Dawn of Apocalyptic*. Philadelphia: Fortress Press.

Hoffman, Frederick J.
    1967   *The Imagination's New Beginning: Theology and Modern Literaure*. Notre Dame, IN: Notre Dame University Press.

Jung, Carl G.
    1955   *Modern Man in Search of a Soul.* Translated by W. S.
                  Dell and Cary F. Baynes. New York: Harcourt, Brace,
                  Jovanovich.

Killinger, John
    1973   *The Fragile Presence: Transcendence in Modern
                  Literature.* Philadelphia: Fortress Press.

Koch, Klaus
    1969   *The Growth of the Biblical Tradition.* Translated by
                  S. M. Cupitt. London: Adam and Charles Black.

May, Henry F.
    1959   *The End of American Innocence: A Study of the First
                  Years of Our Own Time, 1912–1917.* New York: Alfred
                  Knopf.

May, Rollo
    1969   *Love and Will.* New York: W. W. Norton.

Rad, Gerhard von
    1972   *The Message of the Prophets.* Translated by D. M. G.
                  Stalker. New York: Harper and Row.

Ricoeur, Paul
    1967   *The Symbolism of Evil.* Translated by Emerson
                  Buchanan. New York: Harper and Row.

Schneidau, Herbert N.
    1976   *Sacred Discontent: The Bible and Western Tradition.*
                  Baton Rouge: Louisiana State University Press.

Spender, Stephen
    1963   *The Struggle of the Modern.* Berkeley: University of
                  California Press.

Trilling, Lionel
    1968   *Beyond Culture: Essays on Literature and Learning.*
                  New York: The Viking Press.

Via, Dan O.
    1967   *The Parables: Their Literary and Existential Dimen-
                  sion.* Philadelpia: Fortress Press.

Wilder, Amos N.
    1969   *The New Voice: Religion, Literature, Hermeneutics.*
                  New York: Herder and Herder.

Ziolkowski, Theodore
    1972   *Fictional Transfigurations of Jesus.* Princeton: Prince-
                  ton University Press.

IV

American Drama and the Bible:
The Case of Eugene O'Neill's *Lazarus Laughed*

William H. Shurr

Barrett H. Clark once wrote, "It seems, in reading the hundreds of surviving plays of the nineteenth century, that the best of them were the work of more or less ingenious children who lived in a world that had done no thinking since 1620." Clark was in a position to know; he was one of the most eminent historians of American drama and the editor and anthologist of the older "lost plays" of the American theater. The dismal history is, however, worth a few reflections, at least in order to understand the emergence of a truly magnificent native drama early in the twentieth century and some of the conditions out of which it grew.

Some serious drama began to appear in America around the time of the Revolution, as tracts for the times. Some of the plays were stimulants to patriotism and national self-determination; others were loyalist plays attacking the movement for independence, urging the wisdom of remaining in the British orbit. The plays were popular but few today are tempted to read Mercy Warren's *The Group*—in which royalist characters named "Hateall" and "Spendall" pursue their deprecations of Massachusetts in the name of the King of "Blunderland"—or the Tory farce called *The Battle of Brooklyn*—in which American military figures are presented as cowards who need their courage bolstered by alcohol before they can go into battle. Even Royall Tyler's three biblical plays, *The Origin of the Feast of Purim, Joseph and His Brethren*, and *The Judgment of Solomon*, hold little temptation even to the most ardent pursuer of our theme.

If these beginnings, rough but with some wit and some intelligence, seemed to hold out any promise of a great dramatic tradition, that promise was long in being fulfilled. The whole of the nineteenth century seems to the serious reader a vast desert. The few plays that were simultaneously popular and substantial, such as *Uncle Tom's Cabin* and *Rip Van Winkle*, are more rewarding when read in their original forms, in the novel by Harriet Beecher Stowe and the short story by Washington Irving. The drama of the century was farce and melodrama, pirated British plays, or bombastic recitals of the classics.

It has frequently been suggested that the main reason for the slow development of drama in America has been our Puritan tradition. The world of actors and playwrights was too profane and their entertainments too garish for the strictly godly to support or patronize, or even tolerate. In the most popular of the early plays, Royall Tyler's *The Contrast* (1787), the naive Jonathan characterizes the theater as "the shop where the devil hangs out the vanities of the world up on the tenter hooks of temptation." At one performance, he has heard, the devil himself appeared and "carried off one-quarter of the play-house with him."

It is true that audiences at theaters were generally rowdy and brawling. Washington Irving, who had a hand in the authorship of several plays, once wrote pleading for "less grog and better constables" among the audiences in the galleries. An observer later in the nineteenth century wrote that plays were frequently disrupted by "the hard-visaged, the ill-behaved, the boisterous, the indecent," in the top galleries. One member of the clergy believed that Lincoln's assassination by an actor was clear and just retribution for his attendance at a theater.

These are hard words, but recent research has added even more substance to the charge of immorality in the theater. Claudia Johnson of the University of Alabama has shown that the top gallery or "third tier" of the nineteenth-century theater, long a subject of embarrassed silence or alluded to with dark innuendo, was actually the main locale for prostitutes to make their contacts or even to ply their trade.

Theaters in Boston, New York, and Philadelphia included such third tiers explicitly in their plans, even from the late eighteenth century. All theaters for the next hundred years were built with a carefully planned third tier, with its separate entrance and stairway often opening onto a street away from the main entrance. Managers frequently argued that the profits from this section kept their theaters open. One manager who experimented with closing his theater to prostitutes found that he was left with an audience of fewer than fifty people each night and was forced to return to older ways.

As theaters were built in other cities, the same arrangements were made. Professor Johnson describes the scene in the following words:

> The ritual of the third tier was apparently very simple: the entire inhabitants of houses of prostitution would customarily attend the theater in a body, entering the tier by a separate stairway an hour or two before the rest of the house was opened. Unlike the higher class prostitutes who sat throughout the theater and met customers there by pre-arrangement through such means as newspaper advertisements, the lower class prostitutes of the third tier made the initial contacts with their customers in the theater itself. Customers of long-standing took their places with the women in the third tier. Other men were introduced to these prostitutes when mutual friends took them up to the third tier from other parts of the house. A bar was located nearby to serve the upper tier, undoubtedly contributing to the rowdy behavior which was a constant disturbance to the rest of the house.

Johnson's findings go a long way toward explaining why, for most of America's history, a thought-provoking evening of dramatic entertainment was impossible to find. She seems absolutely right in wondering about "the extent to which the third tier . . . directed the types of plays written for and performed on the American stage," why the materials written for the stage were so "unmemorable" in an era when America's greatest literary giants were at work. The theater, she concludes, would have to achieve respectability by banning its prostitutes, before serious writers could find a hearing and a larger public would support them.

Theater managers from time to time tried to attract the sympathetic attention of churchgoers by offering theatrical contributions to morally uplifting crusades. Such temperance tracts as Clifton Tayleure's *The Drunkard's Warning*, H. Seymour's *Temperance Doctor*, William W. Pratt's dramatization of Timothy S. Arthur's *Ten Nights in a Bar Room and What I Saw There* were obvious potboilers; the only memorable line comes from Arthur: "Father, dear father, come home with me now. The clock in the belfry strikes one."

At the end of the nineteenth century and the beginning of the twentieth, drama both in Europe and in America began to be interesting again. Once again the old giant returned to its original classical sources and found a new youth. A renewed appreciation of the power of drama at its origins has always seemed, in the history of the genre, to be the necessary condition for a new drama of any significant magnitude.

The theory of classical drama, which has always made it work so well, converged neatly with the Judeo-Christian religion that came to dominate the West. Judaism already knew of the tragic flaw (discovered in Eden), the regal status of the protagonists (celebrated in the psalms and the prophets), the largest possible "cosmic" stage for action (dramatized in apocalyptic literature), and the inevitability of final cataclysm (once again, the burden of apocalyptic narrative)—before Aristotle became the teacher of the art of drama. When O'Neill came to write his great trilogy, *Mourning Becomes Electra*, the curse on the house of Mannon was obviously derived from classical Greek drama, but "Father Abraham" was the progenitor of the whole Mannon family.

Coupled with these ancient considerations, at the turn of our own century, were a handful of powerful modern thinkers whose ideas came to be seen as eminently dramatizable. At the origins of modern drama are such electrifying thinkers as Nietzsche, Schopenhauer, Marx, and Freud, those early modern explorers into the springs of our individual and collective behavior. It was immediately obvious that their philosophies were materials for immense dramatic skills, with the success of Henrik Ibsen and George Bernard Shaw, the fathers of a new drama that was at once modern, intelligent, and entertaining.

As one speculates on this "New Drama," some clear descriptive lines appear. Worldwide, the drama was stimulated by models from the plays of classical antiquity, by their power to clarify issues and move audiences. In many cases story and setting were both provided by the ancients. The briefest of catalogues suggests this larger picture: Shaw's *Caesar and Cleopatra*; Jean Anouilh's *Antigone, Euridice*, and *Medée*; Jean Cocteau's *Orphée* and *Antigone*; Jean Giraudoux's *La Guerre de Troie n'aura pas lieu* and *Electra*; Jean Paul Sartre's *Les Mouches*; Albert Camus's *Caligula*. Added to the picture to enliven the drama were ideas from modern thinkers and striking applications to the modern situation.

American drama shared the stimulus, to be sure. But as one looks into the complex picture at least some of what distinguishes American drama from European and gives it its own stamp of individuality is the background of another set of materials, narrative lines suggested by biblical stories. In our dramas, perhaps as a link to our Puritan past, a biblical narrative frequently provides the framework, the large field of play for modern speculation.

One must resist such insights if they threaten to become rigid and formulaic, if they are forced to apply to all of our modern plays. But if pursued with some freedom such speculations furnish a theory that may illuminate first the successful practice of Eugene O'Neill and then the power of other representative dramas from the modern American theater.

Concentration on O'Neill in our present context needs no apology, per- haps even no explanation. He was recognized as America's greatest drama- tist when the Nobel Prize in Literature was awarded to him in 1936 and his reputation has not diminished in the succeeding years. Sean O'Casey, an important dramatist in his own right, once summed up the situation in drama thus: "Neither the English nor the American Theatres can ever be quite the same since those giants [Shaw and O'Neill] leaped onto the stage." O'Neill can be taken as an exemplar of one of the major ways in which modern American drama has achieved weight and significance.

O'Neill drew inspiration from a multitude of sources. At one point in his career the New Testament story of Lazarus furnished a vehicle for convey- ing much that was in his mind, a rich and developed narrative that could be pressed into further service. The story of Lazarus was well enough known to provide an audience with easy access to an evening of satisfying entertain- ment. The complexities of the biblical story and the unfinished strands of its narrative allowed further speculation to take place.

The Gospel of Luke tells of Dives the rich man and Lazarus the poor beggar at his door, his sores and his hunger ignored by the rich man. Both die and Lazarus is taken to the bosom of Father Abraham. Dives, in the torment of hell, asks Father Abraham to send Lazarus with a drop of water to cool his tongue. The request is refused and the parable could well end here, with justice firmly restored in the afterlife. But the story continues that Dives then asks that Abraham send Lazarus back to his five brothers to warn them about this place of torment. The last exchange of the parable is memo- rable (Luke 16:29–31):

> But Abraham said, "They have Moses and the prophets; let them
> hear them."
> And he [Lazarus] said, "No, father Abraham; but if some one
> goes to them from the dead, they will repent."
> He said to him, "If they do not hear Moses and the prophets,
> neither will they be convinced if some one should rise from the
> dead."

The parable is unusual for several reasons. It is the only one of the parables of
Jesus in which a character is given a proper name. And, striking and memorable though the parable is, it is found only in Luke. Further, as in John's telling
of the resurrection of Lazarus, the character Lazarus is mute throughout.

According to Luke, Jesus ended the parable with admonitions of personal responsibility for the "offences" of the world, and a warning to those
"through whom they come," but interest has always centered on the dialogue just cited. What if one rose from the dead—how would he look, what
would he say, what entirely unique experiences would shape the words of
wisdom he would have for us? Rich as Luke's parable is, it tempts one to ask
further questions, indulge in further speculations.

In the Gospel of John the temptation proves to have been irresistible.
Lazarus is given full historical reality, a place in a family known to be
devoted to Jesus, even the boon of intimate friendship with Jesus (John
11:3): "Lord, he whom you love is ill," say his sisters. Where Luke's story is
assertion of life beyond death, with justice meting out reward and punishment appropriately, John's story is an advance upon this. John's Lazarus is
the setting for one of the magnificent "I Am" sayings (11:25–26): "I am the
resurrection and the life; he who believes in me, though he die, yet shall he
live, and whoever lives and believes in me shall never die." If Luke has
moved forward with this story to express the new doctrine of justice balanced after death, John's advance is to propose personal belief in Christ as
safety through this judgment. In John, the resurrected Lazarus stands as a
living symbol of the truth and power of Jesus' words.

John's realistic details move the story convincingly. Snatches of conversation are heard throughout the chapter; Martha's "Lord, by this time there
will be an odor" (11:39) seems a consideration of utmost practicality; the
single phrase "Jesus wept" (11:35) has communicated more to believers than
volumes of speculative Christology. The only character who has no words to
speak is, once again, Lazarus himself. When he is led from the tomb his
limbs are still bound and his face tied and hidden by a napkin. Nearly the
last time we see him in the New Testament he is sitting at dinner with his
sisters and Jesus, but he is still mute, still silent about the wonders of both
worlds in which he has lived.

John tantalizes. We have not a single word from Lazarus, who has volumes to tell of what we most want to know; furthermore, we hear nothing
of his subsequent history, his whereabouts during the crucifixion and burial

of Jesus, his role in the postresurrection community, his eventual second death. John leaves us only with these last words: "But the chief priests consulted that they might put Lazarus also to death."/1/ After New Testament times the puzzle quite logically presented itself: since the Gospel of John does not say anything about the second and final death of Lazarus, what then happened to this remarkable man? The temptation to complete the story was too great to resist; where history fails, legend moves in.

According to medieval legend, taking its cue from the plot of the priests to put Lazarus to death, Lazarus was put into a leaking boat, without oars or sails, along with Mary Magdalene and Martha and other followers of Jesus. In an early form of the legend he landed in Cyprus and was made bishop and died there. An eleventh-century legend tells that the boat landed at Sainte-Marie in southern France (sanctifying a point of embarkation for later crusaders going to the Holy Land), that the group dispersed to spread the Gospel in Provençe, and that Lazarus became the bishop of Marseilles and was martyred under Domitian. Several churches—in Constantinople, Cyprus, Milan, Marseilles, and Autun—claim to hold his remains, on the basis of these legends.

The question of the death of Lazarus having been settled, there still remained the questions of what wisdom Lazarus would have derived from his experiences and what his message would be. With Eugene O'Neill's *Lazarus Laughed*, a writer finally arrived to give the mute Lazarus words.

O'Neill subtitled *Lazarus Laughed* "A Play for an Imaginative Theatre," indicating only slightly the production difficulties involved. To begin with, O'Neill estimated that 120 actors would be required for the play. Actually 159 actors appeared in the first production, playing 420 roles. At several points all the actors are on stage. Furthermore, they were all to wear masks, representing the seven periods of life and seven "general types of character." O'Neill feared troubles and difficulties in mounting such a spectacular production, and no financial backers have ever been found for production in New York. The play was first performed in California by the Pasadena Community Players in 1928.

In the play the important biblical number *seven* is prominent from the beginning. In his preliminary stage directions O'Neill gives a list of the masks illustrating seven general types of character, providing the reader a thought-provoking list of human types, perhaps challenging the reader to find a place for himself in this human gallery. The list of masks is interesting: "The Simple, Ignorant; the Happy, Eager; the Self-Tortured, Introspective; the Proud, Self-Reliant; the Servile, Hypocritical; the Revengeful, Cruel; the Sorrowful, Resigned." Some of the human types are balanced by negative and positive characteristics, but the more destructive types have their inner dispositions extended by characteristic actions in the outside world. O'Neill would have us see Everyman, all of our diverse selves, included somewhere among the human types in the play.

The use of masks is also an obvious attempt to recapture the grandeur and solemnity of ancient Greek drama. The use of a chorus throughout the play is a further raid on antiquity signifying O'Neill's sense of the serious materials in the play. The only character who does not wear a mask, who does not need to play a role to his fellows, is Lazarus. The man has seen what lies beyond death; presumably he alone knows the meaning of life; he alone does not need a mask to hide behind. O'Neill's stage direction explains "*Lazarus*, freed now from the fear of death, wears no mask."

The uniqueness of Lazarus is further dramatized by the fact that he grows progressively younger through the play, as if the meaning of his experience grows progressively more life-giving both in his mind and in his body. O'Neill emphasizes this for the reader and the viewer: whenever Lazarus and his spouse Miriam appear together on the stage, O'Neill's directions stipulate that she will have grown noticeably older and that he has grown noticeably younger and more vigorous, more exuberant in his speech.

Though the play has four acts there are only three main locations in which the play takes place: it begins in Bethany in Palestine at the home of Lazarus, moves to Athens for a relatively brief scene in the second act, and then on to imperial Rome for the second half of the play. All of the important religious and political locations of antiquity, O'Neill seems to be saying, are touched and affected by the presence of Lazarus.

When we first see Lazarus he has just been raised from the dead by Jesus and a banquet is being celebrated in his honor. He is a man of about fifty, still stunned and inarticulate in the aftermath of his experience, though even from the beginning "his face recalls that of a statue of a divinity of Ancient Greece in its general structure and particularly in its quality of detached serenity." Where he had been a worried man before, unsuccessful and unlucky, pale though he had worked full days in the sun, now he is hardy, bronzed; he radiates "an all-embracing love" and announces to an eager audience: "There is no death." He here contradicts his father, who has just proposed a toast to his son "whom a blessed miracle has brought back from death."

The main dramatic conflict in the first act—a conflict that would arrest a twentieth-century audience with its iconoclastic modernity—is between Lazarus and Jesus. O'Neill said that he conceived his title, *Lazarus Laughed* in opposition to the phrase in John, "Jesus wept." From the beginning the influence of Lazarus seems to rise, while that of Jesus declines. In the first moments of the play one of the banquet guests recalls the miracle, as Lazarus came out of the tomb at the command of Jesus: "Jesus looked into his face for what seemed a long time and suddenly Lazarus said 'Yes' as if he were answering a question in Jesus' eyes." From the beginning, Lazarus is the man with the superior wisdom and he grows more confident in this wisdom as the play progresses. Though they begin as "brothers," the strong laugh of Lazarus comes to dominate and prevail, to win disciples to himself, as the fortunes of Jesus decline toward crucifixion and death.

During the first act the polarization continues and clarifies. The second scene opens with physical conflict between the followers of Jesus and those who remain orthodox Jews led by their priest. Both groups have disclaimed Lazarus as a renegade; both groups are fanatical in their frenzied loyalties to their own parties and their rage against the others. They soon come to blows. Almost simultaneously Lazarus appears and a messenger comes in announcing the death of Jesus. The fighting is renewed, now with knives and swords, and at its height a Roman centurion enters with a squad of soldiers. When the battle is finished several are dead, including the sisters and parents of Lazarus. He still announces that there is no death. The Roman centurion has orders for the arrest of Lazarus and as he leads him away several of the followers of Jesus as well as orthodox Jews follow after him. Even the Roman soldiers are infected by his laughter. The act ends with the star of Lazarus rising, the cause of Jesus in decline. For the rest of the act O'Neill rewrites New Testament history: Jesus grows sadder and quieter as he approaches his death; Lazarus grows more joyful and energetic and appears as a new messiah to the Mediterranean world after the death of Jesus. O'Neill seems to have had in mind the sad and "Pale Galilean" of A. C. Swinburne's famous poem, outweighed now by a lustier young god.

And as in Swinburne, and in Nietzsche, so also in O'Neill: in the second act the Lazarus who replaces Jesus is taken to be the Greek god Dionysus. The second act opens in Athens, where the Roman soldiers are passing through, leading Lazarus to trial in Rome. Among the soldiers is Gaius, nicknamed Caligula, who will succeed Tiberius as the emperor of Rome. He is apelike and childish, effeminate and cruel at the same time. The Greeks in the crowd have heard that Dionysus has been reincarnated and they expect him in the person of Lazarus.

The interaction between the Greeks and Lazarus serves mainly to amplify the new force of personality that characterizes Lazarus. He now appears younger than in Act One; they acclaim him "Redeemer and Savior . . . a God!" Stories have preceded him that he cures the sick and raises the dead and they expect him to lead Greece in a war of liberation from the Romans. Once again his laughter captivates and transforms the crowd. But a countertheme, suggested in the first act, now grows more prominent and will continue to the end: once people learn the truth they have trouble remembering it. As one of the Greeks says: "But I have heard that when Lazarus has gone people cannot remember his laughter, that the dead are dead again and the sick die, and the sad grow more sorrowful." The message of Lazarus is clear: "Fear no more . . . there is no death . . . there is only life . . . and laughter." Each of his hearers throughout the play immediately catches his meaning and is infected with his laughter. But each then forgets the wisdom that has been revealed. The ironic question intrudes throughout the play: Is Lazarus the embodiment of a wisdom so sublime that the human mind can grasp it only fleetingly, temporarily; or is his "wisdom" only an illusion, another fraud perpetrated on human credulity, one of the "pipe dreams" which O'Neill will unmask so thoroughly in *The Iceman Cometh*?

The interaction between Lazarus and the young Caligula is more subtle. Caligula is calculating and superstitious: he schemes to stay alive to become emperor, yet his peace is shattered by the threat of the supernatural. If Lazarus knows the secret of avoiding death and tells it to Tiberius, then Caligula will never become emperor. If he attempts to kill Lazarus before this can happen, then he risks entanglement with mysterious forces, since Lazarus has already died once.

Caligula is Lazarus's most interesting problem, now and for the rest of the play. The emperor-to-be is obsessed with death. If he becomes emperor he will use the threat of death to subdue his enemies, to add to his power and make others cringe; but to achieve his goal as emperor he must avoid the countless plots against his own life, must himself fear death at every moment. He has learned by experience the power of the fear of death and will use that power to rule. Lazarus thus confronts the power of the fear of death at its fullest in the figure of Caligula and the confrontation produces the most interesting and extended conversations in the play. The arguments almost convince Caligula, the laughter of Lazarus almost infects him.

When the scene shifts to Rome for the second part of the play the action and interaction become more complex still. Lazarus and Miriam are first brought to the senate, where the young Caligula presides. The senators acknowledge their fear of Tiberius's assassins and their degeneracy from nobler times; they chant in chorus about having "no trace of their ancient nobility or courage remaining." In this situation Caligula takes charge and orders the death of the followers of Lazarus who, in their large numbers, their boisterous joy, and their near deification of Lazarus, have become threats to Rome and its emperor. Lazarus intervenes only momentarily to prepare his followers for death; his only message though is his heartening laugh. The stage direction reads:

> He turns, throwing back his head and stretching up his arms, and begins to laugh low and tenderly, like caressing music at first but gradually gaining in volume, becoming more and more intense and insistent, finally ending up on a triumphant, blood-stirring call to that ultimate attainment in which all prepossession with self is lost in an ecstatic affirmation of life.

O'Neill has prepared the reader's edition of his play carefully, to convince us by passages like this that such a laugh is possible. Actually, one of the major production problems is to find an actor with capabilities to produce such sustained and magnificent laughter. O'Neill foresaw the difficulty: "Who can we get," he wrote to a friend, "to laugh as one would laugh who had completely lost, even from the depths of the unconscious, all traces of the Fear of Death?" The play was fortunate at least in its first production in Pasadena. One of the earliest critics to see the play wrote for a San Francisco newspaper of the chilling and gripping qualities of the leading actor's laugh. With obvious wonder he wrote that he had timed one of these laughs (perhaps the one just recorded) at four minutes' duration.

Intoxicated by this laugh of Lazarus, his followers rush onto the spears and swords of the Roman soldiers, who themselves begin to laugh with the same insight: "There is no death." Even Caligula is caught up in the frenzy: "Forgive me! I love you, Lazarus! Forgive me." As the crowd breaks up they have nearly decided to make Lazarus a god. But the recurrent countermotif reasserts itself: Lazarus charges them, "Wait! When you awake tomorrow, try to remember! Remember that death is dead! Remember to laugh!" But they will of course forget this wisdom and the ingrained patterns will assert their old force again.

The rest of the play—the last two of its four acts—takes place at Capri, at the villa of the emperor Tiberius himself. O'Neill stages it so that the old, corrupt, powerful, deceitful, tyrannical forces of empire now confront the new, fragile, spiritual, life-asserting force of the religion of Lazarus. History forces O'Neill to his play's conclusion: the Roman Empire will go on pretty much unchanged. But the irony has already been built into the dramatic lines of the play: one can take the new spark momentarily but it soon dies out.

As the play progresses Lazarus becomes more godlike, in his assertions that there is no death but only "fear of life" and in his strange power over the actions of others. One who is ordered to kill him kills himself, laughing with joy and freedom. The mistress of Tiberius schemes to kill Lazarus's beloved wife, to break his laughter. The plot succeeds, but with the effect that Miriam—who has loved Lazarus but has never really come under the spell of his laughter—finally understands the message. In the most startling dramatic moment of the play Miriam struggles back to life for an instant, for a last word: "Yes! There is only life! Lazarus, be not lonely." The message reassures Lazarus, convinces the characters on the stage, and very nearly convinces the cool reader in the study.

In the last act O'Neill tries to analyze the fear of death as the most profound of human problems. This fear of death is O'Neill's version of original sin, the blight on all human joy and the root of all human evils. It is, as well, the only important threat that tyrants, finally, can wield.

In the last act of *Lazarus Laughed* O'Neill deepens his analysis of this subject. The emperor Tiberius reveals that fear in his case has taken the form of loneliness. Behind his mask is a longing for childlike purity. The courtesan Pompeia, mistress of Tiberius, discovers through her evil deed— the murder of Lazarus's wife—a need for love beyond the flesh, of loyalties that will restore her self-respect. Caligula, in line for the emperor's throne, is convinced that power is achieved and maintained by cruelty. In each case

Death is the mother of fear and the creator of the great loneliness in which each character lives. The message of Lazarus—that there is no death, only life—and the persuasive laugh that accompanies this message, convince each character momentarily. But "men forget."

The play ends, of course, with the death of Lazarus, killed by the mad Caligula who knows that Lazarus's laugh would liberate people from the fear which he needs to use to rule them. As Lazarus is being burned to death the wavering Tiberius addresses him with a catechism of unanswered questions: "Is there hope of love somewhere for men on earth? . . . How must we live? . . . Why are we born? . . . To what end must we die?" Lazarus answers, "O men, fear not life! You die—but there is no death for Man!" As Lazarus is at the point of his second death Tiberius demands to know "what is beyond." Lazarus answers, "Life! Eternity! Stars and dust! God's Eternal Laughter!" The mad Caligula then enters, half convinced by this message but also realizing that the message destroys Caesar's power over men—if he cannot kill them they will not fear and obey him. He rushes with a spear to stop these last words of Lazarus, kills him, and then has another change of heart: "Fool! Madman!" he says to himself. But his last words, and the last words of the play, are "Men forget!"

O'Neill's last act rises to the kind of irony of which only the greatest tragedians are capable. In *Lazarus Laughed* the truth that makes humans free, as the dramatist conceives it, is available by special revelations, but because of flaws and fear the human grasp is a weak one. Human limitations reassert themselves and the saving insight is lost.

One of the early critics who read the play wondered about the repetitiousness of Lazarus's message—there is no fear, only life, and laughter—and declared the play "a bore." Actually, O'Neill worked over the play very carefully, building up the speeches of Lazarus so that they would have an ascending, cumulative effect. Either Lazarus's insight into the truth grows as he ponders his unique experience, or else further insights are stimulated by the people he meets and their personal flaws and individual needs. The characters of the drama are stock figures in the early part of the play; fully developed individuals are introduced only when the scene has shifted to Rome in the second part of the play. As individuals they draw out more of Lazarus's wisdom than he is able to impart earlier to the stock figures.

O'Neill obviously felt the need to go beyond the New Testament, as if drawing out a line of redemptive thought that would be more convincing to a modern audience than the original. Orthodox readers of the New Testament have always agreed on at least one point—that Jesus preached a personal immortality, an afterlife in which the individual Ego would survive intact beyond the grave. The sermon on the Last Judgment in Matthew seemed unequivocal on that point (25:34–45):

Come, O blessed of my Father, inherit the kingdom prepared for
you from the foundation of the world. . . . Truly, I say to you, as you
did it to one of the least of these my brethren, you did it to me. . . .
Depart from me, you cursed, into the eternal fire prepared for the
devil and his angels. . . . Truly, I say to you, as you did it not to one
of the least of these, you did it not to me.

It becomes clear in the second half of the play that this is not O'Neill's
message. He sensed that early twentieth-century audiences could no longer
support this belief and that something must be substituted to fill the gap.
The play was to construct a new religious doctrine. The starting point of his
play, O'Neill wrote, would be "the death of the old God and the failure of
science and materialism to give any satisfying new one for the surviving
primitive religious instinct to find a meaning of life in, and to comfort its
fear of death with."

O'Neill anticipated some difficulties in producing a drama with such an
effect. For *Lazarus Laughed* he envisioned

a theatre that . . . is the legitimate descendant of the first theatre that
sprang, by virtue of man's imaginative interpretation of life, out of
his worship of Dionysus. I mean a theatre returned to its highest and
sole significant function as a Temple where the religion of a poetical
interpretation and symbolical celebration of life is communicated to
human beings, starved in spirit by their soul-stifling daily struggle to
exist as masks among the masks of the living.

O'Neill preaches an alternative kind of immortality, not perhaps as
satisfying, but not as frightening either. The full statement of it is reserved
for the last act, where Lazarus says to Caligula: "What if you are a man and
men are despicable? Men are also unimportant! Men pass . . . Man remains!
Man slowly arises from the past of the race of men that was his tomb of
death! For Man death is not! Man, Son of God's Laughter, *is!*" The individual Ego will not survive, in this conceptualization; the generic *Man* survives
eternally.

It is possible to mistake O'Neill here, to consider his thought to be that
Man survives eternally but merely as a concept. But O'Neill seems to be
taking his stand somewhere between this idea and traditional Christian doctrine. "Man," in the speech of Lazarus, seems more concrete. One seems
close here to the notion of humanity—indeed of all creatures—receiving
temporary individualization from the pool of Being, then returning to and
merging with that pool of Being at death. Still more is indicated. When
O'Neill writes of Man as "Son of God's Laughter" and dramatizes the concept with the ring of Lazarus's laughter throughout the play, he seems to be
further characterizing that pool of Being as joyous and creative.

O'Neill's *Lazarus Laughed* is a play with an enormously strong pulse.
Several sources have been suggested as contributing to or stimulating
O'Neill's thought here. Nietzsche's influence has been recognized almost

from the first appearance of the play. Zarathustra infects his followers with a cosmic laugh similar to that of Lazarus, and Nietzsche's Dionysus, in *The Birth of Tragedy*, transmits life-giving forces to his followers as does Lazarus. One is reassured at least that O'Neill had mastered one of the weightier documents of his trade, but the ambience in O'Neill's play seems still wider.

It has also been said that O'Neill researched Freud and Bergson on the theory of humor but was unable to find in them any similarities to his own perceptions of the kind of spontaneous overflow of joy and energy he wanted to employ in his play. To assess further the accomplishment of O'Neill in this remarkable play it might be better to look closer to home than the critics have yet done, to see him building strongly in the native American tradition. When O'Neill wrote his play, Walt Whitman had been dead some thirty-five years, but his reputation and popularity were growing yearly.

We should perhaps have been able to draw the continuous line from Whitman to O'Neill earlier. *Lazarus Laughed* is a verse play, but written in the same rhythmical lines of verse that Whitman perfected instead of the more traditional pentameters. The closest analogue to Whitman's verse that has yet been discovered is the cadenced line of Psalms and Proverbs, as rendered in the King James Version of the Bible, and there are echoes of the King James idiom throughout *Lazarus Laughed* as well. There are more similarities still. "I know that age and time are but timidities of thought" is a line from *Lazarus Laughed*, but anyone responsive to the idioms of *Leaves of Grass* could easily mistake the line as Whitman's.

Part of Whitman's vast achievement stands behind the more substantial sections of O'Neill's play. Where O'Neill works to develop and deepen his theme, the correspondences with Whitman become more obvious. In Act Two Lazarus sees that Caligula, as the man in line to be emperor, is worth some extra work of persuasion. In the midst of one of his longest speeches yet in the play Lazarus says:

> As Man, Petty Tyrant of Earth, you are a bubble pricked by death into a void and a mocking silence! But as dust, you are eternal change, and everlasting growth, and a high note of laughter soaring through chaos from the deep heart of God! Be proud, O Dust! Then may you love the stars as equals!

Lazarus here takes Caligula through a sequence one can find frequently in Whitman. In "As I Ebb'd with the Ocean of Life" and in "To Think of Time" Whitman succumbs momentarily to the thought of individual annihilation and the despair it produces. But always, for Whitman, salvation comes in a wider and more cosmic view of the life process. Maurice Bucke, a psychiatrist and the friend and biographer of Whitman, called this "Cosmic Consciousness" and believed that Whitman had been the first to evolve a new mental power capable of expanding to this form of conceptualization. Once again O'Neill produces a line that sounds very much like Whitman: "as dust, you are eternal change, and everlasting growth"—the kind of thought Whitman would use as a corrective to the individual's despair, and the kind of rhythm he used to express it.

In the next scene Lazarus expands his thought for Miriam, who has followed him faithfully without fully comprehending his experience or his message:

> Eye to eye with the Fear of Death, did they [the followers of Lazarus who willingly accepted death when the Roman soldiers charged] not laugh with scorn? "Death to old Death," they laughed! "Once as squirming specks we crept from the tides of the sea. Now we return to the sea! Once as quivering flecks of rhythm we beat down from the sun. Now we reenter the sun! Cast aside is our pitiable pretense, our immortal egohood, the holy lantern behind which cringed our Fear of the Dark!"

The achievement is expressed in the idiom of Paul—"O death, where is thy victory? O death, where is thy sting?" (1 Corinthians 15:55)—but the image that justifies it is once again Whitman's. For an expanding and optimistic writer, as Whitman surely was, the great fact to be overcome was death and the thought of annihilation. Whitman faced this most squarely in the poem "Out of the Cradle Endlessly Rocking," where the extraordinary achievement is made, that the word "Death" becomes "delicious." The means for achieving this affirmation are to be found in the image of the sea, here and in many other poems, and likewise in the speech of Lazarus just cited. Ocean produces life, threatens while simultaneously protecting it, and in the end receives back all forms of individual life. As Lazarus says later in the play: "Men pass! Like rain into the sea! The sea remains! Man remains!"

In "Passage to India," Whitman's highest achievement of "cosmic consciousness," all reality is subsumed in the vision of the "vast Rondure, swimming in space, / Cover'd all over with visible power and beauty." But even this is transcended to a still higher vision:

> O Thou transcendent,
> Nameless, the fibre and the breath,
> Light of the light, shedding forth universes, thou centre of them,
> Thou mightier centre of the true, the good, the loving,
> Thou moral, spiritual fountain—affection's source—thou reservoir,
> (O pensive soul of me—O thirst unsatisfied—waitest not there?
> Waitest not haply for us somewhere there the Comrade perfect?)
> Thou pulse—thou motive of the stars, suns, systems,
> That, circling, move in order, safe, harmonious,
> Athwart the shapeless vastnesses of space,
> How could I think, how breathe a single breath, how speak, if, out of
>   myself,
> I could not launch, to those, superior universes?

The poem ends with joyous affirmation:

> O my brave soul!
> O farther farther sail!
> O daring joy, but safe! are they not all the seas of God?
> O farther, farther, farther sail!

It is all here—joy, death, expansive optimism, and the sea—very much as Lazarus would have it when he addresses Miriam toward the end of O'Neill's play:

> But what am I? Now your love has become Eternal Love! Now, since your life has passed, I feel Eternal Life made nobler by your self-lessness! Love has grown purer! The Laughter of God is more profoundly tender!

Our original hypothesis is borne out, then, at least in the case of this play. *Lazarus Laughed* takes a biblical narrative for its starting point. But before he has finished with it, O'Neill has summoned such fathers of our modern sensibilities as Nietzsche, Freud, and Bergson; and the play then further becomes O'Neill's vehicle for elaborating the world views of America's most original and exhilarating poet.

Drama incorporates tradition as perhaps no other art form does. At its best it has always been religious, political, philosophical, and social, with these elements assembled in the figures of memorable characters who are engaged in significant action that can move even mass audiences. It can be taken for granted—since the characters and stories of the Bible, as well as its idiom, have been such a powerful molding influence throughout our history—that dramatists will continue to turn to biblical narratives for stimulus to their creative imaginations, for vehicles for their most challenging speculations.

At least such has been the case in American drama, whether popular or elite. At the turn of the century William Vaughan Moody experimented with a verse trilogy that began with the Incarnation, chronicled the conflicts between God and his creatures, and ended with the unfinished play *The Death of Eve*. Marc Connelley's *The Green Pastures*, a reenactment of Old Testament stories in blackface, prospered while the country slid deep into the Great Depression; it ran for a year and a half on Broadway, won the Pulitzer Prize, and was acclaimed as "perhaps the great religious play of our American times" by a prominent drama critic. In 1942 Thornton Wilder, brother of the noted theologian Amos Wilder, presented the history of civilization in one evening, with biblical episodes inserted appropriately, in *The Skin of Our Teeth*. Archibald MacLeish's *J.B.*, a modern businessman's reenactment of the story of Job, was one of the outstanding stage successes of the late 1950s.

Maxwell Anderson once wrote that the theater should be "essentially a cathedral of the spirit"; in his play on Joan of Arc he amplified this with the

opinion that the theater was "Democracy's temple." He spent his professional career providing liturgies for that cathedral, insisting that the dramatization of the moral virtues and vices most enlivened the theater and that
goodness must triumph at the end of the play.

Anderson was a careful student of Aristotle and he meditated at length on
the theory of dramatic poetry. One of his major contributions to dramatic
theory, and to practice as well, was an extension of what happens in the
traditional "recognition scene." Anderson believed that this recognition should
cause an actual moral change in the main figure, a change in consciousness and
character; the protagonist's soul should be improved by self-discovery. This
invention added both to the scope of his poetry and to the dramatic depth of
his major plays. But in his last work for the stage Anderson seems to have gone
beyond even his own orthodoxies, to probe deeper into the mystery of evil.
This last work was a dramatization of the terrifying novel by William March,
The Bad Seed. In the popular novel March had worked on the ironic
persistence of evil in the little girl who had "inherited" her criminal character
from her murderous mother. Anderson's treatment went far beyond such
dubious theories of criminal psychology and opened up more ancient considerations of the fall of humanity and the effect of original sin.

This also seems to be the area in which Lillian Hellman has done her
deepest probing. We think of her as operating within severely limited
situations—the interactions between blood relations, in small groupings, in
enclosed spaces of the family home—but working intensely within these
limitations. She rarely ranges out toward "poetic" flights or stretches for a sense
of transcendence, but two of the finest drama critics of the recent past have
arrived independently at the same sense of her art. John Gassner wrote in 1964,
"Miss Hellman concerns herself generally with damnation as a state of the soul,
and a case might be made out for saying that her real theme, whether she knew
it or not, is 'original sin' in a modern context." And Robert Corrigan, in the
same year, wrote that "she cannot be considered, as she so often is, a social
writer; rather, she is interested in showing damnation as a state of the soul, a
condition that cannot be reformed out of existence or dissolved by sentimentality or easy optimism."

This story of the fall of humanity, recorded in Genesis 2 and 3, is rightly
taken to be the "first" story of Western civilization, the story that has dominated both its literature and its theology throughout. Once the topic is raised
we are led naturally to a work by one of the finest of the American dramatists,
Arthur Miller. The story was embodied from the very announcement of the
title of his 1964 play, *After the Fall*. Miller himself has given a capsule
description of the play: "it is a way of looking at man and his common nature
as the only source of the violence which has come closer and closer to
destroying the race. It is a view which does not look toward social or political
ideas as the creators of violence, but into the nature of the human being
himself."

In Miller's story the main speaker, Quentin, is awash in a sea of conflicting self-impressions, unable to determine his own identity, whether heroic or cowardly, divine or demonic. His name must come from William Faulkner's Quentin in *The Sound and the Fury*, a character tormented by family sins and hostilities, by the failure of love. The destructiveness in Miller's play is likewise spiritual and psychological: love has turned to contempt or dependency, to some kind of death for those who are loved. Miller's play begins from his main character's puzzlement: "I am bewildered by the death of love. And my responsibility for it." His enlightenment at the end of the play is that finally it was his own ego that was the center of disorder and destruction. The review of his life ends with the damning insight: "I loved them all, all! . . . and gave them willingly to failure and to death that I might live." The Genesis story has been enriched here by the New Testament assertion of the primacy of love and by ironic inversion of the sacrifice of Jesus; but the dynamics of the Fall are by no means weakened. It becomes explicit in the play that human beings are finally condemned to live "after the Fall," in the ruined Eden of the present, to find what salvation they can there.

Similar matters drive the plays of Tennessee Williams, born in the Episcopal rectory of his clergyman grandfather. While critics have described the effect of his plays as "emotional exhaustion" for the audience, rather than the catharsis of pity and terror mandated by classical tragedy, audiences nevertheless have recorded profound and lasting reactions to the great plays of the 1940s and 1950s.

Williams's first professional play, *Battle of Angels* (1940), was shouted to a close during its first and only night in Boston. But his critics and sponsors, and Williams as well, liked it from the beginning, while acknowledging that there was too much matter in it, too many characters, and too many touches of melodrama. And so the play persisted in Williams's mind, through many evolutionary changes, to become seventeen years later *Orpheus Descending*, and then to be filmed as *The Fugitive Kind*. In many ways it can be taken as the archetypal play for Williams, latent in his mind for many years, a repository for many of his most moving themes and characters.

Dominating the play from his room above the store is the dying old husband Jabe—undeniably sharing characteristics of the Old Testament Yahweh, thumping his cane on the floor to bring the actors below to order, slowly dying of incurable cancer. His wife, younger but mature and sensuous, spends her days tending the store below in company with the young writer-drifter she has hired as a handyman. Her name, Myra, is not the least of the items suggesting her identification with the Virgin Mary. The handsome drifter, who immediately attracts all eligible and frustrated females in the area, is named Valentine Xavier, combining the saint of love with the "Savior." His snakeskin jacket suggests the demonic, but also the renewal of life if the old skin can be sloughed. He is Christ seen through the filter of D. H. Lawrence. That he is caught while trying to escape into the "Sangre

de Cristo" country and that he is lynched on a "hanging tree" as the stage
goes up in a final conflagration complete the allegory. Two of the most powerful screen presences of the time, Marlon Brando and Anna Magnani, were
brought in to realize these parts for *The Fugitive Kind*.

In his most recent autobiography Williams has recorded lifelong attempts
to exorcize "puritanical guilt feelings"; his first professional play sets the stage
admirably for that personal *agon*. Like his inaugural play, rewritten as a
mid-career statement, *Battle of Angels* contains much of the matter and
methodology that have come to define the art of Tennessee Williams, his
sense of the problems that infect modern life. It dramatizes as well the
biblical connections with those guilt feelings. Sensuality and sexuality are
disorders in this view of the present fallen world, not to be redeemed even
when the most powerful of our salvation stories is brought in to provide the
narrative foundation for this modern morality play.

In the case of Edward Albee we heard an entirely new voice in his early
plays, especially *The Sandbox* (1959) and *The American Dream* (1960). His
was the drama of tortured family relationships, brought to its highest pitch
in *Who's Afraid of Virginia Woolf?* (1962). Albee's was the voice of incred-
ible hostility between husband and wife, between parents and children.
Those who are linked by marriage and kinship are the special object of a
rage that would annihilate. The corrosive situations seemed so extreme that
Albee was immediately paired with Samuel Beckett, as America's entry into
the Theatre of the Absurd. But so true did the cadenced hostility ring, somewhere in the corners of our souls, that he became America's most "promising" playwright of the 1960s. No one was left untouched by the violence he
uncovered in the national psyche, a violence that was playing itself out in
the public streets as well.

Ruby Cohn of the University of California at Davis has found biblical
echoes throughout Albee's works, beginning with the figures of Peter and
Jerry (Jeremiah, with a suggestion of Jesus), who attack one another with a
combination of love and hostility in *The Zoo Story*, the scope of whose
action and insight ranges from the animality of human beings to sacrificial
altruism and a search for the divine.

Both sets of materials—the stinging injuries of family conversation and
the echo of biblical models—converge in Albee's 1966 play *A Delicate Balance*. In that play the married couple are Tobias and Agnes. Clare, the alco-
holic and seductive sister of Agnes, lives with them. Agnes senses in her own
mind and in the family relationships "a delicate balance" between madness
and sanity, stability and disorder. Tobias faces the terror of emptiness after
retirement from a successful career. Clare "clearly" sees their weakness and
taunts them for it. Into this already unstable situation comes another couple,
Harry and Edna, the best friends of Agnes and Tobias and, as Albee's directions make clear, "very much like them." Harry and Edna have suddenly
become frightened by their loneliness and the horror of their meaningless

existence and their empty home. They have come without warning to move in permanently with Harry and Agnes, like frightened children. The situation is vintage Albee: the action is absurd, but it also thrusts a mirror into the family midst in which the members can more clearly see themselves. Agnes later sees that they have brought "the plague" with them, a contagious "terror," into her own family and home. The final complication of the play is provided by the arrival of Julia, daughter of Tobias and Agnes. Though in her mid-thirties she is fleeing home for comfort after the breakup of her fourth marriage. She becomes childish and mean when she finds Harry and Edna occupying her room.

Names begin to resonate: "Clare" has already been mentioned and "Agnes" is Lamb, though that echo seems submerged. The two most unusual names for contemporary Americans are Tobias and Edna. One experiences the shock of recognition with the realization that these are names featured in the Book of Tobit. This book, prominent among the apocrypha of the Old Testament, has long been a favorite "family" tract for pious Christians. The theme of the story is that simple fidelity to the law of God will work such wonders as the restoration of sight to the blind, the restoration of wealth after adversity, protection from the powerful rulers of this world, banishment of the Demon, and the celebration of a true marriage "made in heaven." All of this is accomplished through the agency of the angel Raphael disguised as a man. One of the morals that later piety would take from the story was that those who show hospitality have sometimes entertained angels in disguise—a moral seriously under question when Harry and Edna arrive to stay in Albee's play.

A Delicate Balance is a careful reconsideration of the pieties in Tobit, an inversion of the ancient story for the discovery of modern truths, for the purging (one hopes) of distempered emotions. The characters are so written that the audience can relate to them more sympathetically than to the characters in previous Albee plays. But to paraphrase one of Herman Melville's most memorable aphorisms, "Surely in no world but a fallen one could such a family exist."

Even when we move to more popular forms of entertainment in America, we must note that they have always tended to be at once biblical and epic. Ben Hur: A Tale of the Christ, the spectacle by General Lew Wallace, was popular as a novel, selling some two million copies after its publication in 1880. It was popular also as a play that ran for several years at the turn of the century, and finally it succeeded in two film versions, in 1925 and in 1959. In any of its forms it still has the power to move an audience.

Although only two of the projected nine episodes of Star Wars are finished, it does not take much probing to discern the biblical quality of the imagination at work there. Darth Vader is a thorough and satisfying embodiment of our most primitive version of the devil. "The Force" by which the Saints combat him is easily recognized as a synonym for "Grace." And the great sage and teacher disappears like Elijah, King Arthur, Jesus; but he is not really dead and will reappear when Israel, England, ourselves most need him to help us through the horrors of the endtime.

Apocalypse Now, to mention one more biblical epic, is a film of flawed grandeur. Its flaws derive from an inconsistent use of one of its models, Joseph Conrad's *Heart of Darkness*. In Conrad the questing character is a lucid moral consciousness probing for the good and evil qualities in his experience, with piercing intensity; in *Apocalypse Now* he is represented rather as a degenerate assassin with no moral awareness of the horrors through which he passes. The viewers are robbed of any solid ground, within the world of this film, in which to anchor their own perceptions and highly stimulated emotions. But the readily acknowledged grandeur of *Apocalypse Now* derives from the inspiration of its other literary model, the Book of Revelation. The horrors of the Vietnam War here represent the triumph of pure evil, where the saints, if there are any, are in great peril, where the rulers of this age are bringing down the world in a rampage of undisguised wickedness.

Much of American drama, in its period of greatest vitality, derives in some way from the stories contained between Genesis and Revelation. But to make the play work, to bring the materials from static to dynamic, some modern element seems also required: the ideas of a powerful thinker, the stories of another modern writer, the deaths of folk figures like Bessie Smith or Marilyn Monroe, facts that have seemed important to the sense of our present times—such as the Vietnam War, the House Un-American Activities Committee, the threat of fascism.

From this point of view O'Neill's *Lazarus Laughed* indeed suggests a formula. It is a prime exemplar of the play where biblical materials are amplified and set into a new kind of motion by powerful modern ideas. The formula has generated much that makes twentieth-century American drama interesting. But if formulization carries the risks of atrophy and predictability, modern dramatic writers continue to surprise audiences with their fresh inventions. In trying to explain the undoubted success of the popular television series *Dallas*, the writers of *Time* magazine recently concluded: "These plot permutations have a biblical resonance: Cain and Abel, Abraham and Isaac, Noah and his sons, Sodom and Gomorrah." These narratives easily suggest the dramatic themes of envy and murderous revenge between brothers, the father who would sacrifice his sons or the father who is driven to create a dynasty bearing his name, and the sense that cities are to be seen as the place where wickedness is most concentrated.

From its beginnings in our own century, American drama has frequently gone back to mine the stories of the Bible, though with some recklessness toward the intentions of its original authors. The Bible remains one of the culture's most prized resources, and its narratives continue to illuminate our modern behavior.

NOTE

Special thanks are expressed to Robert O. Johnson and Georgia Hooks Shurr, who read this essay and offered valuable suggestions.

/1/ Biblical critics disagree on the subject of Lazarus. Some have proposed a more subtle hypothesis than I have described here: in the light of the story of the resurrection of Lazarus in Johannine oral tradition, Luke gave his character the same name and added the second ending (noted above) to show that even the appearance of Lazarus from the dead did not have the effect Dives had hoped for. But the actual relationship between the two stories does not bear on O'Neill's use of the figure.

WORKS CONSULTED

Cohn, Ruby
    1969   *Edward Albee*. Minneapolis: University of Minnesota Press.

Corrigan, Robert Willoughby
    1964   *The Modern Theatre*. New York: Macmillan.

Corrigan, Robert Willoughby, and Rosenberg, James, eds.
    1964   *The Context and Craft of Drama*. San Francisco: Chandler.

Downer, Alan Seymour, ed.
    1965   *American Drama and Its Critics*. Chicago: University of Chicago Press.

Gassner, John
    1960   *Theatre at the Crossroads: Plays and Playwrights of the Mid-Century American Stage*. New York: Holt, Rinehart, and Winston.

Gelb, Arthur, and Gelb, Barbara
    1962   *O'Neill*. New York: Harper.

Gould, Jean
    1966   *Modern American Playwrights*. New York: Dodd, Mead.

Johnson, Claudia D.
    1975   "That Guilty Third Tier: Prostitution in Nineteenth-Century American Theaters." *American Quarterly* 17: 575–84.

Meserve, Walter J.
    1965   *An Outline History of American Drama*. Totowa, NJ: Littlefield, Adams.

Sheaffer, Louis
    1968   *O'Neill: Son and Playwright*. Boston: Little, Brown.

V

American Architecture:
The Prophetic and Biblical Strains

Clifford E. Clark, Jr.

In old Deerfield, Massachusetts, at the end of one of the main streets, sits the Ashley house, built by an Anglican minister in the 1750s. The entrance to the house is through a magnificent door, framed on either side with fluted columns on pedestals and surmounted with gracefully curving scrolls. At the top of each scroll is a pinwheel. In a nearby graveyard, which contains gravestones going all the way back to the seventeenth century, a number of stones have the same shape as the Ashley house door. They too have pinwheels. The remarkable similarity of shape and symbolism between stone and door is not fortuitous, for Americans in the eighteenth century believed that life was transitory. What counted was the future condition of the soul and the prospect of eternal salvation. The gravestone was thus a symbolic door, a door to a new and better world, and the pinwheels were symbols of eternity.

A thousand miles away and thirty years later, Thomas Jefferson wrote to James Madison: "You see I am an enthusiast on the subject of the arts. But it is an enthusiasm of which I am not ashamed, as its object is to improve the taste of my countrymen, to increase their reputation, to reconcile them to the respect of the world, and to procure them its praise" (Jefferson to Madison, 20 September 1785, quoted in Kimball: 9). As the architect of Monticello, the state capitol of Virginia, and the University of Virginia, Jefferson became the early voice for classical revival architecture in America. He not only provided superb designs in this classical revival style but he also established himself as one of the first theorists in what was to become a long tradition of American elite architecture.

Ostensibly there is little connection between Jefferson's innovative handling of classical revival styles and the Ashley door. I mention them simply to highlight what I see to be the two major aspects of the American architectural tradition: the vernacular or folk phase—a set of delightful structures whose styles and forms were shaped by habit and tradition—and the remarkable American phenomenon so well illustrated by Jefferson of the great architect with a philosophy of architecture that influences our perception and understanding of building forms throughout the centuries.

To understand the impact of biblical ideas and motifs on American architecture, we must not only look at both of these traditions, but we must also be aware of their pattern of interaction. Such an examination is especially difficult for the vernacular tradition, because the major assumptions implicit in the structures, which must have been commonplace for the people of the time, are more difficult to understand from a twentieth-century perspective. Still, the great advantage of selectively contrasting the two traditions, as Catherine Albanese (1) has recently suggested, is that it allows us to do for architecture what needs to be done for American religion—that is, to put in a new perspective both the external dimension of American architecture, the evolution of structures created by more elite groups who were explicit about their goals and ideals, and also to discover the inner history of the vernacular tradition—an approach that looks for unconscious, half-hidden, implicit world views and values.

The purpose of this essay is to stand back from these two great traditions within the American architectural experience and to analyze selected samples of the ways in which biblical motifs and ideas have been expressed. The complex nature of American religion and the diverse ethnic, racial, and denominational differences make it impossible to examine the entire field. My hope is rather to analyze a small number of specific examples to illustrate the wonderful innovativeness and diversity of American building and to comment especially on what appears to be a consistent jeremiad tradition on the part of professional architects—a critical, moralistic, messianic philosophy that Americans bring to their understanding of the built environment. The first part of this essay will focus on the evolution of the vernacular tradition in the nineteenth century into a philosophy of architecture reflecting the growing secularization of society. The remainder of the essay will contrast the vernacular tradition with the prophetic stance of major architectural reformers, from Thomas Jefferson and Andrew Jackson Downing in the nineteenth century to Frank Lloyd Wright and Philip Johnson in the twentieth.

Despite the wonderful complexity of the vernacular tradition and the fascinating variation of forms from region to region, certain consistent features characterize its stance over the years. From the Puritans to the Shakers to the house pattern books of the nineteenth century, the vernacular tradition was animated by an in-group perspective, a self-consciousness about each group's own identity, a shared commitment to certain central values, and an uneasiness about and, in some cases, a distinct hostility to outsiders. The Puritans worried about the non-elect, the Quakers, and all those who did not share their convictions; the Shakers feared the grasping materialism and sensuality of American capitalism; and the nineteenth-century plan-book reformers scorned the new Irish Catholic and German Catholic immigrants. By looking at the relationships among these three movements—the

Puritans, the Shakers, and the plan-book reformers—and the structures they built, we can get a new angle of vision on the relationship between biblical motifs and group identity.

To understand the role of the Bible in colonial America, we must recognize that although there were always atheists and nonbelievers in early New England, a religious perspective on the world was generally accepted. Religion was an everyday part of life, explicit in the sermons of clergy like John Cotton or in the diaries of Samuel Sewall but implicit generally in the built world in every community. As several historians have pointed out, most Americans, and especially those in New England, lived in a theocracy—not a rule by the priesthood but one that contained a harmony of ideals between minister, magistrate, and populace. Within this context, the Bible functioned as the great authority, the defender of tradition, the guide to daily life, and the proof of the hierarchy and division within the world (Bercovitch: 3n).

The pervasiveness of religion and the acceptance of it as a central feature of everyday life could be seen in the design and layout of the New England town and meetinghouse. The fact that the church and the meetinghouse were the same building reassured the townspeople that the religious and civil functions were compatible and interrelated. Although in some respects the Puritans enforced the boundaries between church and state by making marriage a civil act and by insisting that offenses against the state could not be punished by the church, nevertheless the structures they built rested on implicit beliefs about the purpose of the community. These assumptions can be perceived in the use of the meetinghouse and its placement in the landscape. Usually positioned on the highest side of the town common, the meetinghouse demonstrated, both by its physical presence and by its central location, that the authority of church and town was unitary, tangible, and hierarchical. The principle, dramatically proclaimed by John Winthrop on board the *Arabella*, that "God Almightie in his holy and wise providence hath soe disposed of the Condicion of mankinde, as in all times some must be rich some poore, some highe and eminent in power and dignitie, others meane and in subieccion" (Winthrop, 1630, quoted in Miller and Johnson: I, 195; see also Walsh: 79–95) was made tangible in the layout of the church. Seating was arranged by social standing with the wealthy and educated in the front, the poor in the rear, and the indigent and criminal segregated in the galleries. The pulpit was given a commanding position above the rest of the congregation.

If the Bible reinforced traditional attitudes toward obedience and authority, churches and domestic houses in the seventeenth and early eighteenth centuries tended to be simply constructed, functional, and plain. The lack of frills or ornate decoration was characteristic of the Puritan attitude toward religious observance. For example, the Old Ship Meetinghouse in Hingham, Massachusetts, which dates to 1681, has a plain interior that stresses the reliance on the spoken word. The vernacular tradition in colonial architecture reflected the implicit values of a biblical commonwealth—homogeneity, order, hierarchy, and conformity. From village to village the patterns were similar; tightly knit, well-defined communities worked and worshipped together in architectural structures that mirrored the harmony and directness of the Puritan vision.

This vernacular tradition, with its simple, direct placement of religion at the center of life, did not die out with the end of the eighteenth century. It has lived on in the simple austerity of the folk traditions in many parts of this country. One of the prime examples of the power of this tradition is the Shakers. Founded in 1773 by "Mother" Ann Lee and brought to Niskayuna, near Albany, two years later, the Shaker faith stressed the principles of chastity, community of goods, simplicity, confession of sins, and separation from the world. Called "Shakers" because of the frenzied shaking that they exhibited during their religious services, this group built twenty-five settlements between 1780 and 1826, mostly in the northwest part of the county.

The great innovation of the Shaker style, which was reinforced by the angularity of their designs and by the layout of their communities, was the direct sense of separation of this world from the next. The functional hierarchy of Shaker buildings was color-coded; barns were dark red and the meeting-house was white. The structures were oriented at right angles to reinforce the rigid divisions they saw in the everyday world between men and women, between their society and public "worldlings." Even stovepipes ran in right-angled segments and meal signs warned: "Bread and meat are to be cut square." Heavenly space, in contrast, was spherical and mystical. If the orderly arrangements of buildings and systematic interiors gave the Shakers a sense of identity and purpose, the twirling dances gave the members a sense of the freedom to be gained in the heavenly sphere (Hayden: 65ff.; also Andrews).

There were two prerequisites for the continuation of the vernacular architectural traditions; both were fulfilled by the Shakers. The first prerequisite was the preservation of an unusual religious tradition apart from the mainstream of society. The Shakers, through their simple, direct craftsmanship and their clear conception of the differences between heavenly and earthly space, deliberately set their communities apart. They even built special offices where they could meet and do business with the public, thus preserving their own interior world. The second prerequisite was isolation. As Henry Glassie (5ff.) has pointed out in his study of folk culture in the eastern United States, certain styles of houses persisted in the mountains and among social classes that were less influenced by new fashions, popular trends, or elite, academic culture. Basic structural continuities in terms of room design and use of space have continued for generations in parts of the South, the Mid-Atlantic states, and New England.

While the vernacular tradition, with its accepted standards, was the dominant tradition in the seventeenth and eighteenth centuries, it was surpassed in the nineteenth by a set of new, mass standards. The new architectural ideals, and particularly the revival of earlier historical styles such as the

Gothic and the Italianate, were popularized for a much larger audience through the publication of thousands of house-plan and house-pattern books. Even churches, which had earlier followed traditional European styles, were designed from pattern books. Implicit in these structures were new assumptions about the nature of religion, the role of the church, and the understanding of the Bible. Nineteenth-century builders displaced the vernacular tradition from its central position in popular culture and created an entirely new way of applying biblical motifs and standards to mass-produced buildings.

An early example of the pattern-book style and the assumptions that surrounded it was the magnificent First Congregational Church (1806) in Old Bennington, Vermont. Like the meetinghouses, the First Church is situated on the top of a hill, overlooking the town. The white, wood church, built in the neoclassical style with three doors topped by a Palladian window and finished off with a delicate spire with oval lights and tall slender columns, is very much like Plate 33 in Asher Benjamin's *The Country Builder's Assistant*, published in Greenfield, Massachusetts, in 1797. The proportions of the church, the symmetrical façade, and the magnificent oval ceiling in the interior demonstrate the period's new faith in rationality, which is also confirmed by the lessons in plane geometry at the beginning of the pattern book. The world view is still hierarchical, as indicated by the explanations of classical orders in the plan book and the seating arrangements in the church; the most prominent families sat on the main floor in front, and criminals and blacks were segregated in the rear balcony. It is also instructive that the early plan books carried no direct references to the Bible. Rationality was the key to understanding the underlying laws of the universe, whether they be applied to religion, the laws of physics, or the laws constructing buildings. Although the Bennington Congregationalists did not subscribe to the extreme use of reason that led William Ellery Channing and others to found the Unitarian Church in 1819, their church did reveal a more rationalistic approach to the world. The marvelous interior circular ceiling symbolized the sense of unity and harmony they felt with the underlying principles of the universe.

It was only a small step from the early plan-book celebration of classical revival styles to the more complete expression of the new attitudes toward religion and the Bible which were dramatically demonstrated in the Gothic revival. The new rage for Gothic revival styles that swept the country between the 1830s and the 1860s and found expression in churches, schools, prisons, domestic houses, utopian communes, and cemetery gates rested on the major reorientation of religious outlook that took place during the Second Great Awakening and on the aesthetic assumptions of the romantic movement (Clark: 33–56).

In many ways, the waves of revivals that swept the nation in the 1830s and 1840s served as a catalyst for extensive social and intellectual changes. Not only did vast numbers of new converts enter the churches, but these

Christians also brought with them a new sense of the immediacy of religion and of the urgent necessity to change traditional patterns of behavior. Since the revivals were sparked by a strengthened sense of the erosion of morality caused by the new immigration, the sprawling uncontrolled growth of cities, and the dynamic expansion westward across the continent, they brought with them a renewed sense that individuals ought to play a more direct role in their own salvation. This more positive attitude toward human nature also brought with it a missionary zeal to perfect the world. Mass revivals, with their intense emotional experiences, caused many to rethink their lives and to rebuild their social environment.

Under the impact of revivalism, religion came to play a more aggressive role in people's lives. If church members in the late eighteenth century had seen the erosion of religion's impact on everyday life and had interpreted the First Great Awakening as a miracle, an exception to daily routines, nineteenth-century church leaders like Lyman Beecher and Charles Grandison Finney turned revivals into planned events, a conscious strategy to increase church membership. So, too, the Bible after 1830 was viewed not as a repository of values and authority that reinforced tradition and the entire social structure but as a new instrument for dealing with contemporary moral issues—a change in keeping with the gradual shift in attention from the seventeenth century's preoccupation with life after death to the nineteenth century's concern about the immanence of Christ in the present world (McLoughlin).

It is ironic that revivalism not only stimulated a new interest in building styles like the Gothic that would strengthen and reinforce building standards but also produced a counterreaction among the church leadership that stressed the need for appropriate family environments. The leader of the new movement was Horace Bushnell, a minister in Hartford, Connecticut, who was upset by the emotionalism and stress of revivalism, which pressured each individual to make an immediate decision to transform his or her life. Expressing his views in 1847 in a book entitled *Christian Nurture*, Bushnell argued that a child should grow up in a Christian environment and never need the radical shift in outlook demanded by the revivalists. How might this be accomplished? Simply raise the child in a Christian home and surround him with people who would set the proper example. In a sermon entitled "The Organic Unity of the Family," Bushnell asserted that the child "breathes the atmosphere of the house. He sees the world through his parents' eyes. Their objects become his. Their life and spirit mold him." Such a position was to reinforce the religious self-consciousness of many mid-century Christians.

Closely related to the changing attitudes toward revivalism and the Bible that were reflected in the Second Great Awakening and its aftermath were the new aesthetic standards that emerged from the romantic movements in the arts. The romantic movement rested on four premises. The first was that people could best be moved and persuaded by an appeal to feelings and intuition. Rejecting the earlier view that reason was humanity's greatest tool, the romantic stressed the emotional and spiritual sides of life. The second premise was a belief in a series of moral laws and ideals lying beneath surface reality. Thoreau, in his fascination with the seasons and his ability to draw analogies between the pond and the eternal verities of life, was appealing to this Neo-Platonic conception of the world. The seasons represented the eternal cycle of life—birth and death, rebirth, fulfillment, and decline. This pattern of death and rebirth, sacrifice and resurrection, which was central to the romantic outlook leads to the third and fourth premises—that nature was a source of refuge and inspiration and that the natural world, because of its eternal truths, was a reflection of the divine presence. This "Christianized Naturalism," as the historian Perry Miller has called it, was perhaps the central premise of the nineteenth-century American outlook. Most middle-class Americans believed that nature was a holy text, open for interpretation to any who would explore its meanings (Novak).

The pervasive identification of God in nature and of the divine presence in the material world held by nineteenth-century Americans may be difficult for us to understand today. Yet such an identification was real for millions of people. As art historian Barbara Novak (1980) explains, in terms that might equally apply to architecture at mid-century,

> the unity of nature bespoke the unity of God. The unity of man with nature assumed an optimistic attitude toward human perfectability. Nature, God, and Man composed an infinitely mutable Trinity within this parareligion. . . . And in the mutability which landscape presents, God's moods could be read through a key symbol of God's immanence—light, the mystic substance of the landscape artist.

From these convictions about the importance of feelings, underlying moral laws, and a Christianized naturalism, conclusions followed. One was a pervasive belief that individuals were shaped by their environment. We all are, the romantics asserted, products of habit, shaped by the experiences of our youth. Hence, if one could transform the individual's environment, one could redirect and reform that person's life. Another was the belief that art and architecture, because they played on the feelings and emotions like the natural world, should be viewed as divine forces, vehicles for spiritual understanding. This aesthetic theory, which associated architectural forms with spiritual ideals, taught that taste and the perception of beauty were inextricably related to the moral development of the individual.

By the 1840s, these two streams of thought—the changing attitudes toward religion that developed out of the Second Great Awakening and the romantic convictions about art, nature, and the pervasive influence of environment—came together to give new meaning to the role of the Bible in architecture.

Attention focused on the Gothic style. The Gothic, or "pointed" style, as it was known, was described by one contemporary as "a building, the character of whose architecture is distinguished by the upward direction of its leading lines, and by such curves as may be introduced meeting, or having a tendency to meet in a point." In its most popular form as a rural cottage, the Gothic style stressed verticality by its steep pitched roofs, board and batten siding, sharply peaked dormers, and ornamentation on the gables. The rural Gothic style not only harmonized well with natural surroundings which gave it a picturesque look, but because of its origin in a more religious time, it was also thought to symbolize an eminently Christian form of private dwelling. In such a rural home, isolated from the evils of urban life, the Christian family could "worship God, with none to molest us or make us afraid." The early Gothic revival reached the height of its popularity for domestic architecture between the 1840s and the 1860s and fell from favor in the 1870s, except for large civic and educational buildings. The reasons for the rise and fall of its popularity help to shed light on the influence of religion and the Bible on architecture at mid-century (Clark).

Gothic architecture was first popularized in England by A. Welby Pugin, who stressed its symbolic importance. Gothic churches with their cross plans, three-part divisions, and thrusting towers and spires symbolized perfectly the basic elements of Christianity: the redemption of humanity by Christ's sacrifice on the cross, the Trinity, and the resurrection of the dead. American plan-book architects were quickly captivated by the symbolic potential of Gothic structures. William H. Rawlett, in his book *The Architect*, published in 1847, set forth his own rationale for adopting the Gothic style:

> There is so intimate a connection between taste and morals, aesthetics and Christianity, that they, in each instance, mutually modify each other; hence whoever serves to cultivate the taste of the community, will be likely to improve their morals; and whatever promotes their knowledge of beauty, will give to Christianity increased opportunity and means of charming the heart and governing the life.

This quotation indicates that architects saw the Gothic style not only as an instrument for stimulating the emotions but also as a mechanism for social control. It would curb ambition, limit the contemporary preoccupation with material goods, and establish a truly Christian family world. One reformer commented wistfully, "Would that parents could understand what a nursery of all that is best and of immortal worth home is capable of being. . . ." Some architects saw the utility of Gothic for urban row houses because it would supply a sense of verticality which would overcome the boring repetition of horizontality. Others, like the landscape architect and designer of Central Park, Frederick Law Olmsted, suggested that the style was perfect for the new suburban development of Riverside, Illinois, because "the fact [is] that the families dwelling within a suburb enjoy much in common, and all the more enjoy it because it is in common—the grand fact, in short, that they are Christians . . . and not Pagans" should be reflected in their physical surroundings.

Still others, like Catherine E. Beecher and Harriet Beecher Stowe, saw the "Christian House" as a vehicle for women to develop their special talents and abilities for working with with children. They wrote:

> It has been shown, that the best end for a woman to seek is the training of God's children for their eternal home, by guiding them to intelligence, virtue, and true happiness. When, therefore, the wise woman seeks a home in which to exercise this ministry, she will aim to secure a house so planned that it will provide in the best manner for health, industry, and economy, those cardinal requisites of domestic enjoyment and success.

Women, who were prevented by the church from entering the priesthood, could now turn their talents to "ministries" at home. As household experts, they could ensure that the children were properly raised and religiously instructed.

In short, by the 1850s, architects were convinced that the Gothic style could meet the protective and nurturing needs of Christian Americans. Quickly adopting Horace Bushnell's vision of supportive Christianity, they set out to design the ultimate Christian dwelling. The result was the conception of the house as a church. No efforts were spared in giving their designs the proper associations. One of the most important symbols was the cross. The house was often designed in the form of a cross plan, and crosses were usually attached to the tops of the gables. One pattern book even supplied a full page with twenty different designs of crosses that might be applied to houses. In addition to the crosses, stained glass became popular for providing accents in the windows and some of the guide books suggested that the primary colors be used to symbolize the Trinity. For the front parlor, a pump organ could be purchased upon which the family's favorite hymns could be played. Even stoves, machines, and bedroom furniture could be designed following Gothic standards. All in all the Gothic house became the perfect place for Christian nurture (Beecher and Beecher Stowe, quoted in Gifford).

Americans' love affair with the Gothic style, however, did not last long. As the ritualistic and sacramental approach to faith present in the Oxford movement in England and in Bushnell's Christian nurture at home began to wane, many people came to view the Gothic style as overly formalistic and restrictive. One writer in *Harper's New Monthly Magazine*, in May 1865, called it the "gilded idol of fashion" which deceived the lady of the house:

> The whole structure commands her ceremonious reverence; she bows down before the lofty walls and columns of stone, and on entering, while muttering the formula of the breviary of fashion, fixes her eyes in pious ecstasy upon the rose-wood and ormolu idols of her adoration.

Clearly, here was the traditional Protestant dislike of Catholic ritual. Other critics complained of the Gothic style's functionality or of its association with the rich, such as its use in the construction of Memorial Hall at Harvard in 1866.

In some ways, the shifting influence of the Bible in this period is best summed up with a statement made by Henry Ward Beecher, the Congregational minister, abolitionist, and social reformer.

> Art, natural scenery, literature and buttresses that hold up the tower and spire of [my] theology, God has written voluminously and not in one department alone. *My theology* requires me to search out truth in ten thousand places besides the Bible. I think that the Bible is but God's finger, pointing the direction where truth is to be found. (To a friend, 1851)

For Beecher as for many other Victorian Americans the Bible was less a repository of truth and a guide to action and more a source of inspiration, one of many sources reaffirming the eminence of God in the universe.

In addition to the vernacular architectural tradition of the eighteenth century with its implicit assumptions about hierarchy and authority and the nineteenth-century popular culture's use of the Bible for inspiration and social control, the American architectural tradition has another strand that has been equally powerful and persuasive: the jeremiadic and prophetic strain. From Thomas Jefferson on, American architects, though they have not recognized it themselves, have functioned within what historians Perry Miller (1964) and Sacvan Bercovitch (1978) have called the jeremiad tradition. In Miller's original conception, the term "jeremiad" referred to the long tradition of political sermons in Puritan Massachusetts that judged and castigated the colony for failing in its mission to create a city on the hill, which was to serve as an inspiration for Christians worldwide. The earliest settlers saw themselves as being on an errand, both in the sense of undertaking a journey for someone else (English Protestantism) and in the sense of having as their own purpose (errand) the establishment of a new faith. Miller's brilliant insight into the duality of the mission—creating new standards both for oneself and for the rest of the world—pointed to one of the central elements of the jeremiad tradition. Like the prophet Jeremiah, the Puritans were taking a moral stand, judging the degenerate behavior of the people, bewailing the preoccupation with materialistic concerns, and promising divine retribution if these erring ways were not stopped.

While Miller saw the jeremiad tradition as essentially negative and pessimistic, Bercovitch has persuasively argued that the Puritans' cries of declension and doom were part of a strategy designed to revitalize the errand. From the jeremiad tradition, the Puritans developed a driving sense of mission that fused sacred and secular history and developed a prophetic vision of the future. What became important was the process of striving for new standards and higher ideals. Anxiety became the motivating force; self-discipline and social control served as the instruments of social change and progress. Bercovitch follows this jeremiad tradition from the Puritans to the present, showing how the Puritan preoccupation with religious mission was gradually transformed into a quest for an American identity. The debate over the meaning of America, he argues persuasively, placed an enormous stress on consensus and controlled progress, essentially ruling out any basic challenges to the system. Almost by definition, too, the search for an American identity has been an ongoing one and will continue to be so.

Although neither Miller nor Bercovitch thought of American architects when they analyzed the nature of the American jeremiad tradition, the similarities are striking. As Herbert Schneidau (10ff.) has argued in his book on the Bible and the Western tradition, part of the biblical tradition has always been critical of the status quo and skeptical of the dominant culture's ideology. In this respect, American architects have followed in a long tradition, decrying present standards and searching for a "truer" theory for architectural practice. Although architects from Jefferson to Andrew Jackson Downing and Frank Lloyd Wright have espoused widely different styles, their arguments follow a consistent style—a style that owes much to the jeremiad tradition and the biblical skepticism about contemporary values.

In many ways, Thomas Jefferson stands as the initiator and cornerstone of this tradition. His lifelong interest in architecture, including the continual remodeling of his own home, Monticello, provides an insight into some of his central ideals and concerns. Jefferson faced major problems in his work as a designer. There was a general lack of knowledge about and standards for building. Writing his thoughts on the state of Virginia to the secretary of the French legation in Philadelphia in 1781, he was scathingly critical of present American structures. Many houses, he commented, were simply huts made of logs. The only public buildings worthy of mention were the capitol, the palace, and the college in Williamsburg. Even they lacked proportion and misused ornament. "The College and Hospital," he scornfully added, "are rude, mis-shapen piles, which, but that they have roofs, would be taken for brick-kilns. . . . The genius of architecture seems to have shed its maledictions over this land." Impermanent, poorly constructed American buildings failed to come up to European standards.

Related to the lack of standards was the problem that large building design was traditionally associated with the aristocracy. A newly freed nation had no inclination to be innovative; it tended simply to continue older patterns and practices. This lack of imagination at home was matched by the tendency to look to Europe for our architectural standards and styles. Like the biblical prophets, Jefferson bemoaned present practices. Retribution would come not from God but from the loss of credence in the outside world and from unsanitary and unhealthy building practices at home.

What could be done to change present practices, establish new standards, and overcome contemporary prejudices that associated impressive designs with aristocratic pretensions? How could we create artistic excellence and still assert a distinctive American identity? Jefferson's answer was both original and paradoxical. The solution was to turn to the universal standards of science, "to isolate and exhibit in their art the external and universal principles of reason and nature." And, while developing a "science" of architecture, we should also return to the classical standards of early Greek and Roman republics. History and science, the past and the future, would be combined to support the new experiment in republican government.

Thus, for Jefferson, architecture had a moral purpose. It was to uplift and inspire the people. As he confided to Madison in 1785, "how is taste in this beautiful art to be formed in our countrymen unless we avail ourselves of every occasion when public buildings are to be erected, of presenting to them models for their study and imitation." Neoclassical designs, like Jefferson's capitol of Virginia, with symmetry, balance, and dignified simplicity, would stand in marked contrast to the jaded decadence of Europe. The open porticos and arcades in his design for the University of Virginia also reflected the nonconspiratorial quality of democratic government. American architecture, like American government, would represent a purer and freer version of English standards. Thus, the classical virtues of honor, duty, patriotism, dedication to the state, simplicity, and frugality would be reborn in the new American republic. Charles Lee, a friend of Jefferson, spoke for many when he said that he once regretted "not being thrown into the World in the glorious Third or Fourth century of the Romans but now it seemed that the ancient republican dreams at length bid fair to being realized" (Adams).

If Jefferson was an advocate of neoclassical standards, he also thought of himself as a scientist. His *Notes on the State of Virginia* contains a section comparing the differences between wooden and brick structures in terms of their impact on owners' health. Beneath Jefferson's idealism was the practicality of a man of science. Monticello, with its practical dumbwaiter, two pen-copier, swivel chair, and bed in the wall bespoke the practical inventor. Yet all these gadgets, as the historian Garry Wills (epilogue) has pointed out, were less important than Jefferson's vision of the future—his fascination with the universals of design, whether it be for a government or for a house. Unbeknown to himself, Jefferson fulfilled the jeremiad tradition, attacking the present, looking to the future, identifying the destiny of the American arts and nation with the future good of humanity.

The tradition begun by Jefferson in the eighteenth century of establishing a sense of prophetic vision was picked up in the nineteenth century by many architectural reformers. Perhaps the most popular and influential of these at mid-century was Andrew Jackson Downing. Downing, who was born in 1815 and brought up in Newburgh, New York, had the great insight to combine a theory of landscape gardening with architecture. The owner with his brother of a successful nursery business, he codified the new theories of Victorian architecture in four books before his tragic death at the age of thirty-seven in a steamboat fire on the Hudson River. Downing's books, the most famous of which was *The Architecture of Country Houses*, published in 1850, went through six editions before the Civil War.

Downing's study of country houses, like the books of the other major American architects who wrote in the jeremiad tradition, begins with a dichotomous view of the world. Writing on the real meaning of architecture, Downing argues that architecture should be both an instrument of progress and a means of social control. Architecture would add moral significance to people's lives; it would elevate and purify their feelings. But, alas, Americans lacked the proper training. Like a conservative romantic, Downing argued that "correct taste is only the result of education: the feeling must be guided by the judgment." Enthusiasm, in Downing's view, must be checked by reference to the proper authorities. Hence the purpose of his book. Speaking from within the prophetic tradition, Downing argues that he is providing nothing less than a new insight into the eternal principles of architecture.

In the lengthy essay that follows, Downing points out that the very best architecture combines beauty and utility. An interest in the Beautiful is instinctual. "It is a worship, by the heart, of a higher perfection manifested in material forms" (1850). Beauty includes harmony, symmetry, and unity. Absolute beauty was an expression, in material form, of those ideas of perfection that are universal, inherent in nature as well as art.

In contrast to this ideal, Downing paints a gloomy picture of the state of architecture in America in 1850. Buildings were ill-proportioned and poorly constructed, lacking in taste and inappropriate to their locations. The forms of Greek and Roman temples, in particular, while suitable for lecture halls and philosophical rooms, were horribly inappropriate for private dwellings. Even worse, Downing warned, were structures that revealed the vices of the occupants.

> A house built only with a view to animal wants, eating and drinking, will express sensuality instead of hospitality. A residence marked by gaudy and garish apartments, intended only to dazzle and impress others with the wealth or importance of the proprietor, will express pride and vanity instead of a real love of what is beautiful for its own sake. (Downing: 9)

The state of American architecture may have been dismal, but the future held promise. Architecture could be truthful; wood could look like wood and stone like stone. Houses could represent the tastes and aspirations of their inhabitants. For those few great individuals who aspire for more, the picturesque villa was appropriate. Downing's enthusiastic language here bears repeating:

And, lastly, there are men of imagination—men whose aspirations never leave them at rest—men whose ambition and energy will give them no peace within the mere bounds of rationality. Those are the men for picturesque villas—country houses with high roofs, steep gables, unsymmetrical and capricious forms. It is for such that the architect may safely introduce the tower and campanile—any and every feature that indicates originality, boldness, energy and variety of character. (Downing: 24, 263)

The appropriateness of this argument, in an age of Jacksonian individualism, can easily be imagined. One can clearly see why Downing's architectural business, while he was still alive, grew rapidly into one of the largest firms on the East Coast.

Like Jefferson, and in keeping with the facet of the jeremiad tradition that tended to identify the mission of the church with that of the state, Downing saved his most important arguments to suggest that Americans needed to develop their own distinctive building forms and not copy those of others. "One would suppose," sighed Downing, "that a cultivated American would exult and thank God for the great Future which dawns on him here, rather than sigh and fondle over the great Past which remains to Europe." Americans should form their own "free and manly school of republican tastes and manners," and not waste their time on meaningless foreign conventions. Conceding that some conservative individuals who help check the excesses of democratic governments have a natural interest in the past, Downing allowed such individuals to build in the appropriate historical revival styles. But he went on to warn that the great family estate that was handed down over the generations in Europe was simply inappropriate in a republic. In the place of the great hereditary home, Downing lauded the greater hereditary institutions in America. Nationalism and the mission of America were to be built on equity, justice, and the wisdom that comes from knowing the universal principles which animated nature and architecture (Downing: 264).

Like the Puritans who used the covenant of grace as a vehicle of social control, Downing saw architecture as a stabilizing force in a hectic, rapidly growing, democratic society. Like the Puritans, too, who yoked social identity to a claim to election, Downing stressed the benefits of the American republican tradition that avoided the pitfalls of aristocracy. Lastly, the path to glory had to begin with appropriate preparations. As the Puritans had stressed incessant activity on the part of the believer, Downing stressed the adoption of a new philosophy and set of architectural standards. Rhetorical exhortation, particularly in terms that avoided "the dry and barren manner in which architects have usually written" would be the new vehicle for salvation.

With Andrew Jackson Downing as its great popularizer and daring critic, the center of innovative design in the mid-nineteenth century remained in a few key firms on the East Coast. By the turn of the century, however, this center had shifted to Chicago and the Midwest. Certainly there were still important firms in the East like Mead, McKim, and White, who designed the Boston Public Library in 1888, but the greatest architectural innovators were part of a major artistic renaissance taking place in Chicago. A center of trade and commerce, Chicago grew rapidly after its great fire in 1871 and became the home of two new styles of architecture, the "Chicago School" for commercial buildings, and the "Prairie School" for private residences. Using a simpler, less historically oriented design, architects of the Chicago School, such as William le Baron Jenny, John Wellborn Root, Daniel Burnham, and Louis Sullivan, put up tall office buildings that were supported by internal steel frames floated on iron and concrete rafts in the mushy Chicago soil. One of the hallmarks of the later structures was the "Chicago" window, a large picture window flanked on each side by narrow, double-hung sashes. The other great innovation, of which the leading exponent was Frank Lloyd Wright, was a new house design of the Prairie School that stressed a low, horizontal silhouette, flat pitched roofs with large overhangs, bands of windows, and imposing, centrally located fireplaces. It is not surprising that the great architectural renaissance in Chicago revitalized the jeremiad tradition. One of the leading early representatives of the Chicago School was John Wellborn Root (1850–1891). A Georgian by birth, Root had studied architecture, art, and engineering in England and had followed this education with a degree in civil engineering from New York University. Perhaps better than anyone else, Root represented the new philosophy of efficiency. Although Downing and others had recognized the importance of utility and functionality in their designs, Root elevated that concern into an obsession. Arguing that the tall Chicago office building was expressive of the complexity, luxury, and vitality of modern life, Root asserted that he had found the underlying eternal principles of building. The key to good architecture, he insisted, was that the internal structure of the building must absolutely dictate the external design:

> I do not believe it is possible to exaggerate the importance of the influence which may be exerted for good or evil by those distinctively modern buildings. Hedged about by many unavoidable conditions, they are either gross and self-assertive shams, untrue both in the material realization of their aims and in their art function as expressions of the deeper spirit of the age; or they are sincere, noble, and enduring monuments to the broad and beneficent commerce of the age. (Root, quoted in Monroe)

Here was the classic jeremiad position, a descendant from the original Puritan position that divided the world into the inner, spiritual covenant of grace and the exterior covenant of works. Inner spirit versus exterior manifestations, faith versus behavior, true dedication versus false pretenses—these themes run through most of the American experience. The Victorians in the nineteenth century were preoccupied with this issue. They constantly worried about "false appearances." If, as John Ruskin the English critic observed, what you like is an expression of what you are, then it was exceedingly important that the inner and outer sides of life corresponded. Hence Downing's obsessive concerns with the appropriateness of the house to the social standing of the one who inhabited it and to the values prized by a democratic society. Like the American Victorians who were fascinated by disguises, mistaken identities, and false appearances (see the cases of false appearances in songs like "After the Ball is Over" and "She's Only a Bird in a Gilded Cage"), the new Chicago School architects like Root and Sullivan transferred the same preoccupations with truth and integrity to their discussions of architecture.

In his *Life and Thought*, Root (quoted in Monroe) gave full expression to the hatred and disdain he felt because contemporary designs displayed no connection between external and internal forms. Attacking the "seductive" and "criminal" blandishments of the renaissance revival styles, he pictured his generation as victims of "crimes against Beauty and Truth. . . ." His references to the "Queen Anne" or "stick" style, which was known for its turned spindle decorations on porches and irregular silhouette, are particularly acerb. Calling it the "Tubercular Style," similar to a disease, Root explained that "its eruptive tendencies manifest themselves in all sorts of things, from wens to carbuncles and ringworms." Other styles were equally bad. The classical revival was dubbed "The Cataleptic Style," and the renaissance revival was called "dropsical," "distended," and "bloated." All these debaucheries, he argued in an essay called "A Utilitarian Theory of Beauty," should be replaced by the laws of utility (Gifford: 477–80).

Root's prophetic attack on past traditions represented the opening salvo in the position of the new "Chicago School" of architects. His ideas were further articulated and developed into a more far-reaching theory of architecture by Louis Sullivan, a graduate of the Massachusetts Institute of Technology and the École des Beaux-Arts in Paris, who has been justly called both "creator and prophet of the modern commercial skyscraper" (Roth). Known for his design of the Chicago Auditorium (1886–90), a complex structure that combined an opera house, a hotel, an office block, and the Wainwright Building (1890–91), in St. Louis, Missouri, Sullivan is most famous for his slogan, "form follows function" and his use of organic decorative motifs. The Wainwright skyscraper was divided into three parts—the first-floor store area, the middle section of offices, and the upper section for mechanical equipment. Yet all the parts were held together by an ornate terra cotta sheathing in a naturalistic design.

The major themes that Sullivan was to express in his later writings appeared in a talk he gave before the American Institute of Architects in 1894. Sullivan combined a Darwinian sense of the natural world, full of beauty and power, with an idealistic conception of man as seer and prophet. Like John Dewey, who was running his Chicago Laboratory School at the same time, Sullivan was fascinated by the openness and creativity of children. (One of his famous later books was entitled *Kindergarten Chats*, 1918.) The vision of the child and his natural sympathy with the physical world were the inspiration Sullivan wanted to recapture. As he explained to the delegates, "Let us not forget our little man, for he is to companion me in spirit through this discourse. I believe he exists somewhere, has in his breast the true architectural afflatus and will someday come forth the Messiah of our art." This prophetic sense of his own role and his messianic concern for the future were to lie at the base of much of Sullivan's work. In fact, biblical references are a continual substratum in most of his essays.

In this talk, for example, Sullivan speaks first of the "trinity" of inspiration, thought, and expression. He next moves to the position that great architecture must possess a soul. The best structures, which vibrate to an inner spirit, become an overpowering reality. The architect, in touch with this reality, ". . . goes straight to the unfailing bounty of nature, and there, by virtue of his passionate adoration, passing the portals of the objective, he enters that extraordinary communion that the sacred writers called to 'walk with God.'" Sullivan's visionary language, his sense of America's future greatness, with his violent attacks on the "murky materialism" and "fanatical selfishness" of his own generation, set him apart as a prophet in his own time (English: 13–19).

When public preferences turned back again to neoclassicism after the 1893 World's Fair and Sullivan's own boldly ornamental buildings were themselves no longer in style, his own sense of prophetic detachment and alienation increased. In *The Autobiography of Idea*, which he published in 1924, Sullivan, or "the child," as he refers to himself with a strange detachment in the early part of the book, attempts to achieve a synthesis of the artistic and scientific imaginations. In this work, he arrives at his great conclusion, "that function creates form." But this great insight was destroyed by the classicism of the World's Fair, "a veritable Apocalypse, a message inspired from on high." This "appalling calamity," this "naked exhibitionism of charlatary" had "overwhelmed the land with a pall of desolation" and had killed creative American architecture. "From the height of its Columbian Ecstasy, Chicago drooped and subsided with the rest, in a common sickness, the nausea of overstimulation" (Sullivan: chap. XV). Still, Sullivan was not entirely without hope. The younger generations still had the opportunity to come along and redeem the nation. The instincts of the child might yet be reborn. Although he was a prophet scorned in his own time, Sullivan, like his Puritan predecessors, retained his faith in the errand and in the particular mission of American architects. Later generations, fascinated by Sullivan's vituperative language and mystical visions, transformed him into a saint—the spiritual predecessor to the movement in modern architecture.

Among those who canonized Sullivan and called him his "*Lieber Meister*" was Frank Lloyd Wright. Considered by many the most creative and original

American architect of the early twentieth century, Wright left the School of Engineering at the University of Wisconsin in 1887 to become a draftsman in the offices of Adler and Sullivan in Chicago. Although Wright left Sullivan's office in 1893 after Sullivan reprimanded him for working as a consultant outside the firm, Wright later paid tribute to him in his autobiography (125, 130). The "Master's" writings were too sentimental for Wright, but Wright liked "his radical sense of things." He also recognized that much of Sullivan's egocentrism, like his own, was a defense against criticism.

If Sullivan sentimentalized the outside world, so did Wright. Both looked to nature for comfort and inspiration. Both saw the patterns of growth and interrelatedness, but while Sullivan stressed nature as "power," Wright tended to emphasize the moral and human qualities of the natural world. Wright was also more willing to see the machine as an agent of civilization and progress.

The sentimentalism at the heart of Wright's vision could be seen in a book he illustrated in the 1890s (Wright and Gannett). A limited edition of William C. Gannett's sermon, *The House Beautiful*, tacitly confirmed Wright's Victorian image of the family, complete with its sense of domesticity and spirituality. The house was a sacred space:

> "I heard a voice out of Heaven," says another Bible verse—"A Great Voice out of heaven, 'Behold, the Tabernacle of God is with men, and He will dwell with them, and they shall be His people.'" Call the great power "God," or by what name we will, that power dwells with us in so literal a fashion that every stone and rafter, every table, spoon and paper scrap, bears stamp and signature to eyes that read ought: "The House in which we live is a building of God, a house not made with hands."

Like Gannett, Wright recognized that houses had symbolic and spiritual values for their owners. The dining room table and chairs that he designed for the Robie House in 1909 resemble a communion table, suggesting perhaps both the spiritual and communal qualities of a family's coming together at mealtimes.

If many of the ideas and concepts implicit in Wright's houses were traditional, the designs themselves were part of a radically new style that came to be known as the Prairie School. Wright was the prophet and codifier of these new designs. The Prairie School design reduced the number of parts of a house to a minimum, eliminated basements and attics, and used a series of parallel windows and low overhanging roofs to create a sense of horizontality, integrating the house with its building site. As Wright explained: "We of the Middle West are living on the prairie. The prairie has a beauty of its own and we should recognize and accentuate this natural beauty, its quiet level. Hence, gently sloping roofs, low proportions, quiet skylines, suppressed heavy set chimneys and glistening overhangs . . ." (Gutheim: 123).

Using the latest building technologies such as pre-stressed concrete and steel beams, Wright and the Prairie School architects opened up the interior spaces and created a more unified design. Even furniture and other interior furnishings were designed by the architect. The house thereby became more than an ordinary structure; it became a work of art. Although this idea was difficult for some clients who wanted to select their own furniture, Wright soon built up a dedicated following that supported his ideal.

Following in the jeremiad tradition, Wright attacked his opposition and set forth his own ideals in a series of articles published in the *Architectural Record* between 1907 and 1928. Criticizing the feebleness of historical revival styles, which he dubbed "Colonial Wedding Cakes" and "English Affectations," Wright went on to assert that "the sins of the Architect are permanent sins." In place of these earlier falsehoods, Wright insisted on maintaining the organic integrity of the house, thus creating a new American architecture. Like the country, its architecture should be democratic and progressive, true, and honest. Machine standardization would allow for new industrial buildings, "Shimmering iridescent cages of steel and copper and glass in which the principle of standardization becomes exquisite in all variety." In place of the sham of the past, Wright proposed the realization of the kingdom on earth. His vision is of the millennium. "To be good Gods of Earth *here* is all the significance we have here. A God is a God on Earth as in Heaven. And there will never be too many Gods." His plea was for every architect to be himself: "For yourself, by yourself, within yourself, then, visualize it and add your own faithful building to it, and you cannot fail."

Wright's sense of alienation and persecution, together with his messianic vision of the future, his clear-cut principles, and his idealism, made him a powerful force within the American architectural tradition. Like Jefferson, Downing, and Root, Wright was a skilled draftsman, and he provided a new set of principles, using machines, steel, glass, and concrete to develop a general theory of modern architecture. As Sullivan had done before him, Wright saw a new transnational mission for the architect. Where the earlier generation had stressed the development of a distinctly American style of architecture, Wright in later life talked about universal human needs. Still, he valued most the particularly American view of nature and freedom. He criticized materialism and advocated a return to earlier American truths. In his autobiography in 1934, Wright explained that there was a direct connection between architectural truth, nature, and democracy:

> I believe that once we do establish ourselves as organic on organic foundations and are therefore independent of external props and braces, we can afford a far more flexible, natural and free social *FORM* than has ever been known. And architecturally, therefore we will have the practical social-basis for the great, beautiful, healthy buildings of genuine human Freedom. Actual Democracy will be ours.

Salvation, defined in American terms, was still possible.

As Wright's most recent biographer has suggested, Wright deliberately created the role of the harassed prophet and seer. Antisocial and professionally unorthodox, perpetually seeking to perfect his own designs, Wright, like the prophets of old, was a prickly personality, difficult to get along with. Like them, too, he was constantly critical of his surrounding society. Even his designs were never fixed. Shortly before he died in 1959 he was working on yet another alteration of Taliesin. In all this, he provided what has come to be one of the basic hallmarks of the American architectural tradition—a sense of prophet vision. The vision was powerful, and the celebration of Frank Lloyd Wright at times turned from a mainstream religion into a narrow cult. Nevertheless he retained a sense of mission that made him an inspiration to architects and architectural historians alike.

In the twentieth century, Frank Lloyd Wright's prophetic stance, though imitated by many other major architects, has been matched by only one—Philip Johnson. In the 1930s, while Wright was battling against the return to historical revival styles, Philip Johnson jolted the architectural world with a book entitled *The International Style*, which he published with Henry-Russell Hitchcock. Johnson was not only a great architectural theorist, but in 1943 after working as the director of the Department of Architecture and Design at the Museum of Modern Art, he took his degree at Harvard and entered into practice himself. Because of his witty and dramatic writings and a number of highly influential designs—including the "Glass House" in New Canaan, Connecticut, the Kline Biology Tower at Yale, and the IDS Center in Minneapolis—Philip Johnson has to be considered one of this century's most important architectural interpreters.

Like a true disciple in the jeremiad tradition, Johnson, who has admitted to holding doctrinaire opinions, begins *The International Style* with a list of the nineteenth century's stylistic failures. Searching for the true principles of architecture—the one dominant style—he sets forth the new orthodoxy for the architectural faith in terms of three basic principles. The first principle considers buildings as volume instead of mass. The surfaces of the building should appear as a "skin tightly stretched over the supporting skeleton." The second principle is that designs also should be based on regularity, particularly that produced by machines and materials such as plate glass windows, rather than on axial symmetry. Finally, all applied decoration should be avoided. The structure should be its own ornament. The watchwords of the movement were pure form and pure functionalism.

Johnson's condemnation of general public building standards, while more restrained than that of Sullivan and Wright, has the same contemptuous stance. "So bad in every way have been the facades of most American commercial edifices," wrote Johnson, "that their rear elevations, which are at best merely sound building, seem by contrast to possess architectural quality." The book also reflects optimism about the future. The millennium was still a long way away, but the plans laid in the 1930s, argued the writer, would set the pattern for the future. Americans were learning slowly from the Europeans. There was still hope that the new principles could indeed be practical universally (Hitchcock and Johnson: 81).

What stands out about Johnson's position is the secularization of the jeremiad tradition, particularly in the 1970s, when Johnson and others had abandoned the older universals of *The International Style* and shifted to a new eclecticism (postmodern architecture). Looking back now, he sees the book as part of an earlier "conversion" and a youthful "evangelical" crusade. Reflecting on his own work and on the present concerns, he finds much of what he believed in to be dated. "We live in a time of flux. . . . There are no regional prides, no new religions, no new puritanism, no new Marxism, no new socially conscious morality that can give discipline, direction, or force to an architectural pattern. Today we know too much too quickly. It takes moral and emotional blinders to make a style" (Johnson: 271).

The passing of the prophetic tradition that we witness today in the writings of Philip Johnson provides a useful perspective on part of the American architectural tradition. The prophet vision, so useful for inspiring and explaining the meaning of architectural forms, which ran from Thomas Jefferson to Philip Johnson, has had at its center a sense of fixed purpose and absolute values. The sense of being chosen, on an errand to redeem the world, has been crucial to these architects' self-identity. If contemporaries missed the message, if the common people overlooked the eternal principles underlying the architect's ideals and turned instead to the alluring deceits of tawdry materialism, then the prophetic vision was reinforced and confirmed. After all, that is what had happened to the prophets of old.

As individuals, the great representatives of American architecture have often been an egotistical and self-centered lot, difficult to get along with and constantly at odds with friends and acquaintances over what appear to be minor differences of opinion. Nevertheless, they represent a sense of vision that has inspired and shaped American architectural practice. In fact, this biblical sense of mission has been their most clearly defining feature. Perhaps it is precisely the biblical and prophetic sense of otherness that has given to this tradition its great force and power.

Ultimately, when one looks back on the shape of the American architectural tradition and compares the great architectural exponents with the implicit vernacular tradition, one finds an interesting convergence. What identified much of the later vernacular tradition was both its sense of continuity with the regional past and its growing sense of isolation and estrangement from popular commercial styles. So, too, the elite architects tend to see themselves as prophets, set apart from present standards and critical of popular culture. The sense of mission, the biblical stance of criticizing contemporary standards, and the queasiness about others who do not share their vision, continue to influence their outlook. Like the West Virginia farmer who builds his house in the traditional way because that's the way it ought to be built, the major architects still judge "good" and "bad" architecture. If their standards are less fixed and a new orthodoxy has not yet arisen, nevertheless they take an extraordinarily judgmental attitude toward the world. Perhaps, as Michael Kammen, a historian from Cornell, has suggested, both traditions are simply part of the American tendency to view the world in terms of dualisms and polarities. Like the Puritan sentiment of old, Americans assert that they have the correct vision of the future. Yet there is always the nagging fear that, indeed, they may not be a part of the elect.

WORKS CONSULTED

Adams, William Howard, ed.
  1976   *The Eye of Jefferson*. Washington: National Gallery of Art.

Albanese, Catherine L.
  1979   "Research Needs in American Religious History." *Bulletin of the Council on the Study of Religion* 10: 1.

Andrews, Edward Deming
  1963   *The People Called Shakers*. New York: Dover Press.

Beecher, H. W.
  1851   "H. W. Beecher to ?, Nov. 29, 1851." *Beecher Family Papers*. Yale University.

Bercovitch, Sacvan
  1978   *The American Jeremiad*. Madison: University of Wisconsin Press.

Clark, Clifford E., Jr.
  1976   "Domestic Architecture as an Index to Social History: The Romantic Revival and the Cult of Domesticity in America, 1840–1870." *Journal of Interdisciplinary History* 7: 33–56.

Downing, Andrew Jackson
  1850   *The Architecture of Country Houses*. New York: Dover Reprint.

English, Maurice, ed.
  1963   *The Testament of Stone: Themes of Idealism and Indignation From the Writings of Louis Sullivan*. Evanston: Northwestern University Press.

Gifford, Don, ed.
  1966   *The Literature of Architecture*. New York: Dutton.

Glassie, Henry
  1968   *Pattern in the Material Folk Culture of the United States*. Philadelphia: University of Pennsylvania Press.

Gutheim, Frederick, ed.
  1925   *In the Cause of Architecture*. New York: Architectural Record.

Hayden, Dolores
1976   *Seven American Utopias*. Cambridge, MA: M.I.T. Press.

Hitchcock, Henry-Russell, and Johnson, Philip
1966   *The International Style*. New York: W. W. Norton.

Johnson, Philip
1979   *Philip Johnson Writings*. New York: Oxford University
                        Press.

Kammen, Michael
1971   *The Contrapuntal Civilization*. New York: Thomas Y.
                        Crowell.

Kimball, Fiske
1915   Jefferson to Madison, 20 September 1785. In "Thomas
                        Jefferson and the First Movement of the Classical
                        Revival in America." *Journal of the American Institute
                        of Architects* 3: 9.

McLoughlin, William G.
1979   *Revivals, Awakenings, and Reform*. Chicago: University
                        of Chicago Press.

Miller, Perry
1964   *Errand into the Wilderness*. New York: Harper
                        Torchbook.

Miller, Perry, and Johnson, Thomas H., eds.
1938   John Winthrop, "A Modell of Christian Charity." In *The
                        Puritans*. New York: Harper Torchbook.

Monroe, Harriet
1896   *John Wellborn Root: Architect*. Boston: Houghton,
                        Mifflin.

Novak, Barbara
1980   *Nature and Culture, American Landscape and Paint-
                        ing, 1825–1875*. New York: Oxford University Press.

Roth, Leland M.
1979   *A Concise History of American Architecture*. New
                        York: Harper and Row.

Schneidau, Herbert N.
1976   *Sacred Discontent: The Bible and the Western
                        Tradition*. Berkeley: University of California Press.

Sullivan, Louis H.
1956   *The Autobiography of an Idea*. New York: Dover Press.

Walsh, James P.
1980   "Holy Time and Sacred Space in Puritan New England."
                        American Quarterly 32.

Wills, Garry
1979   *Inventing America*. New York: Vintage Books.

Wright, Frank Lloyd
1937   *An Autobiography*. New York: Horizon Press.

Wright, Frank Lloyd, and Gannett, William
1896   *The House Beautiful*. Chicago: privately printed.

VI

The Bible and American Music

Edwin M. Good

The problem of identifying the presence of the Bible in music is different from that of identifying its presence in other artifacts of culture. In representational art, a biblical scene can be readily recognized, though in nonrepresentational art a title may be needed. In fiction, drama, and poetry, the words themselves may allude to or quote from biblical passages; specific reference may be made to the contents of the Bible; and patterns of plot, character, or structure may be derived more or less explicitly from the Bible.

Music has no such system of built-in references to allow indubitable recognition of a biblical allusion. There are, to be sure, musical conventions of reference. A flute, an oboe, or an English horn (or an instrument with that kind of timbre), playing at a relatively slow tempo in 6/8 time with certain kinds of dotted rhythms, conventionally refers to pastoral contexts. Heavily rhythmic patterns in marching tempo suggest military allusions, and certain slow progressions of chords may suggest liturgical meaning, especially if the composer has taken care to mark them "religioso." Such conventions are extremely general, and nothing in them permits direct identification or explicit allusion to biblical shepherds, Philistine marches, or Passover rituals.

We can determine the presence of the Bible in music in three ways: (1) by recognizing biblical texts in vocal music; (2) by noting a composer's provision of a biblical title or program; (3) by hearing quotations of melodies unambiguously associated with biblical words or figures, such as "Go down, Moses" or "Joshua fit the battle of Jericho." Even the latter cases may in specific instances refer less to the Bible than to contexts in which the Bible was used. When Charles Ives (1874–1953) quotes nineteenth-century revival hymns, the references are not to the Bible but to the emotions attendant upon recollections of revivals. On the other hand, R. Nathaniel Dett (1882–1943) uses both the words and the tune of "Go down, Moses" in his oratorio *The Ordering of Moses* to interpret the biblical text itself.

One fact may be stated at the outset. No major American composer has written a major work involving the Bible. Some major composers have written, for them, minor works, and many minor composers have written, for them, major works in which the Bible is present in one of the three ways outlined above. The Bible has been a fecund source of inspiration in American music, but its inspiration has not so far issued in music of the highest stature. I have sought to use as examples music of high quality that is representative of its period and type or inventive in influential ways. The American past has produced quite enough dreary music, biblical or not, and, admitting the fact, I have not felt the necessity of calling attention to its exemplars.

American Music

It is not easy to define American music. Wilfrid Mellers considers everything before Charles Ives as the "prehistory" of American music, and he holds that "the first authentic American composer" was Ives (37). It is a dubious distinction if only because it depends on a determination of characteristics that distinguish American from other musics, something in the music itself necessitating the attributive adjective "American." Mellers seems to me, moreover, to ignore Ives's remarkable conservatism, the fact that his music is so thoroughly nostalgic and recollective, quoting revival tunes and patriotic songs that were already old hat when Ives was a boy, proposing programs redolent of a man's memory of boyhood experience and emotion, trying out of boyhood memory to reconstruct his father's experiments with sonority and texture. I think, therefore, that Mellers is simply wrong when he claims that Ives "showed us, creatively, what the pioneer world was really like, not what it might have been" (37). No, it is not the pioneer world that Ives shows at all; it is the settled world of decayed New England Puritanism of the late nineteenth century. What is distinctively American about Ives is his programmatic allusions to those earlier American scenes, experiences, and persons. But he was by no means the first American composer to do that, and on that ground no clear dividing line can be drawn between Ives and the eighteenth-century figure of James Hewitt (1770–1827), the composer of *The Battle of Trenton*. The dividing line is the astonishing tonal imagination that Ives had and Hewitt did not, the distinction, namely, between a mediocre composer and a great one—some will deny the latter adjective to Ives—not between a non-American and an American one.

The defensiveness of American musicians about their art is a motif to be noticed from well back in the nineteenth century. While eighteenth-century music stores advertised and eighteenth-century performers placarded their performances of "the most approved European masters," Americans in the latter part of the nineteenth century were attempting to declare their musical independence of the European tradition. Very important in that effort was a famous article by the Czech, Antonin Dvořák (1841–1904), published in *Harper's* (February, 1895) while he was the director of the National Conservatory in New York from 1892 to 1895. In it he urged Americans to emulate European musical nationalism by establishing their own nationalism. Dvořák did not put it just that way, but as a certified Bohemian nationalist, he was in fact advising Americans to do as he did. Nationalism in music, then and later, was to be achieved by using as musical materials the indigenous folk and popular music of the nation, which Dvořák conceived to be the black folk music in America. He even showed American composers how to do it with his "American" String Quartet, op. 96, using spiritual tunes, and the Symphony "From the New World," op. 95, which intended an expression of American folk culture without actually quoting from it (although the melody of the slow movement to the words "Goin' home" has nearly achieved the status of an American folk song). The irony of this way of achieving nationalistic expression is that it depends so much on specified programs or on allusions to what is external to the music itself. That approach introduces "subject matter" into the consideration of the music, but it does not assure that the music, taken in itself, is nationalistic in substance, style, or form. Had Dvořák titled his symphony "From the Old World," no one would have thought anything amiss, and analysts would have raced up and down the score to find old Czech and Bohemian tunes. The program a composer alleges of a work *is* external to the work, and without knowing what it is, most listeners are unable to guess it. (I give the following useful experiment to demonstrate this allegation: gather a group of people who are not put off by modern music but who do not know a great deal specific about it. Tell them that you are about to play a work in which the composer intended to draw a specific picture and that they are to describe the picture. Then play them a decent recording of Ives's "Central Park in the Dark in the Good Old Summertime" without allowing a glimpse of the record jacket or any hint of the title. My prediction, based on having done it several times, is that of any forty people perhaps two will guess something not ridiculously distant from Ives's title.)

My point is that the American musical tradition derives from the European in ways so determinative that we could not extricate ourselves from it if we wanted to. It was not for nothing that Aaron Copland (b. 1900), perhaps the most "American" of modern American composers, had his most important training in the Paris studio of Nadia Boulanger (b. 1887). Nor was he the only American composer to do so. Though in some periods American musicians freely acknowledged their indebtedness to Europe's music and in others they were scrapping with knives and bottles to dissociate themselves from it, the music they have written, taken in itself, has always been demonstrably at one with the European tradition. In recent decades art music has used idioms from jazz, but that is no evidence to the contrary. American composers have used jazz as dialectical embellishment, not as fundamental diction, and European composers have freely done the same.

What, then, is the "American music" to which the title refers? I know of no way to define it except as music written in America (including Canada). And I immediately turn around inconsistently and exclude from this discussion works of modern expatriate European composers who spent parts of their careers on this continent, such as Paul Hindemith (1895–1963), Igor Stravinsky (1882–1971), Arnold Schoenberg (1874–1951), and Béla Bartók (1881–1945). The somewhat lame excuse for this exclusion is that these composers had all reached musical maturity in Europe. Their presence in America had more to do with the accidents of politics than with their musical careers, and they would doubtless have written no differently had the political situations allowed them to stay in Europe. That is a lame argument, and I state it only to show why every line I try to draw around American music seems doubtful on one basis or another. That bona fide American composers have been heavily influenced by all of these massive modern figures changes nothing. It only demonstrates once more how thoroughly the American musical tradition rests on the European. In saying that, I neither criticize American music nor glorify European; I happen to prefer much of the music of Ives, Elliott Carter (b. 1908), and Lukas Foss (b. 1922) to most of the music of Bartók, and I evaluate them on the same grounds.

One other distinction needs to be drawn. In this article I am dealing with "art" music as distinguished from "popular." The modifiers are less than perfect, but alternatives seem to me even more imperfect. "Classical" will not do, because the term is a technical one in music history for the style of the period from about 1750 to about 1810. "Serious" is inappropriate, because some of the music in the category I wish to discuss is comic, sometimes even trivial, and some of the music in the category I distinguish from it is solemn if not tragic (e.g., "the Blues"). H. Wiley Hitchcock distinguishes the "cultivated" from the "vernacular" tradition (51). The terms are usable, but I think that "art" and "popular" are simpler and more descriptive. "Art music" suggests some tinge of the elite, or a higher cultural level, a more complex technical mastery of musical means than is necessary in "popular" music. Even that becomes ambiguous in the light of the technically breathtaking virtuosity of some contemporary "popular" composers and performers. The borderline cases are difficult to decide, and I shall leave them that way. If in what follows I trespass into the territory staked out in Daniel Patterson's essay, I plead that I have been unable to find clear boundary markers./1/

The Colonial Period

Nearly all the music known from the colonial period is religious. There was doubtless "secular" music about, but it consisted mostly of folk songs, popular ballads, dances, marches, and the like—folk or popular music, not art music. It seems ironic that the musical life of the English colonies was so low when one thinks, as Irving Sablonsky has pointed out (4), that colonization began just after the highest musical peak that England has ever known, the age of Thomas Tallis (ca. 1505–1585), William Byrd (1543–1623), Thomas Morley (1557–1602), John Dowland (1562–1626), and others. But

Sablonsky goes on to note rightly that the English who came to this continent were neither of the religious persuasions for which the great English
church music of Henry Purcell (ca. 1659–1695), Byrd, and Orlando Gibbons
(1583–1625) was written nor of the gentle classes for whose amusement and
entertainment at home Morley wrote his *Plaine and Easie Introduction to
Practicall Musicke* (1597), a means for gentlemen and ladies to learn enough
to carry their parts in the madrigal singing that was a popular form of leisure in upper-class England. The Puritan and lower-class cast of the early
English Americans led them to emphasize spiritual songs, not madrigals, and
to shun what they thought "popish" ostentation in the greatest of Anglican
church music.

The sturdy Puritan psalm tunes formed the musical staple in New England and the Atlantic colonies, while in French Canada the only art music
was the somewhat decadent plainchant that French Catholics knew. To be
sure, the Moravians in Pennsylvania and the Carolinas had the chorale and
instrumental traditions from their German background, and the Swedes in
Delaware doubtless possessed something very similar. The New York and
New Jersey Dutch were psalm-singing Calvinists as thoroughgoing as the
Puritan New Englanders, whereas the Pennsylvania Quakers seem to have
avoided religious music entirely. Still, the music was not, in the sense I have
sketched above, American. The tunes were those that Puritan congregations
used in England, though it is difficult to know exactly which ones they were
in the early days, since the first psalm books contained only words and no
tunes.

The Pilgrims, coming to Plymouth from Leiden, had their own metrical
Psalms, done by Henry Ainsworth in 1612 (he also chose the tunes) in order
to avoid the liberties with biblical text and true doctrine permitted by the
standard English Psalm version of Sternhold and Hopkins (1562). The Leiden group, of course, were purist radicals, but even the Massachusetts Bay
Puritans, though they used the good tunes from Sternhold and Hopkins and
from Ravenscroft (1621), wanted words that accorded better with scripture
itself. Thus it was that a committee prepared for the Massachusetts Bay
colony a new metrical version of Psalms which, when published in 1640, was
the first book printed in North America—*The Whole Booke of Psalmes
Faithfully Translated into English Meter*. It quickly became known as the
Bay Psalm Book and went through many editions. The translations were
restricted to six different metric patterns, corresponding to the most commonly used tunes, but the *Bay Psalm Book* had no music in it. One was
expected to know the tunes—an expectation that soon enough fell afoul of
reality.

As the quality of congregational singing deteriorated, some thought the
fault was a failure of religious appreciation for singing itself. John Cotton
(1584–1652) took the second edition of the *Bay Psalm Book* as an opportunity to defend the orthodoxy of good singing: "As we are to make melody in

our hearts, so in our voices also" (*Singing of Psalmes a Gospel-Ordinance*, 1647). But it soon became clear that the problem was not that the New Testament injunction about "singing and making melody in your heart to the Lord" (Eph 5:19) was interpreted to mean that one should *not* sing aloud; it was that there were as many versions of every tune as there were singers. Thus came to pass the astonishing practice of "lining out" the Psalms (it was used in England too), in which the deacon would sing a line, and the congregation, after its fashion and depending on its collective confidence, would imitate it—and so on through all the verses of the Psalm.

Scholars have debated the proper interpretation of this practice. One finds in primary sources references to "reading" the Psalm line by line, to "lining out" the Psalm, and to "setting the tune." Several scholars take the first two terms to mean enunciation of the words alone and only the third to singing the tune line by line. It seems to me unlikely that both a spoken and a sung line by deacon and precentor would intervene before each line sung by the congregation. John Endecott (ca. 1589–1665) described in 1652 a meeting of native American Christians, who sang a Psalm in their own language "but to an *English tune*, read by one of themselves, that the rest might follow, and he read it very distinctly without missing a word as we could judge, and the rest sang chearfully, and prettie tuneablie" (quoted in Stevenson:10; italics original). Here it is clear that "read" means to sing with the words.

"Lining out" may have improved the relative unity of the singing, though deacons were known to modify tunes by inspiration, forgetfulness, or lapsing from one tune into another. The practice slowed the pace of the singing to a crawl. At least "lining out" gave some access to the words of the psalm for the increasing numbers of illiterates coming to the colonies. Not until the ninth edition of the *Bay Psalm Book* (1698) were tunes published with the words—thirteen of them, borrowed from *Introduction to the Skill of Music* (London, 1667) by John Playford (1623–1686), eight in the "common meter" (8, 6, 8, and 6 syllables in a quatrain verse). That was also the regular ballad meter. Texts set to it could have been sung to most of the secular ballad tunes making the English rounds, and perhaps some of them were. Of that we have no knowledge.

From 1721 comes the earliest evidence of music *written* in the British colonies. In that year in Boston appeared two books: *An Introduction to the Singing of Psalm-Tunes in a Plain and Easy Method* by John Tufts (1689–1750) and *The Grounds and Rules of Musick Explained, or An Introduction to the Art of Singing by Note* by Thomas Walter (1696–1725). It appears that Tufts's book was printed before Walter's, and it is unfortunate that the earliest extant copy of Tufts is of the third edition of 1723 (see Finney). The 1721 edition of Walter contains a tune, "Southwel New," that cannot be traced to any earlier English publication. Tufts, who enlarged his book after the first edition, clearly used Walter in the enlargement, and the third edition includes "Southwel New." But it also includes a tune, "100 Psalm Tune New," that is not in Walter, nor is it derived from earlier English sources. Although it is not certain, it is reasonable to suppose that Walter composed "Southwel New," that Tufts composed "100 Psalm Tune New," and that these are the earliest art musical works written in British North America. If, moreover, a copy of Tufts's first edition were found to contain "100 Psalm Tune New," the palm could more definitively be awarded. We will return shortly to Tufts and Walter.

Canadian pride, it turns out, can boast the first art music written in North America. The Canadian, Charles-Amador Martin (1648–1711), wrote a plainchant melody to the "prose" section of the office at some time between 1674 and 1684 (Kallmann: 22–23). The Latin words of the text have biblical reference: "Sacrae Familiae Felix spectaculum, / Nascentis gratiae Dulce cunabulum / Se nobis reserat. / Castis visceribus Quis flos egreditur! / Pannis terrestribus Deus involvitur, / Cunis et accubat. / Quis natum cogitat Intactae Virginis? / Visum ne territet, Sol puri luminis /Nube se temperat," etc. (part of text and music in Kallmann: 24). For our subject, it is interesting that the first musical works written in North America, modest though they were, were composed for words related to the Bible.

One of the outcomes of Tufts's and Walter's books and of sermonic pleadings by clergy members like Thomas Symmes (1677–1725) and Cotton Mather (1663–1728) was the "singing school" movement, which spread all over the colonies. Mather lent his presence to an early form of it with a sermon as early as 1717. His diary for 16 March of that year notes: "In the Evening I preached unto a large Auditory, where a Society of persons learning to Sing, began a quarterly solemnity." The diary of Mather's nephew, Samuel Sewall, gives the sermon's text (Rev 14:3): "No man could learn that Song" (Fisher: 8). The subtitle of Walter's book gives the clue to the nature of the singing school. It was a project to teach people to read music (Tufts devised a system of notation by letters to the same end) and to practice the music to be sung in church in order to improve the wretched state of congregational singing. The response to the idea, predictably, was mixed. The singing schools caught on especially with the younger folk, for whom they were not only a challenge and a musical pleasure but an excellent occasion for socializing. Those who had grown up and lived their lives with "lining out" the Psalms could see only a dire prospect. Thomas Symmes, perhaps the most voluble proponent of the new method (he styled himself "Philomusicus"), characterized the objections with a certain amount of sarcasm in a pamphlet, *Utile Dulci, Or, A Joco-Serious Dialogue, Concerning Regular Singing* (1723):

1. It is a new way, an unknown tongue.
2. It is not so melodious as the usual way. (!)
3. There are so many tunes we shall never have done learning them.

4. The practice creates disturbances and causes people to behave indecently and disorderly.
5. It is Quakerish and Popish and introductive of instrumental music.
6. The names given to the notes are bawdy, yea blasphemous.
7. It is a needless way, since our fathers got to heaven without it.
8. It is a contrivance to get money.
9. People spend too much time learning it, they tarry out nights disorderly.
10. They are a company of young upstarts that fall in with this way, and some of them are lewd and loose persons. (Ellinwood: 20)

To each of these objections (one does wonder how one can be both Quakerish and Popish at the same time), Symmes replied vigorously and with a certain amount of humor. Other clergymen of the same persuasion were a bit easier on tender consciences, but congregations were occasionally split over the issue—as has not been unknown in more recent times.

The singing school movement was finally successful, and it continued as an aspect of the American scene in cities until after the Civil War, in rural areas longer still. Singing schools spread throughout the colonies, which suggests that the old method of "lining out" the Psalms was used elsewhere than in New England. We know very little of the psalmody of the colonies outside of New England. Psalms were sung by Anglicans, Puritans, and Baptists alike, but the metrical versions that were popular in centers like Charleston, Baltimore, and New York have not been discovered. A somewhat ambiguous reference to psalm-singing in the diary of William Byrd (1674–1744) of Westover, Virginia, suggests a similarity to the New England scene. On 15 December 1710, he relates that he went to church "to hear the people sing Psalms and there the singing master gave me two books, one for me and one for my wife." The books led to a quarrel between him and Mrs. Byrd, the contents of which he did not state save to say that "she was wholly in the wrong." A week later, 24 December 1710, he remarked, "We began to give in to the new way of singing Psalms" (Stoutamire: 19). The way in which Byrd refers to this episode suggests that the notion of singing schools may have been imported to Virginia from England rather than from New England. His mention of a singing master predates by several years any indication of the start of singing schools in New England and by over a decade the two works by Tufts and Walter that were so influential in the New England movement. It seems to me possible, though no evidence demonstrates it, that the books with which the Byrds were presented might have been the English forerunners of Tufts and Walter, such as Playford or *Compendium of Practical Musick* (1665 and later editions) by Christopher Simpson (ca. 1610–1669), to which Lowens refers as "standard works of reference" (49). However that may be, Byrd's giving in to "the new way of singing Psalms," along with his saying that he went "to hear the people sing Psalms" (not, by inference, to sing them himself), strongly suggests that the argument between him and his wife had to do with "lining out" the Psalms and the legitimacy or propriety of singing from notes.

The long-range results of the singing schools were multiple. They certainly led to more unity and, perhaps, better tone in congregational singing. By providing a corps of trained and practiced singers in a congregation, the singing school led directly to the church choir and its rendition of anthems and other choral music in churches. It must be remembered that the singing school, although it developed from the needs of the church, was separate from the church (Lowens: 281). In the cause of art music in America, the growth of the choir was undoubtedly significant. That the church choir has over the decades also inflicted told and untold suffering upon the pious is a mere side effect. The singing school movement coincided to some extent with the introduction of organs into American churches, and that in turn affected typical church architecture. As the eighteenth century went along, churches were frequently built with the organ and a choir gallery in the rear, where the voices of those trained in the singing school could encourage the less able in the congregation to sing more loudly if not more "tuneablie."

The musical life of the colonies was becoming more complex in the eighteenth century. We begin to hear of secular art music. The first notice of a public concert in North America was on 30 December 1731, in Boston (Sonneck: 250–51), and only a few months later, the *South Carolina Gazette* in Charleston announced "a *Consort* of Musick at the Council Chamber, for the benefit of Mr. [John] Salter" on Wednesday, 12 April 1732 (Sonneck: 11). We have no idea what might have been performed on either occasion, nor is it certain that these were the first concerts on these shores. They are simply the first of which we have knowledge. Since a sharp distinction was made in that period between sacred and secular music, I shall not pursue the subject of secular concerts in the colonial period. Perusal of Sonneck's exhaustive researches of concert programs before 1800 shows that music with a sacred cast to it very seldom appeared, although there were occasional sacred concerts.

The distinction is important, though it was always sharper in the minds of ecclesiastics than in the minds of musicians. In looking over the history of musical styles, one can see that in any period sacred music developed along the same lines as secular music but tended to be more conservative. Mozart and Haydn were still writing sections of their Masses in the older polyphonic style when that style had virtually disappeared from symphonies and string quartets. The distinction rests finally on the Greek assumption that the different modes had different musical qualities and exerted different ethical effects on the listener. Following St. Augustine, Christians were often worried about the ill effects music might have because of its appeal to the sensual. Pope John XXII objected to the Ars Nova with its decorative embellishment of simple melody precisely because the additions "heighten the beauty of the melody" (McKay and Crawford: 5). For the same reasons, Calvin would have no harmony in music sung in Geneva, and the Puritans went for simplicity of line and, once it was allowed, of harmony. Even Thomas Symmes, the clergyman so eager for the success of the singing schools, warned in *The Reasonableness of, Regular Singing, or, Singing by Note* (1720) about the wrong use of singing: "Is there not great reason to fear that you mistake the *Pleasing Impressions* made on your *Animal Spirits*, by the *Tune*, to be the *Melody* you ought to *make in your heart unto the Lord*? Do you not mistake the natural Effects of *Musick*, for the Comforts of the Holy Spirit, and Actings of Grace in your Souls?" (quoted in McKay and Crawford: 4–5; italics original). But to sing a Psalm in a secular concert would have been as thoroughly out of place as to play an oboe concerto in church. Still, the same musicians who played and sang in secular concerts sang, played, and led singing in churches. The young American society was not so replete with musical achievement that it could afford specialists.

Another effect of the singing schools was to call forth demands for more and better music for the newly confident choirs and congregations to sing. A series of American composers emerged in the latter part of the eighteenth century to fill the need. Among a fair number of composers who compiled and contributed to collections of tunes, such as Daniel Read (1757–1836), Timothy Swan (1758–1842), Supply Belcher (1751–1836), Justin Morgan (1747–1798—famous as the breeder of the Morgan horse), Andrew Law (1749–1821), Jacob Kimball (1761–1826), Samuel Holyoke (1762–1820), Oliver Holden (1765–1844), and a good number of others, perhaps the best and most famous was William Billings (1746–1800) of Boston. It is worth pausing over Billings as the exemplar of the Bible-related music of the late eighteenth century. He stands out as perhaps the most talented of the group and one of the most articulate about his hopes for music. Still, Barbour is surely right when he says that, though Billings "was a much better composer than any of the English composers performed in 18th-century America . . . this is not to say that he was a great or even a near-great composer" (138). Billings may be the one exception to my statement above that no major American composer has written a major work involving the Bible. Among American composers of the late eighteenth century, Billings was major; among American composers in general, in my opinion, Billings is not major. Still he was a fascinating character, tanner turned composer, a Bostonian from birth, "a singular man, of moderate size, short of one leg, with one eye, without any address, & with an uncommon negligence of person" (diary of William Bentley of Salem), an inveterate taker of snuff who "every few minutes, instead of taking it in the usual manner, with thumb and finger, would take out a handful and snuff it from between his thumb and clenched hand" (Gould: 46).

Billings's Psalm tunes, like most others, were in four-part harmony for male and female voices, with the melody in the tenor. Ordinarily some sopranos doubled the tenor melody an octave higher, and some tenors doubled the soprano harmony an octave lower, thus making for a rich choral texture of six parts. He also wrote more complicated anthems for use by choirs. Whether these works were performed with accompaniment of organ or other instruments is debated. Boston churches were seldom equipped with organs, even in the latter eighteenth century (the Brattle Street Church turned down an organ bequeathed to it by Thomas Brattle in 1713, wanting no part of such Popish novelties), but Billings is credited by some with introducing the cello into the service. The attribution is almost certainly mistaken, as references to bass viols, violas, and other stringed instruments precede him in New England by some years. But some of his anthems have organ interludes.

Compared with most of his contemporaries, Billings is subtle. Compared with high-level composers of his time, he is crude, and for a long time Billings was criticized by historians of American music such as Louis C. Elson and John Tasker Howard. When American musicians began to take notice of their past as it differed from the elite European tradition, Billings came in for something of a revival. There is in him a freedom and vigor of melody, rhythm, and harmony that most of his contemporaries lack, a musical enthusiasm that can be quite refreshing even in its crudeness. He does things in voice leading over which theorists cluck sadly: parallel fifths and octaves between parts, odd leaps within parts where stepwise progressions would make smoother writing, cross rhythms that completely abrogate the natural rhythm of the words. He has been called "illiterate" (Lindstrom) and "uncouth" and "utterly untrained" (Elson). For almost any opinion about Billings, from the most negative to the most enthusiastic, phenomena in his scores can be quoted in support.

In his Psalm tunes, Billings used metrical Psalms from available sources, such as the versions of Isaac Watts, the New Version of Tate and Brady (1711), Charles Wesley, and James and John Relly. It is interesting how often he was drawn to versions using uncommon meters. Three regular meters account for nearly all of the eighteenth-century Psalm versions and tunes, and, indeed, for 80 percent of Billings's own (Barbour: 2): Short Meter (6, 6, 8, 6 syllables in a quatrain), Common Meter (8, 6, 8, 6), and Long Meter (8, 8, 8, 8). Billings frequently used a 6, 6, 6, 6, 4, 4, 4, 4 meter, often called the Hallelujah Meter because "Hallelujah" fit the four-syllable lines of the second quatrain, and other meters for stanzas longer than quatrains, e.g., 8, 8, 6, 8, 8, 6 and 7, 8, 7, 8, 7, 8 for sestet stanzas and 8, 5, 8, 5, 7, 7, 8, 5 and 7, 7, 7, 7, 5, 7, 7, 7 for octave stanzas. In two poems from the Relly versions, both poet and composer outstripped themselves. Billings wrote his tune "Restoration" to a meter of 4, 4, 4, 6, 6, 2, 4, 4, 4, 6, carried through eight stanzas: "Greatly beloved / Of God approved / Ere time began / Jehovah's darling, man, / Possessed his nature, love, / Above. / There man is known / Whilst angels own / Above them far / This bright and morning star." Another, more complex in rhythm and rhyme scheme, is the text of Billings's tune "Baptism": "O how doth God our souls surprise / When he our conscience doth baptize / Into the holy nature. / Where free from all offense and blame / We now possess in Christ the Lamb / The fulness of his stature. / Now free / Are we / And shall ever / In our Savior / Stand perfected / With him to this grace elected." It is a nearly unbelievable 8, 8, 7, 8, 8, 7, 2, 2, 4, 4, 4, 8. As Barbour says, these texts "offer rich possibilities for asymmetry in melody" (8), which Billings took. That he would be drawn to such texts is an indication of his free musical spirit and also of his willingness to try anything.

The anthem texts, for choir only, are more varied. Here Billings took prose texts from the Bible, including extracts from Isaiah, Jeremiah, Joel, and the Song of Songs. (The King James Version, which he used, like the scholars of the day, did not count these works as poetry.) But Billings's free spirit shows more clearly in the anthems than in Psalm tunes. He freely combines texts from here and there in the Bible, as in the anthem "Retrospect," in which he has stitched together some original words with lines from Jer 4:19; 47:6; 48:10; Isa 2:4; 52:7; Luke 2:4; and Rev 19:6 in a kind of pastiche. He was quite prepared to add to the biblical text for effect. In "Universal Praise," after the first verse of Psalm 150, "O praise God, praise him in his holiness," Billings was carried away by his own verse: "Praise him propagation; / praise him, vegetation, / and let your voice / proclaim your choice / and testify / to standers-by / with ardent fire / your firm desire / to praise the Lord. / Let the leading bass inspire, / let the tenor catch the fire, / let the counter [alto] still be higher, / let the treble join the choir" (as the individual parts enter).

Perhaps Billings's most famous anthem is the *Lamentation over Boston*, in which he parodies various Old Testament texts to shift their references to revolutionary New England: "By the rivers of Watertown we sat down and wept, when we remembered thee, O Boston" (cf. Ps 137:1). He picks up Jer 31:15, 20: "A voice was heard in Roxbury which echo'd thro' the Continent, weeping for Boston because of their danger" (Barbour mistakenly identifies the source as Jer 3:21 [p. 11]) and "Is Boston my dear Town, is it my native Place? For since their Calamity, I do earnestly remember it still." These quotations do not exhaust Billings's paraphrases in this anthem, but they demonstrate the ardor with which he applied biblical texts to his own times.

One musical device, with which Billings has frequently been identified, though he neither invented nor monopolized it, is the "fuguing tune." Often turning up not only in anthems but also in Psalm tunes for congregational singing, the fuguing tune—there is some indication that people pronounced the word as "fudging" (Mellers: 8)—used imitative entry in different parts to add variety to the singing. Usually beginning in straight, four-part harmony, the fuguing section gave way after a few measures to a concluding homophonic section. Billings himself thought the device a grand one, saying in the introduction to his collection, *The Singing Master's Assistant* (1778), that "the audience are most luxuriously entertained and exceedingly delighted" by it. Ecclesiastics were doubtless irritated at the thought that entertainment might be any part of the point, but Billings had liberal leanings. The device pretty much disappeared from American hymnic practice, though a rather pale shadow of it can be observed in the usual arrangement of "Adeste Fideles" at the words, "O come, let us adore him."

The period of the Revolution and immediately afterward was a certain high-water mark for native American musc. Singing school masters tramped the countryside and compiled collections of tunes for their charges to learn (and to buy). If Billings's own patriotism, which verged on jingoism, be taken as representative, there was a distinct feeling for the religious rightness of the American cause, and the tunes of Billings and his contemporaries were eagerly sung in churches. Indeed, there is plenty of indication that, although traditional Anglican chant was used in Anglican churches in America and plainchant in Catholic ones, even those congregations were not infrequently exposed to the works of the Yankee tunesmiths (Lowens's term: 178ff.; see also Ellinwood: 31–46). But as the ardors of the Revolution receded, reaction in musical matters took their place.

The Early Nineteenth Century

Even some earlier practitioners of the fuguing tune turned against it. Samuel Holyoke (1762–1820), publishing his *Harmonia Americana* (Boston, 1791), explained the omission of fuguing tunes because of "the trifling effect produced by that sort of music; for the parts, falling in, one after another, each conveying a different idea, confound the sense, and render the performance a mere jargon of words" (Stevenson: 74n). The same sentiment was expressed by Elias Mann in 1807, whose preface to *The Massachusetts Collection of Sacred Harmony* deplored "those wild fugues, and rapid and confused movements, which have so long been the disgrace of congregational psalmody" (Stevenson: 75).

The older tunes did not entirely lose place; they were contained especially in Psalm collections for use in the West and in rural areas, where they were not infrequently adapted to the "shape-note" format. But their continuance in collections made for the urban East depended on their being "corrected" and reharmonized in order to remove the crudities that the newer generation of composers and compilers felt so keenly. For the American scene saw a considerable influx both of European musicians and of the high tradition of European music. The native tunes began to look very shoddy as opportunities increased to hear works of Handel, Haydn, Mozart, and Beethoven. Those American composers who took the lead in providing music for American churches now explicitly declared their allegiance to the European tradition, adapted melodies from the great masters of the baroque and classical eras to religious words, and, when they composed their own, imitated the melodic and harmonic usage of Europe.

Two names stand out above the rest, both influential in American sacred music until well after the Civil War: Thomas Hastings (1784–1872) and Lowell Mason (1792–1872). Hastings, who is said to have been an albino (Ellinwood: 218), was located at first in upstate New York and later in New York City. Teaching himself music, he began rather early to compile books of tunes in which he was drawn more to English than to German models. *Musica Sacra* (Utica, 1815 or 1816), Hastings's first collection, had tunes by American composers, including himself, and such Europeans as Giardini, Purcell, William Croft, Handel, and Burney. In a few years, Hastings changed his allegience. Writing *Dissertation on Musical Taste* (Albany, 1822), he inaugurated an explicit allegiance to the German musical tradition, which has continued in American practice to this day and has occasioned frequent complaints from adherents to other tastes and to the claims of American music: "We are decided admirers of *German* musick. We delight to study and to listen to it. The science, genius, the taste, that every where pervade it, are truly captivating to those who have learned to appreciate it: but such, we presume, are not yet the *majority* of American or English auditors or executants" (quoted in Hitchcock: 54; italics original). Two motifs from that forthright statement deserve comment. One is Hastings's characteristic use of the term "science," an unqualified term of praise and an implicit condemnation of the self-taught crudities, as Hastings saw them, of the eighteenth-century tunesmiths. The cultivation of "scientific" music is a leitmotif of the ideology pursued by the American elite throughout the nineteenth century. The other motif reflects a critical point in Hastings's entire career: "captivating to those who have learned to appreciate it." We saw the point being pressed by Thomas Symmes at the beginning of the eighteenth century with the establishment of the singing schools, and it is the point, as we will shortly see, of the movement of music education in the United States. As the American nation began to feel itself approaching adulthood—whatever the apprehension of Europeans, who continued to see it as awkwardly adolescent—the state of higher culture in the country worried many of its leaders from Thomas Jefferson on down. To the musically cultivated in the early nineteenth century, the American model was execrable, utterly unfit for imitation and development. The European and especially German model provided a long tradition for emulation, and that tradition came to the fore partly with the fact that in the national period immigrants with musical training were more likely to come from Germany, where political and social unease was high, than from England and France. But the taste for the high musical tradition of Germany had to be cultivated; its appreciation had to be learned.

Hastings himself wrote some six hundred hymn texts and one thousand tunes (Ellinwood: 218). He is now known chiefly, if not entirely, for the tune

"Toplady" to the text, "Rock of ages, cleft for me," a curious pastiche of biblical allusions, which was published in *Spiritual Songs for Social Worship* (1832), compiled by Hastings and Lowell Mason. (This is the only instance I can find of collaboration between these two dominant figures; other evidence suggests that they considered themselves bitter rivals [Stevenson: 81–82].) The production of metrical Psalms virtually died out in the nineteenth century, since religious poetry began to be used for singing. To be sure, especially in Protestant practice, such verses were likely to have roots in biblical phrasing, but hymn texts were no longer paraphrases or translations of biblical texts, as the old metrical Psalms had been.

Lowell Mason's name is undoubtedly more familiar now than Hastings's for such tunes still in hymnbooks as "Missionary Hymn" ("From Greenland's icy mountains") and "Olivet" ("My faith looks up to thee"). He sought a "devotional" style in hymn writing, a style heavily indebted to German rules of harmonic progression, which he learned from F. C. Abel in Savannah, Georgia. Of Abel little or nothing is known, save that he was German in origin (Hitchcock and Ellinwood both call him F. L. Abel). But Mason acknowledged his influence and followed it so thoroughly that his hymnic style could almost be called the prototype of the "religioso" convention in later music. Immensely productive, Mason made a fortune from the royalties of his collections of sacred and church music, beginning with the most famous of all, the *Boston Handel and Haydn Society Collection of Church Music* (1822), compiled while he was a bank clerk in Savannah. Some of his production was less ethical; the *Manual of the Boston Academy of Music* (1834), purporting to be an original work on music education derived from principles of Pestalozzi, was actually a translation of Georg Friedrich Kübler's *Anleitung zum Gesang-Unterrichte in Schulen* (Stuttgart, 1826), minus any acknowledgment of the original (Stevenson: 78).

Perhaps Mason's more lasting influence was not from his publications but from his educational activities. Probably without thinking of the connection, he took the singing school movement from itinerant singing masters and put it into the schools. A long campaign culminated in the inclusion of music as a subject of instruction in the Boston public schools in 1838 and the appointment of Mason as superintendent of music for the whole system. Whether or not he had cribbed the *Manual*, he now had to put his ideas on the line, and he responded with the greatest energy and effectiveness. Music has been dealt with in American classrooms ever since. But Hitchcock well delineates the problem it has caused (64–65). The folk and popular music was, of course, ignored by teachers (and by Mason) as beneath notice, but the highest levels of the European art music tradition were beyond the reach of those without special training and qualifications, both students and teachers. The result was a mediocre musical curriculum, the attempt to teach pupils to "appreciate" the blandest, most innocuous, least inventive and adventurous music coming out of the European tradition. Allen Britton has characterized the music used for schoolroom education as "polite," which is as good a tag as any to describe the entire effect of Lowell Mason (see Mellers's references to "Bracebridge Hall music": 25). By his ideology, Mason could not tolerate the popular, but by his own musical training and sensibilities he was unable to aspire to the level of the genuinely elite. Thus the American experience of music in schools and churches has seldom tapped resources more impressive than the most banal levels of Mendelssohn—not even rising to the kind of music Mendelssohn wrote that persuaded his European contemporaries of his rare genius.

Of biblical music up to the Civil War there is little. With the decline of the metrical Psalm and its being supplanted by the devotional hymn and without a sufficiently rich musical culture in the churches to support the performances of larger works like oratorios or cantatas, the musical scene was relatively grim right up to the Civil War. To be sure, there were such organizations as the Handel and Haydn Society of Boston, founded in 1815 by the immigrant musician (German, of course) Gottlieb Graupner (1767–1836). That society, formed "for cultivating and improving a correct taste in the performance of sacred music, and also to introduce into more general practice the works of Handel, Haydn and other eminent composers," was no refuge for an aspiring American composer, for no American composer, nearly by definition, was "eminent." Nor were there any whom we might attempt to reinstate. Perhaps the best composers of art music were George Bristow (1825–1898) and William H. Fry (1813–1864), both of whom essayed operas in the Italian style—that European domination again (Fry's *Leonora* ran for sixteen performances in Philadelphia in 1845, but he could not get the Paris Opera even to give it a rehearsal). I find no record of biblical or other religious works by either. The age of the later Beethoven, Weber, Schubert, Schumann, and Mendelssohn in Germany and Austria; Berlioz, Chopin, the earlier Liszt in France; Rossini, Donizetti, Bellini in Italy—a time of musical invention and adventure, whatever we may now think of its general quality—produced imitators of mediocre quality in this country.

The situation in Canada was similar if not even further behind. The urban areas of Canada were more isolated from each other than in the United States. But some of the same phenomena were to be observed. Stephen Humbert (1767–1849), who fled from the United States to St. John, New Brunswick, in the Revolution, put out a collection of tunes in 1801, *Union Harmony, or British America's Sacred Vocal Musick*. In the introduction to the second edition (1816), he especially advocated the fuguing tune, of which he had many examples—and that at a time when the fuguing tune was disappearing from new U.S. collections. As for other art music, it came from European, not Canadian, pens for some time to come (Kallmann: 27–90). We will pick up the Canadian story again at the middle of the nineteenth century.

The Late Nineteenth Century

During the latter half of the nineteenth century, we begin to see the production of music of some quality by American composers. As aspirations toward something better were to some extent nurtured by the public schools under the influence of Lowell Mason and others, the lack of facilities for training professional musicians became a more urgent problem. It was sometimes masked by the fact that many musicians immigrated in various European crises, especially at the Revolutions of 1848, which saw a flood of solidly competent German musicians appear from across the Atlantic. The German bias on the American scene was only furthered by these immigrations. The first native American piano virtuoso, Louis Moreau Gottschalk (1829–1869), a native of New Orleans and French by training and tendency, is quoted as saying in 1862, "It is remarkable that almost all the Russians in America are counts, just as almost all the musicians who abound in the United States are nephews of Spohr and Mendelssohn" (Hitchcock: 56). The large number of these musicians available for performance and teaching made it seem sometimes unnecessary to have facilities to train Americans to take their places. And the musical profession has always proceeded on an apprentice system, in which one's piano, voice, violin, or composition teacher as an individual is the most significant influence on one. In the meantime, budding American composers and performers usually made the pilgrimage to the great centers of Europe for their training.

That began—but only began—to change in the latter nineteeth century. The year 1860 saw the founding of the first conservatory in the United States, the Peabody Institute in Baltimore (not completed until 1868); in 1865 the conservatory at Oberlin College, Ohio, was founded; and in 1867, the Boston Conservatory, the New England Conservatory in Boston, the Cincinnati Conservatory, and the Chicago Musical College. The lack of such an institution in New York, the musical center of the nation, is surprising, but the National Conservatory was founded by Jeannette Thurber in 1885 (it was granted a national charter in 1891), the Institute of Musical Art in 1904 (merged with the Juilliard Foundation in 1926), and the Mannes School of Music in 1916. For many more decades most of the important musical figures in the United States spent two to five years or more in Paris, Berlin, Weimar (where Liszt taught), Leipzig, or Vienna.

One of the results of this increase in educational activity was the wish on the part of church musicians to be a bit more ambitious in their productions. If the singing schools and the public school music education had taught many people to read notes and to "appreciate" music better than the jigs and quadrilles of contemporary dance music, then conductors and organists took the opportunity of putting their choirs to more challenging anthems than the standard tune books contained, sometimes to longer works such as cantatas or even oratorios for special liturgical seasons, sometimes to

combination with choirs of neighboring churches for such seasonal extra-
vaganzas. Where did they get such materials? The music publishing business
was not a leading growth industry. The English firm of Novello began a
monthly magazine in 1844, *The Musical Times*, with an anthem as an insert
in each issue, and in 1846–47 it began to publish cheap editions of oratorios,
masses, cantatas, and the like. These editions became more easily available
when the firm established a New York office in 1852, though only after
1894, when H. W. Gray in New York became the American agent for
Novello, did real accessibility come about. Meanwhile, a few American
magazines catered to the church choir trade, such as the monthly *The Par-
ish Choir* (1874–1887, weekly 1887–1919), the fortnightly *The American
Choir* (1896–1898), and the various enterprises of E. S. Lorenz, *The Choir
Leader* (1894), *The Choir Herald* (1897), *The Volunteer Choir* (1913), all
aimed at a less ambitious clientele than the others and containing anthems
mostly written by Lorenz's own staff, with results of predictable quality
(Ellinwood: 70–71).

For the time being, music with biblical contents continued, then, to be
ecclesiastical music. What could qualify as art music came in this period to
have relatively high quality. American composers, however imitative they
might be, were not badly served by their European training. One of the most
prolific church composers was Dudley Buck (1839–1909)—a student for three
years in Leipzig under, among others, Moscheles—an organist (one of the
founders of the American Guild of Organists) and composer of anthems, often
on biblical texts. For some time Buck's anthems were in great demand, but he
allowed himself to fall into formulas, and one Dudley Buck anthem sounds
much like another. Buck's best known student was Harry Rowe Shelley (1858–
1947), also an organist and anthem composer, whose "Hark, hark, my soul" is
occasionally heard even now. On the whole, composers of that school wrote in
ways hardly distinguishable from such contemporary English composers as Sir
John Stainer (1840–1901) and Sir Arthur Sullivan (1842–1900), works heavily
influenced by Mendelssohn, harmonically competent, a bit slick in the use of
choral textures, often with solo sections that allowed the church soloist,
whether volunteer or paid, to whip up a bit of emotion, to be followed by
soothing, devotional harmonies from the choir. They are not *bad* music, but
neither do they challenge any but the incompetent.

For music with biblical content, we must turn to someone like John
Knowles Paine (1839–1906), Dudley Buck's contemporary but a composer of
a quite different stripe. Paine studied early in his native Portland, Maine,
with Hermann Kotzschmar (1829–1909), a German immigrant. Returning
from three years in Berlin in 1861, he took an organist's post in Boston and
began the next year to teach a noncredit course in music at Harvard. In
1875, Harvard took the plunge and appointed Paine to the first university
professorship of music in the United States. He remained in the post until
his retirement in 1905.

Paine's output was large, and his position allowed him the luxury of hearing his compositions performed. Though the works of American composers have never bulked large on American symphony programs, the Boston Symphony was not inhospitable to Paine. Like everyone, he wrote in the small forms—songs, short organ and piano pieces, hymns, and anthems—but he also ventured into the large forms of symphony, symphonic poem, overture, opera, Mass, and oratorio. The oratorio *St. Peter*, op. 20 (1872), may be taken as the best instance of Paine's use of biblical texts. On the negative side, it must be said that *St. Peter* is very nearly a clone of Mendelssohn's *St. Paul*. It has the same form: biblical narrative in recitative, arioso solos for quotations of biblical characters, chorus parts for the apostles, arias to biblical texts that expand on and interpret the emotions of St. Peter and others in particular episodes, choral pieces on biblical texts at important interpretive and structural junctures, and even the use of accompanied German chorales, which Paine himself notes in the text as exemplified in Mendelssohn's *St. Paul*. The form is an extension of the traditional German form of the Passion, as in J. S. Bach's from St. Matthew and St. John. Paine's style is also Mendelssohnian, using in the choruses the same mixture of chordal, harmonic writing and imitative style (a double fugue, for example, in no. 8 on the words, "Repent, and believe the glad tidings"). One could believe, if one did not know the source, that the melody of the soprano aria, no. 3, "The spirit of the Lord is upon me," was Mendelssohn's own, and Paine uses the same kinds of descriptive orchestral accompaniments for such natural phenomena as wind and storm (e.g., the interlude after "vapor of smoke" in the bass aria, no. 30, and the portrayal of the Pentecostal wind in the accompanied recitative, no. 27). On the positive side, Paine was a serious musician, and the work is a careful setting of the texts with real competence in vocal and orchestral writing. And some of it is Paine's own: at the words, "The sun shall be turned into darkness, and the moon shall be turned into blood" in Peter's Pentecost speech (no. 30), the bass soloist is accompanied at the unison two octaves below by lower strings, with a single note tremolo in the upper strings, a hollow and foreboding effect of which Mendelssohn would never have thought, and Paine modulates from F minor to a triumphant C major in marchlike rhythms for "the great and notable day." One must say that, if Mendelssohn's *St. Paul* is worth performing now and again (and it is), then Paine's *St. Peter* is also worthy of an occasional performance as no more a mere historical curiosity than its predecessor.

One finds similar phenomena among Canadian composers. A certain isolation obtained between the French-Canadian composers of Montreal and Quebec and those of the English tradition in the Maritimes and Ontario. The French were nearly all Roman Catholic and produced service music for their churches as well as more ambitious works. Perhaps primary among them was Calixa Lavallée (1842–1891) of Montreal, a composer in small and large forms from etudes to operas. One of the latter is *Le Jugement de*

Salomon, presumably based on the incident in 1 Kgs 3:16–28. Kallmann says that the work is either lost or—what comes to the same thing—not yet located (239). This is, by the way, the earliest North American opera on a biblical subject to which I have found reference. Guillaume Couture (1831–1915) wrote an oratorio, *Jean le Précurseur* (1914), which Kallmann (243) considers more than worthy of revival. Of composers in the English tradition, Charles A. E. Harriss (1862–1929) wrote a large number of works, including the dramatic cantata, *Daniel before the King* (1890), and Angelo M. Read (1854–1926) wrote a cantata, *David's Lament* (1903), doubtless on the poem in 2 Sam 1:19–26 (I could not locate the score or a description). Canada has always had the problem that careers in the United States frequently beckoned its top-flight musicians with the promise of more prestige and higher salaries. Our scholars and historians are too provincial in supposing that discussions of "American" music need not include that of Canada. At the same time, Canadian scholars should be encouraged to seek out and publish the works of earlier Canadian composers, so that the rest of us may help to evaluate them as they deserve, and the works of the deserving may enter the international repertoire.

The Twentieth Century

Something quite new can be observed of the presence of the Bible in American music during the twentieth century, and I wish to concentrate on it here. Though biblical music for liturgical use continued to be composed, sometimes by leading composers (Masses, for example, by Roy Harris [b. 1898] in 1948, by Lou Harrison [b. 1917] in 1962, by Roger Sessions [b. 1896] in 1955, by Randall Thompson [b. 1899] in 1956), the most interesting biblical music in this century has been written not for the church but for the concert hall or the opera house. Even when the work carries a liturgical title, such as the *Mass* of Leonard Bernstein (b. 1918), it may not be intended for ecclesiastical liturgy. Bernstein's work, frankly called a "theater piece," including dancers and dancer-singers and composed only partly on the Latin text of the Mass, was written for the opening of the John F. Kennedy Center for the Performing Arts in Washington, D.C., in 1971. Ceremonial, ritual, the occasion was; ecclesiastical, public worship, it was not. Even a work that was written for an ecclesiastical occasion, Randall Thompson's *The Nativity according to St. Luke* (1961)—composed for the two hundredth anniversary of Christ Church, Cambridge, Massachusetts—is called a "Musical Drama," has stage and lighting directions in the score, and is rather a drama taking advantage of the setting in a church sanctuary than a liturgical work. That, indeed, is typical of twentieth-century works using biblical texts.

I do not mean that liturgical music of high quality has not been written. One need only mention the names of such composers in the U.S. as Leo Sowerby (1895–1968), Normand Lockwood (b. 1906), Daniel Pinkham

(b. 1923), T. Tertius Noble (1867–1953), and the Canadians Healey Willan (1880–1968) and Violet Archer (b. 1913). It is nearly impossible simply to characterize twentieth-century liturgical music, for as the century has matured, the variety of music written for worship has ranged from jazz, rock, and country styles to complex vocal works with orchestral instruments and even, occasionally, prerecorded tape. The quality of the most recent of these experiments is not yet assessable. Proponents hail the use of popular idioms or of avant garde art music media; opponents curse it as opponents always have, ever since John Tufts tried to teach people to read notes. One who wishes to wait and see how engaging it may turn out to be in ritual contexts must all the while fend off both enthusiasts and naysayers. The problems with popular forms are that they are not well suited to convey the sense of transcendence that worship entails and that their performance styles, requiring rhetorical distortions of words that irresistibly remind a hearer of settings entirely different from ritual ones, often jar the aesthetic integrity of a liturgy. The more avant garde idioms have something of the reverse difficulty, that a congregation is called on to assimilate a musical diction so unfamiliar as to be, for most members, meaningless and uncommunicative, if not negatively communicative. A problem faces the musician in liturgy that is absent from the concert room: the audience at a concert has voluntarily paid for the privilege of being there. The religious congregation has other motivations, not necessarily including the compliant acceptance of musical experiments. I mean to suggest, gently, to musical experimentalists in liturgy that they should temper the wind to the shorn lamb.

I turn to some twentieth-century works that are not liturgical, in several different forms. With the first pair, two Psalm settings by Charles Ives, there is ambiguity about their origin and the composer's intent. Ives, in many ways the most original composer America has produced, was a student at Yale of Horatio Parker (1863–1919), one of the leading lights of the late nineteenth century, but he chose to go his own way in experimenting with tonalities, textures, and idioms that reflected his vision of the American character and that would enlarge the hearing capacities of attentive listeners. Ives was capable of profound scorn for the "nice" music of composers like Paine and other "learned" writers. He never heard most of his works performed, for musicians would not take the trouble to penetrate his seemingly chaotic style. I have argued early in this essay that Ives was really a conservative at heart, and I think that characterization is not damaged by his musical experiments. The Psalm settings reflect a conservatism of liturgical atmosphere that, nevertheless, may exceed the capacities of any but the most nearly professional choir. Whether "67th Psalm" (1898) and "Psalm 90" (1923) were actually intended for performance in church is uncertain. A memo Ives wrote at an unknown date about "67th Psalm" (Kirkpatrick: 178) says: "Father, I think, succeeded in getting a choir in Danbury to sing this without an organ—but I remember I had difficulty in the New Haven choirs. The two keys gave trouble." Either Ives's recollection that his father had conducted the anthem (George Ives died in 1894) or his consistent dating of the work in 1898 was mistaken. "The two keys" refers to the method of composition. The alto and tenor parts are divided to give a basic six-voice chord, and the other parts are occasionally divided so that there may be as many as eight voices at a time. The men, in the opening and closing sections, sing basically in G minor, the women in C major, with an occasional foray elsewhere (e.g., at measure 6 the men go to A major, the women to E minor). A contrapuntal middle section, beginning with a strict canon between men's and women's voices, provides a very different texture and more complex harmonic combinations. Ives says, in the same memo quoted above (Kirkpatrick: 178), that "this is a kind of enlarged plainchant." In itself, the remark suggests a liturgical intent to the work, whatever the success or its opposite Ives may have had in getting it sung in church. But the chordal texture of the opening and closing reminds one more of Anglican chant (the last measures are written in that form) than of the Gregorian chant that is usually meant by "plainsong" or "plainchant."

"Psalm 90" is quite different; it is longer, a more carefully conceived interpretation of a very complex Psalm, and involves organ and bells as well as a choir capable of singing more than eight parts. The entire work unfolds over a constant C pedal in the organ, and that utterly solid, continuing sound suggests the underlying assurance in the Psalm. In the five measures of introduction, Ives gives and marks the musical motifs interpreting the text: the first organ chord is marked "The Eternities," the second, "Creation," and the third, a thirteenth-chord, "God's wrath against sin." A melodic motif of a falling fourth in measure 3 is marked "Prayer and humility," and measures 4 and 5, in which the bells enter, have the legend, "Rejoicing in Beauty and Work." These musical motifs are the material of the anthem, so that the music of v. 1 of the Psalm is sung over the same chord as the first of the introduction. At v. 2, the second chord of the introduction, transposed up, interprets the "creation" statement, and v. 3, "Thou turnest man to destruction," contains the "wrath" chord, extended to a fifteenth in an upward sequence that Ives also used at the end of v. 1, measures 13–15, of the progression of generations. He uses the same "wrath" phrase several times elsewhere, e.g., slightly modified with v. 5, with v. 7 ("we are consumed by thine anger, and by thy wrath are we troubled"), and with v. 11 on the words "anger," "fear," and "wrath." The melodic "prayer and humility" motif opens the setting of v. 4, "For a thousand years in thy sight," while the "rejoicing" bell accompaniment enters at v. 14 and continues to the end. One astonishing musical device may show Ives's characteristic heedlessness of the problems singers might have in actually singing his notes and his striving for an effect that he hears. In measures 60–65, with the words "For all our days are passed away in thy wrath: we spend our years as a tale that is told," Ives moves the sopranos up from middle C to high G and the basses down from middle C to low E-sharp by whole tones, each ending with a half-tone interval. As this separating process continues, the voices are constantly dividing, with altos following sopranos up and tenors following basses down until the final upper chord on "wrath" is a dense, 22-part tone cluster, *fortissimo*. In the second half of the couplet, he brings them all back the same way to the softest unison middle C. Tonally the effect is stunning. But Ives adds a rhythmic effect by writing the successive upward chords increasingly quickly—the first in the time of nine 16th-notes; the second, eight; the third, seven; and so on until "in thy wrath" has successive 16th-notes. In the downward movement, the same is done in reverse so that "we spend our years as a tale that is told" is sung ever more slowly. Well sung, "Psalm 90" is a very moving work. It seems doubtful that any but a professional concert choir could sing it well, and it should probably be supposed to be a concert, not a liturgical, anthem.

One would have to say the same of Aaron Copland's "In the Beginning" (1947), a setting of Gen 1:1–2:7 for mezzo-soprano and unaccompanied chorus. Indeed, the work's premier was given by the Collegiate Chorale, a concert choir conducted by Robert Shaw. Taking the King James Version of the biblical passage, Copland set it relatively straightforwardly, following the diction and rhythm of the words themselves, and only at particular places, especially in choral passages, repeating words and using imitative devices. Formulae in the text, such as "And God said," "And it was so," and "And it was evening, and it was morning the ——— day," Copland set formulaically, the latter in particular with an identical, chantlike phrase each time it appears. The texture of the work is rather austere with a modal flavor imparted by Copland's characteristic open chords moving polytonally. Emotionally, the piece comes to its climaxes at the putting of the lights into the sky (1:14–18) and at the creation of the human race (1:26–28), with a closing of restrained but powerful feeling on 2:7. On the whole, Copland avoided pictorial writing, though when the firmament divides waters from waters (1:7), the voices divide and imitate each other, and for "and over every creeping thing that creepeth upon the earth" (1:26 and its echo in 1:28) he wrote a somewhat humorous downward sequence of parallel chords in absolutely even rhythm.

A very different kind of work is the *Eight Bible Vignettes* for piano solo by R. Nathaniel Dett (1882–1943). I have discovered no other music from this side of the Atlantic with a biblical program for piano solo. Dett may have known of the biblical sonatas of Johann Kuhnau (1660–1722), narrative, descriptive music for harpsichord on biblical stories, including a very dramatic one on David and Goliath. Born in Drummondville, Quebec, Dett very shortly moved to the United States and spent his entire career here. He was one of a very few American black composers of art music before the present generation, along with Harry T. Burleigh (1866–1949) and William Grant Still (1895–1978). None of these three has an entry in the indexes of Mellers, Hitchcock, or Sablonsky, though John Tasker Howard (278–82) discusses all three at some length, together with two lesser lights, William

Levi Dawson (b. 1898) and Clarence Cameron White (1880–1960).

Dett was not an innovator, and all of his piano music shows the melodic textures of late romanticism, though he occasionally ventured beyond its harmonic limits. The *Eight Bible Vignettes* were his last piano work, written from 1941 to 1943, with the single movements published separately until the completion of the whole. For most of the movements, Dett has provided a written program, identifying Gen 21:14 as the specific "Desert Interlude" of no. 2 and 1 Sam 18:1 as the situation of no. 3, "As his own soul." In the first, "Father Abraham," Dett has woven together the Hebrew tune "Leoni" (he quotes the usual words, "The God of Abraham praise," in his "legend" to the movement) and the spiritual "Father Abraham Sittin' beside the Holy Lamb," proposing a simultaneous involvement in Abraham by the oppressed, both Jews and blacks. And the movement begins with a melodic motif derived from neither tune but very reminiscent of the spiritual "Sometimes I feel like a motherless child." With several movements, the main melodies are clearly conceived as vocal settings of particular biblical words, though I know of no evidence that Dett had first thought of these works as potentially vocal. No. 5, "I am the True Vine," is a fugue in three voices—Dett refers in the "legend" to the Trinity—on a theme with words brought together from John 15:1 and 5: "I am the true vine, ye are the branches." No. 7, "Other Sheep," is likewise based on a melody, received from an African student of Dett, setting words from John 10:16: "Other sheep I have, which are not of this fold: them also I must bring." In no. 6, "Martha Complained," the parts of the story portrayed are shown as melodic lines with words spoken in the text, along with pictorial elements such as a sharp, very dissonant chord where, Dett imagines, Martha's feelings rose to the climax of her breaking a dish in anger. But with no. 4, "Barcarolle of Tears," and no. 8, "Madrigal Divine," we have no clue to the biblical source of the musical conception. The work as a whole is of uneven quality, but it is worth including on piano programs, especially if there is value (and in my opinion there is) in deliberately performing works of earlier and contemporary black composers.

Surprisingly few operas have biblical settings, and of the few a small proportion is American. Such better-known European examples as Rossini's *Mosé in Egitto*, Saint-Saëns's *Samson et Dalila*, Richard Strauss's *Salome*, Arthur Honegger's *Le Roi David*, and Arnold Schoenberg's *Moses und Aron* (never finished) are joined by fewer than ten American operas on biblical themes. The earliest of these is *Judith*, a "lyric drama" by George W. Chadwick (1854–1931), performed in 1901. The story of Judith, by the way, is one of the few biblical themes that recur among operas. I find five other Judith operas in the whole history of opera, and aficionados may know more: Serov's *Judith* (1863), Reznicek's *Holofernes* (1923), Honegger's *Judith* (1926), Goossens's *Judith* (1929), and John Powell's *Judith and Holofernes* (after 1954). The story of Jephthah's daughter seems the next most popular subject, with four exemplars (Montéclair [1732], Meyerbeer [1812], Chapi [1876], and Lou Harrison [1963]), and Salome and John the Baptist next with three (Massenet, *Hérodiade* [1881], Richard Strauss [1905], and Mariotte, *Salomé* [1908]). Otherwise there are two Queens of Sheba (Gounod and Karl Goldmark), two Moseses (Rossini and Schoenberg), and assorted single entries such as the Prodigal Son (Ponchielli), Joseph (Méhul), Samson and Delilah (Saint-Saëns), and Deborah (Pizzetti). I would classify *Amahl and the Night Visitors* (1951), by Gian-Carlo Menotti (b. 1911), as quasi-biblical.

The one successful American biblical opera is *Susannah* (1955) by Carlisle Floyd (b. 1926). Called a "musical drama," *Susannah* is a transplantation to the Tennessee mountains of the apocryphal Susanna, one of the additions to the book of Daniel (Floyd added the *h* to the usual spelling in English Bibles). Floyd himself wrote the libretto, a rather loose adaptation of the story. While in the original the charge of adultery against Susanna is proved false by Daniel's intervention, in the opera the evangelist, Olin Blitch, actually does commit adultery with Susannah and repents in heartfelt agony. While the justice done to the false accusers in the original is acclaimed by the assembly of Jews, the opera ends on a sardonic note. Susannah's brother, Sam, shoots the evangelist in cold blood, and the townspeople come after Susannah as a lynch mob, ordering her to get out of the valley. She refuses, standing off the mob with a shotgun. Though Floyd's opera revolves around the dramatic problem of lust by old men for a beautiful young woman, the shape of his plot is quite different from that of the apocryphal story. The opera closes with a perception of unending injustice coming out of closed-minded' religiousness and the bitter, hopeless hatred of a woman for her entire community. The adaptation of an old story is very modern indeed. Floyd's music is melodically expressive (Susannah's aria "Ain't it a pretty night?" often finds its way to recital programs of ambitious sopranos) and always texturally apt for the mood of the scene. The work received the Music Critics Circle of New York Award for 1956 as the best opera staged in New York that year.

My theme, that biblical music in the twentieth century is moving out of the church and into the concert hall and opera house, is underscored by the American biblical operas. All but two to which I can find reference date from the 1950s to 1970s, the earlier instances being Chadwick's *Judith* and the still earlier *Le Jugement de Salomon* by the French-Canadian Calixa Lavallée. If, as has sometimes been argued, America is moving into a post-Christian era, one of the results is that the Bible has begun to be accepted into the general culture as a cultural artifact transcending its purely religious setting and interpretation. It is, then, no longer a document to be left entirely to the sphere of "religious" music but can freely be taken up for "secular" music with no thought of impropriety.

An instance is my last example, the "Jeremiah" Symphony, Leonard Bernstein's first symphony, written in 1942, first performed in 1944, and the winner of the Music Critics Circle of New York Award for that year. It is in three movements, titled respectively "Prophecy," "Profanation," and "Lamentation." In the last movement, a mezzo-soprano sings the Hebrew text of Lam 1:1–3, 8; 4:14–15; 5:20–21. Bernstein himself explained the sequence of the movements in a program note in 1944. "Prophecy" suggests the "intensity of the prophet's pleas with his people"; the Scherzo, "Profanation," portrays "pagan corruption within the priesthood and the people"; and "Lamentation," with the text, is Jeremiah's mourning over destroyed Jerusalem (quoted in liner notes to Deutsche Grammophon recording 2530 968), closing with a "kind of comfort, not a solution" (quoted in the same liner notes from remarks at a press conference, Berlin, 1977). The setting of the text is very much in the style of traditional synagogue chant, and, indeed, Bernstein himself referred to its source as a liturgical chant used for Tisha B'Av, the festival of mourning for the destruction of Jerusalem. Jack Gottlieb has argued its derivation from motives in the traditional *kinnot* for that festival and has shown the derivation of themes in the first and last movements from synagogue chants for Rosh Hashanah (292). The use of the chant style gives the lament a certain atmosphere of objectivity, keeps it within a rituallike discipline, with a quiet, slow ending on an ambiguous, unresolved E-minor seventh chord (E-G-B-D).

I am aware of the necessary speed with which the surface of American music has been skimmed in this essay. One could, I suppose, write a book on the subject. Yet I come back to the perception with which I began: the works embodying the Bible are not the greatest works of the tradition they represent. Perhaps the problem has been the ambivalence with which the American musical community has seen the Bible, traditionally ascribed overwhelming potency by the religious traditions on the one hand, subject to restrictive dogmatic interpretation on the other. Any composer wishes to tackle the problem of dealing with potent texts, and yet too powerful a text can overwhelm the music, subordinate it to its own effect. As the power of ecclesiastical restrictiveness recedes as a factor in American culture, perhaps the Bible's intrinsic potency can be even further released for musical settings that do not depend on liturgical contexts or ecclesiastical approval. There is surely a tremendous amount of profoundly meaningful material in the Bible awaiting composers' attention without requiring overt or conventional religiosity in the setting. One can imagine magnificent operas on Abraham, Saul, Isaiah, Jeremiah, St. Paul, and splendid settings of the Song of Deborah (Judges 5), the Song of Songs (which has already had some attention from Lukas Foss and Mario Davidovsky), and other poetic texts.

One may at least hope for the day when a major American composer writes a major work on the Bible. We whose profession is the interpretation of that book must at the very least rejoice if other means of interpreting it, including musical ones, exceed our interpretations in depth and communicative power.

NOTE

/1/   I am indebted to Susan Kwilecki, a graduate student in Religious Studies at Stanford University, for bibliographic and research assistance for this essay, especially for the colonial period.

WORKS CONSULTED

Barbour, J. Murray
    1972   *The Church Music of William Billings*. 1960. Reprint. New York: Da Capo Press.

Britton, Allen
    1961   "Music Education: An American Specialty." In *One Hundred Years of Music in America*. Edited by Paul Henry Lang. New York: G. Schirmer.

Ellinwood, Leonard
    1970   *The History of American Church Music*. Rev. ed. 1953. New York: Da Capo Press.

Elson, Louis C.
    1925   *The History of American Music*. New York: Macmillan.

Finney, Theodore M.
    1966   "The Third Edition of Tufts' *Introduction to the Art of Singing Psalm-Tunes*." *Journal of Research in Music Education* 14: 163–70.

Fisher, William Arms
    1918   *Notes on Music in Old Boston*. Boston: Oliver Ditson.

Gottlieb, Jack
    1980   "Symbols of Faith in the Music of Leonard Bernstein." *Musical Quarterly* 66: 287–95.

Gould, Nathaniel Duren
    1853   *Church Music in America*. Boston: A. N. Johnson.

Hitchcock, H. Wiley
    1974   *Music in the United States: A Historical Introduction*. 2d ed. Englewood Cliffs, NJ: Prentice-Hall.

Howard, John Tasker
    1941   *Our Contemporary Composers: American Music in the Twentieth Century*. With the assistance of Arthur Mendel. New York: Thomas Y. Crowell.

Kallmann, Helmut
    1960   *A History of Music in Canada, 1534–1914*. Toronto: University of Toronto Press.

Kirkpatrick, John, ed.
    1972   *Charles E. Ives: Memos*. New York: W. W. Norton.

Lindstrom, Carl E.
1939   "William Billings and his Times." *Musical Quarterly* 25:
                             479–97.

Lowens, Irving
1964   *Music and Musicians in Early America.* New York:
                             W. W. Norton.

Marocco, W. Thomas, and Gleason, Harold, eds.
1964   *Music in America: An Anthology from the Landing of
                             the Pilgrims to the Close of the Civil War.* New York:
                             W. W. Norton.

McKay, David P., and Crawford, Richard
1975   *William Billings of Boston: Eighteenth-Century
                             Composer.* Princeton: Princeton University Press.

Mellers, Wilfrid
1975   *Music in a New Found Land: Themes and Develop-
                             ments in the History of American Music.* New York:
                             Hillstone.

Sablonsky, Irving
1969   *American Music.* Chicago and London: University of
                             Chicago Press.

Sonneck, Oscar J.
1907   *Early Concert-Life in America (1731–1800).* Leipzig:
                             Breitkopf & Härtel.

Stevenson, Robert
1966   *Protestant Church Music in America: A Short Survey
                             of Men and Movements from 1564 to the Present.* New
                             York: W. W. Norton.

Stoutamire, Albert
1972   *Music of the Old South: Colony to Confederacy.*
                             Rutherford, Madison, Teaneck. Fairleigh Dickinson
                             University Press.

VII

The Bible in American Painting

John W. Dixon, Jr.

The problem of "The Bible in American Art" must be distinguished carefully from the larger problem of "religion in American art." They are not the same thing nor is the smaller question rightly understood as a special case of the larger; they are in some degree different problems, however much the areas overlap.

There is a still more inclusive problem. There is often danger and always presumption in carrying every immediate problem back to first principles; it would be perfectly possible to chronicle the role of the Bible in American art without resorting to any large cultural generalizations. Such a procedure, however, would fall a good deal short of the need for understanding that such a subject requires.

American culture is very nearly unique in the development of human history. Other cultures have developed from one of two kinds of backgrounds. The earliest cultures (Egypt, the Mesopotamian cultures, India, China, the ancient Mexican cultures) developed slowly from the soil of prehistoric cultures. They had, therefore, leisure for the slow, organic development of the various modes of their symbolic speech. Their formal language developed naturally in communion with their natural setting. Their technology was congruent with the land, and the imagination that the technology served could work within the limits—or just enough beyond the limits—determined by technological possibility. When they arrived at the late, reflective, self-consciously intentional stage of their development, they did so with a fully developed, mature symbolic imagination.

There is no recovery of such original culture innocence; all later cultures of necessity grow up in the context of their predecessors, of necessity inheriting the forms of an earlier symbolic speech. What they achieve is, therefore, necessarily shaped by their own symbolic imagination, by their own history, economics and technology, and by the imagination of others who have imprinted their hopes, their fantasies, their sense of the real on the surviving artifacts. Nevertheless, the process is not essentially different. Even in the case of the Byzantine culture, perhaps the most dramatic illustration of the mutation of one culture into another, there was leisure for the slow, organic development of a coherent symbolic speech.

In art, this has meant the natural manifestation of the symbolic imagination in the forms of materials which themselves shaped the symbolic
imagination. One of the most vivid impressions sensitive travelers carry
away from their visit to ancient sites is the coherence of art and the land.
Partly, of course, this is adventitious; every landscape has its climate and the
workings of weather have made human monuments into something closer to
a natural object than might have appeared to be the case when the cathe-
drals were white. Even so, the Parthenon, even if it retained its color and
gilding, belongs on the Acropolis as a completion of a landscape that is a
singular union of stone, sea, and sun. The temples of Khajuraho or Bhuva-
neshvar fused the mythical presence of the Himalayas and the swarming
fecundity of subtropical India into an image that is peculiarly Indian and
not achievable anywhere else.

Obviously, the landscape is not the only formative element in the making of the symbolic imagination. Of equal importance is the city, which of
course itself developed in and out of the landscape. Civilization is, by definition, a product of the city, and it is not easy for the American mind, part of
a culture widely dispersed over the land, to imagine the cultural dominance
of the city in the older cultures. The city is the center, the heart, the source.
The provinces are defined in terms of their relation to the city.

Such cities do not develop by design. They are an intersection of the landscape (literally, since they develop at the intersections of roads and rivers, and
imaginatively) with political and economic necessities. The imagination is,
therefore, shaped by the most elemental forces of human existence.

This is "natural" humanity and the natural unfolding of symbolic
speech. The impact of the Bible and of the biblical imagination on such
cultures is difficult to trace, precisely because it is one force among many
and makes its own way organically. Very occasionally the impact can be
seen dramatically when a people possessing a developed formal symbolic
language is converted to Christianity. Perhaps the most dramatic example of
this is the Celts, who had developed, in the interlace, one of the great symbolic forms. Once Ireland was made Christian this form became the repository of an imagination that had at first been shaped by wholly different
forces. The interlace, which had been the decoration for weapons, orna-
ments, and tools, became both the setting and the interpretation of the Holy
Book, an idea quite outside the Celtic imagination earlier.

Usually the Bible is more nearly a part of the original fabric in its slow
weaving. The Gothic imagination is inseparable from the social and economic
order of feudal France and the distinctive shapes of the Île-de-France. To that
extent it is one of the forms of "natural" humanity. Nevertheless, we can still
wonder if such a "natural" human, working within the images of shape, order,
and energy that were a part of land and society could have developed the
intoxication with light that grew out of New Testament imagery and sent
arches high and thin to turn interiors into images of Christ, the light of the

world. The facades are covered with the grave, majestic, serene figures of the apostles and other biblical characters. It is not difficult to trace this sense of severe majesty to the singular character of the French landscape and the French society. But visibly the figures derive their qualities from the figure of Christ in the center. The "image of Christ" is highly complex and varied; the tone of thirteenth-century France made possible the choice the sculptors made among the many elements of that image. But the act of choice was bounded by the biblical possibilities, and only a short time earlier, Romanesque artists had made a very different kind of choice. Neither form is normatively biblical; both are demonstrably French; neither is comprehensible without the biblical idea at its core.

Late medieval Italy was bound to produce the intense and powerful individualism that is so characteristic of the Italian Renaissance. The landscape encouraged and even compelled the independence of cities. The balanced contention of the papacy and the empire made it possible for small cities, willing to guide their behavior by the skill of their intellect without any regard for honor or morality, to survive and flourish. The decisions to be made within those cities were habitually decisions whose wage was victory or defeat, life or death, a circumstance that compels the development of strong, distinct personalities.

Much of the individualism of Renaissance art is no more than a representation of the individuality that, in truth, existed in Italian cities as nowhere else in the world. And yet the whole tonality of the great treatments of this theme is not traceable to a simple record of existing personality. There is no way at all to *prove* that it developed under biblical influence. Nevertheless, it is demonstrably faithful to the complexity of personality and of purpose that is, indeed, so much a part of the Bible.

These are samples, but they will serve their purpose if they suggest the modes of interaction between the imagination in the Bible and the cultures that have developed with the Bible as one of their formative ingredients. American history and, correspondingly, the American imagination are wholly different.

There is no precedent in history for the distinctive character of the American development. There have of course been many colonial settlements, but normally they remain extensions or provinces of the originating country. Greek settlements in Sicily and Italy were pure Greek and in every way part of Greek culture. "Indian Asia" was and is a cultural province of Hinduism and Buddhism, however much colored by indigenous traditions. Even such major cultures as Rome and Japan, whose histories can be compared, had a very different development. Each had an indigenous culture with roots in the prehistoric period. Each came to be dominated by another culture; yet there was a distinctively Roman and Japanese character to their works of art that was never effaced by the foreign influence.

The American experience was wholly different, and the impact of the

Bible on American art is not understandable except against the background of the singularity of that experience. The first thing to note is the distinctive character of the American landscape and climate. All cultures are intimately bound up with their landscapes, for it is the landscape that first forms the imagination of artists and poets. American painting and poetry are no exception, deriving much of their imaginative energies from nature (Novak). The problem arises in the movement of these shapes back toward the people. Traditionally, American painting has had no prestige outside America and little within America; it is not a part of the imaginative furnishing of the American mind. In a different mode, a number of poets and novelists have established the imaginative reality of certain landscapes (Hawthorne's New England, Faulkner's Mississippi). Others that are both visually and culturally rich (e.g., the Southwest, the Pacific Northwest) have barely been touched. In some ways the Aegean, the Roman Campania, and the English midlands are more actively a part of the American imagination than America's own landscape.

Yet it is one of the world's great landscapes, badly needing to be given its place in the world's imagination by artist and poet. It is one landscape because, for better or worse, America is one country, but it has great variety. It is a fierce landscape, yet the fierceness itself is characterized by variety. Many cultures have grown up in landscapes that have single, powerful personalities. Egypt, the Near Eastern cultures, Greece, and India each developed in a landscape that is often fierce and always intense in the assertion of a single powerful personality. Only Europe and China among the major cultures developed in landscapes and climates sufficiently restrained and benign to permit the development of personality outside the domination of a natural setting. Even so, both the variety and intensity of the Chinese climate may, indeed, be more like America than like Europe, leaving Europe alone as a climate conducive to the extraordinary range of personality that has been so much a part of European history.

The American landscape is in every sense enormous. Even those sections of the country with a climate as nearly benign as Europe's have a size and a proportion that are decidedly greater than Europe's, and always beyond these are the great plains, the deserts, and the vast forests. All are characterized by large changes in temperature, sudden and violent storms or floods, or cold.

Yet only some of this has been transmuted into imaginative realities by art—and only for some people; most Americans have had to confront their great mysterious land directly. The Americans who confronted this land were themselves singular, as varied as the weather and the land itself. Thief and idealist, entrepreneur and preacher, learned and ignorant, they nevertheless, in a very general way, showed certain traits. Whatever their own social position, they came from socially and technologically developed societies into a wilderness that had no foundations for any of the institutions that are required by such a society. Everything had to be, literally and figuratively, built. This required the possession or the rapid development of a high degree of social and technological self-consciousness.

America has been consciously *made*, while the older cultures have *developed* much more organically. Thus, the American imagination valued the ability to solve the problems of moving as rapidly as possible from the primitive state of the colonies to technological sophistication. From the first there was a premium on skill and on practical intelligence; the history of some of the early eastern settlements is often an account of the clash between those who assumed class privilege and those who in fact did the work and had no intention of supporting parasites. There was also the drama, especially in New England, of the clash between ideology and concrete reality in a world in the making.

By and large, the idea of emigration did not attract the culturally advanced people in Europe; there was no particular reason for artists, poets, novelists, philosophers, and scholars to make the move. Fanatics, ne'er-do-wells, idealists, and those who were clever, skilled, ambitious, and adventurous could find a place in the new world. What they did *not* bring with them was any sense of symbolically powerful artistic forms or even the idea that the forming of matter is central to humanity. An example of art in early America is the rude chapel at Jamestown. There is evidence that the builders of this simple hutlike structure chose bent timbers for the doorway so that it might have the *appearance* of a Gothic arch. The paradigmatic value of this does not lie in the fact that the chosen form was Gothic. (The dogma that Gothic was dead by 1500 at the latest is true enough for the creative parts of European culture, but it was still very much alive in the villages from which the colonists came.) Rather the significance lies in the fact that a great form—the Gothic arch—had become a *sign* rather than a true symbolic form. There was no sense of the structure of the form or the function of the structure. Without this reality, a form is no longer a true symbol but a nostalgic sign.

It should not be necessary to point out the paradox to which this argument leads. The symbol has been converted into the sign, and so the sign does not proceed from the deep symbolic need that inspired the original symbol. But there is a deep symbolic need involved, the need to absorb the symbolic speech of the past even if in the process the original symbolic energy is lost. This point needs elaboration, for it is both complex and central to the argument. It is necessary to remember the traditional distinction between symbol and sign: the sign points to something other than itself, whereas the symbol is in some way fused with ("participates in" was Tillich's phrase) the reality it symbolizes. The forming of symbols is the essential act of contending with reality; we never know "reality" directly, but only by means of our symbolic forms. Signs as such have a different function. They may be purely useful ("This is the way to the exit"). They may point to some idea or act that is itself the symbol; doctrines about the Eucharist point to the Eucharist without in any way being a part of the Eucharist. At the same time, signs are sometimes symbols within another order of experience. Doctrines about the Eucharist may be signs in one order of discourse while they may have a powerful symbolic role in the order of propositional rationality. Thus, untangling Reformation debates about the nature of the Eucharist is very difficult, since sometimes the debate is about the Eucharist and sometimes it is about the symbolic acts of the human mind and it is not simple to tell which is which.

Captured in this problem, the American imagination adds the further complication of treating true symbols as signs, and again it is not simple to tell which is which or to untangle one from another. A Gothic arch is a sign of a church. A Gothic arch can also be a sign pointing to the symbolic act which was genuine in the act of Gothic forming. Yet calling this "nostalgia" is too simple. It often is that. But not only does the symbol-as-sign carry with it something of its old symbolic authority, it also is a true symbol in another symbolic system, one that gathers up a variety of other symbols and incorporates them into a new type of symbolic system. This is complicated still further by the possibility of genuine symbolic thinking in the old languages. Richardson's Trinity Church may appear to be another essay in symbols as signs and presumably has been experienced in much the same way St. Patrick's Cathedral has. Yet it is a genuine and creative act of thought in the symbolic forms of Romanesque architecture, even though art historians are convinced that the Romanesque style is irrevocably dead. The problem of American forming is precisely this unmastered complexity of American symbolic speech.

Of all the varied characteristics of American church architecture, this has been the most common from its first manifestation to the present. The forms of churches do not emerge from true symbolic need but are chosen arbitrarily as signs—sometimes nostalgic, as at Jamestown, but more often sociological. Usually the chosen form is quite incompatible with what actually goes on in the church and especially with what the church thinks it stands for. This creates a curious psychological situation which may be indescribable. Forms never entirely lose their symbolic energy, even when they are transposed into signs. Those energies may, indeed, become destructive if they are so divorced from the context that once gave them symbolic wholeness.

In addition, *no* form lacks symbolic meaning, symbolic effect. A form divorced from its true symbolic relevance becomes a symbol of a wholly different form of consciousness. It is a peculiarly American consciousness that can treat the great symbolic modes so instrumentally, to act as though the symbolic process were accessible to the practical intelligence. It is not altogether, but there is profound symbolism in thinking that it is. It accounts, at least in part, for the profound split in the American soul, the psychic discontinuities in American life that provide a most desirable openness of possibility but make it extremely difficult to achieve symbolic, cultural, or psychic unity.

That great achievement of the American imagination, the Constitution, is great because of its profound, fully American, symbolic integrity. The eminently practical intelligence that was essential in the early development of the new world expanded to include the events of the past (particularly of Roman and British history), the thinking about those events (particularly in Greek philosophy, Roman and English law, and the plays of Shakespeare), the modes of political organization, and the actualities of the American situation. The resulting document not only has extraordinary practical usefulness; it also has an equally extraordinary symbolic depth and range that are distinctively American. It is, therefore, a singular fusion of theory and practice, respectful of both while yielding sovereignty to neither. It joins an extraordinary idealism with an acute awareness of human vagary and fault. It fuses sign and symbol into a coherent whole. Similarly, Abraham Lincoln, the most "constitutional" of American leaders, is also the most powerful single symbol in American public life because of his fusion of the energies that give symbolic shape to language and act with the singularities of the American situation. Lincoln is singular and universal in the richness of his American particularity. Thomas Jefferson, on the other hand, for all his equally rich Americanness, was essentially at home in the European Enlightenment and thus not fully able to cope with some central characteristics of American reality. One has only to imagine the two men in Paris or at the Court of St. James.

The American imagination is perfectly capable of functioning with full symbolic integrity in certain very important areas. It has not been able to do so in art. There are three indigenous church forms in American architecture. The mission churches of the Southwest raise the difficult question of the Hispanic element of American life. I have been talking as though the eastern settlements represent America, and this has been intentional. The Spanish settlements were far in advance of the English. They were consciously and deliberately governmental–ecclesiastical projects and from an early time used architects, artists, theologians, and poets for the same propagation of the faith that was a calling of the Catholic powers in Europe. Not many years after the crude settlement at Jamestown, the first library in the Americas was built in Puebla, Mexico, a beautiful, structurally and formally coherent baroque room. But the great Mexican churches, distinctively Mexican, are *baroque* churches and baroque is a European idea.

The mission churches are very nearly the only American forms that show a true influence of the indigenous Indian formal imagination. The idea of the space may be conventionally Spanish baroque, but economic necessity simplified it to a pure geometric form. The technology is Indian and the resulting forms have considerable symbolic integrity. Yet, like most of the potential American symbols, they are too simple and too limited to function fully in the development of an American symbolic imagination.

Books travel more easily than churches, and so the landscapes of

Hawthorne, Melville, and Faulkner are parts of the equipment of the literate imagination. The mission churches deserve to be. Yet there is always something alien about them for most Americans, with their usually tawdry, incompetent altars, poor imitations of their baroque exemplars. Always there is the motif Stephen Vincent Benét identified: "Black-robed priests who broke their hearts in vain / To make you God and France or God and Spain" (Benet: 4). Theocracy has been a regular ingredient of American fantasy, but it has never become permanently rooted in American polity.

On the other hand, the infamous Akron plan, with its square room dominated by large folding doors opening into a Sunday school auditorium, is a purely American invention and a possibility only within the American imagination. It may represent the nadir of Christian church architecture as far as style is concerned, but it has a certain symbolic charm. There is, at least for those who grew up in them, a certain casual amiability, a certain naive confidence in technical solutions, a true lack of pretension that shares to some degree the quality of the third form, the only true invention of the American symbolic imagination in church architecture—New England meetinghouse. Significantly, this is the only genuinely biblical form in American architecture.

Like most true symbols, the meetinghouse is multivalent. It was literally a meetinghouse; as the only auditorium in the village it was the normal place for the town meeting. It was the place people went to "meet" their neighbors, a social idea but one not incompatible with biblical principles. Most particularly, it was where one met God.

This, in itself, is not an American idea or even a new one. It is, in fact, one of the oldest. Ancient temples were not for congregational worship. They were the habitations of the gods, and the people, through their representatives, the priests, went to the temples to meet the gods. In the meetinghouse the whole people believed that they were gathered to meet God who was present among them in the iconic book. More particularly they succeeded in that very difficult task of finding a form that not only made their ritual act possible but also was a formal manifestation of what they stood for. Thus, the form became a true symbol. It is a great achievement, a rare achievement that has never happened in painting.

The Forms of Paint

For better or worse, every culture not located in an absolutely benign climate must develop an architectural language of some kind. This is not true of painting and sculpture. In the slow arduous journey from the primitive beginnings, the old organic cultures required the aid of images for their symbolic organization. America was an intentional culture. The organizing images in the development of the American mentality were legal, theological, and technical, but not formal.

There was, nevertheless, a hunger for forms as there is in all people, but it was a hunger to be fed in odd and sometimes peripheral ways. Itinerant portrait painters could make something of a living, but their products hardly rank among the world's significant images. In the decorative arts, women developed designs of more than passing interest. As the culture progressed in wealth and sophistication it was more and more possible to adapt European visual language to American purposes. But none of this went to the heart of the American symbolic imagination.

Emphasis on the inevitable domination of technology required by the transplanting of a developed society into an unorganized land should not suggest that symbols played any smaller part in America than they do in every human society. The technical requirements themselves became a symbolic order of the highest importance. The intentionality of the society itself compelled another kind of symbolic act. Institutions, social and legal processes, had to be *constructed*. They had to be thought about and they were deliberately and carefully thought out. The reflective intelligence developed in the closest possible relation to immediate conditions, rather than in the construction of pure theory.

Beyond these the images that dominated the American imagination were biblical—the pilgrim people, the chosen people set apart, the city set on a hill, etc. Yet whatever the authority of such biblical images and the iconic book itself, no one developed any visual equivalent or succeeded in translating them into anything like an adequate visual statement. It is entirely possible—though impossible to demonstrate—that one of the reasons such images were drained of their authority or translated into purely secular forms is the failure to state them in compelling visual forms.

The impact of the Bible on a visually inchoate culture tended to equal inchoateness. Where there is a coherent symbolic order, including those shaped by biblical symbols, the visual structures become instruments of interpretation and of proclamation. A particular manifestation of biblical symbolic order is implanted in the visual imagination of the people and is made a living part of their process. In American painting, religious subjects in general and biblical subjects in particular tend therefore to be idiosyncratic images of no great significance as interpretations of the subject or as works of art./1/

At one level there are the works variously termed "folk" art or "naive" art, paintings done by self-taught or amateur artists (Dillenberger and Dillenberger: 19). These have a great deal of charm for sophisticated tastes and they are an interesting social record, but their significance is not great. The most famous of these painters is Edward Hicks, who did an estimated eighty versions of the Peaceable Kingdom, illustrating an image from Isaiah. He is much like greater American artists in his obsessive concern with one subject, but the importance of his work is slight. It is tempting to suspect that he would not have gotten the attention he has were it not for a faint resemblance to a greater man—Le Douanier Rousseau.

Those among the naive artists who were less naive than the others or who, for one reason or another, had access to images from parent European cultures, produced some rather strange, interesting provincial adaptations of European styles. Some of these have considerable interest, even a certain visual authority, but are incomparably less significant than their models.

An altogether different problem appears with the painting of the major professional painters of the early republic. To what extent these painters— John Singleton Copley, Benjamin West, Washington Allston, and others—were American and to what extent they were, in style, European is a debatable question that might best be left to the specialists. The nonspecialist eye—or this one at any rate—can see them only as essentially formed by European styles yet with an accent that is tangy with Americanism. Be that as it may, what comes through to me from their paintings with biblical themes is the singularity of the personality. It is not a personality or a style formed on the Bible or a style that has anything penetrating to say about the Bible; the style is the American version of the Enlightenment. The subject is some particularly dramatic moment in a biblical narrative, one that lends itself to a certain nobility of presentation. Yet the resulting images have the character of calculation. It is calculation that is both serious and sincere; calculation does not necessarily imply insincerity and these were serious artists—serious about their subject and about their art. Even so, the subject is at a distance, and the presentation is cinematic. Compositions are not a little like Cecil B. De Mille, and actors are reminiscent of Charlton Heston.

It is probably worth saying that the problem is not simply in American art. A greater contemporary, Ingres, was no more successful with his biblical paintings, which have exactly the same characteristics. The problem is one of the mentality of the late eighteenth and the nineteenth century, which is rather more than this essay can handle beyond a few general comments.

In my judgment, John Singleton Copley is the finest of these early American painters. His *Ascension* (plate 1) is a serious, skillful, and impressive painting. Yet, to the twentieth-century eye, the figures appear posed as though in a tableau. They assume the posture or make the gesture that the intelligence of the artist has determined should represent the inner spiritual state. There is not the sense of a continuous flow from the inner life of the represented person to the external expression or manifestation of that inner life. To the modern eye (or to *some* modern eyes—too often art historians are tempted to preface their own opinions with an inclusive "we") the result is curiously lifeless and formal./2/

This is dangerous. Our own taste is formed by a romantic expressionist epoch, and we have no right to impose it judgmentally on the artistic language of other people. The grand gesture, the emotional cipher of pose, was the vocabulary of the eighteenth-century visual language, and such paintings would have "said" something to those people that they no longer "say" to many of us. Nonetheless, I still have some suspicion of the validity of my prejudices; the kind of strong, ordered intelligence that is manifest in such works is not itself biblical.

Copley's *Ascension* is representative of an important type of interaction between art and the Bible. A number of artists through the nineteenth and even into the twentieth century have seen the Bible as a treasury of dramatic events. They vary, obviously, in the degree of their commitment to the overt content of the stories. Perhaps the greatest painting of a biblical subject done in America in the nineteenth century, Thomas Eakins's *Crucifixion*, was done by a professed agnostic. This painting (plate 2—a color plate of a preliminary study is in Jane Dillenberger and Taylor, Pl. 100) may be a subtype significantly different from those represented by the Copley painting. Many of the others, whatever their seriousness, are weakened by their striving after a "spiritual" expression that the style is not equipped to carry. It may be that Eakins is a paradigm of an approach that, precisely by the dimensions of its distance from biblical intention, is more faithful to biblical principles.

There is no real way of tracing Eakins's motives or of determining his intentions by any investigation outside of the work itself. It was not a commission (many an agnostic has painted a religious subject because it was a job). It was apparently something Eakins wanted to do for his own purposes. Eakins is distinguished as one of the great realists of the American tradition. "Realism" is a dangerous term. It does not mean that reproductive representation of details so beloved and admired by popular taste. In Eakins's case, it means an absolute fidelity to the appearance of surfaces. Too great detail would dissolve the integrity of the surface. Too sketchy an impressionism moves the experience of actuality from the object to the perceiving mind. Rather, in Eakins's paintings, it means the varied but integrated singularity of particular forms disposed in a light that is itself the principal means of their revelation.

Only those who have not meditated deeply on Velázquez and Eakins can ever think that surfaces are superficial. Colored surfaces are the means of interchange in the world; it is only by extrapolating from colored surfaces that we construct the space and the mass that are the world we inhabit. Where most painters seek to set out some idea of that space and mass or what that space and mass symbolize, Eakins and Velázquez give the lighted surfaces as fully and as directly as they can. We then are compelled to use those surfaces, as we are too often too lazy to do in our ordinary life, to reconstruct the mental or spiritual world that lies behind them and gives them their quality. For this reason, Eakins is not simply the greatest American portrait artist but one of the greatest portrait artists. At the same time he is intensely American with a Lincolnian Americanness. It is the remorseless actuality of physical things radiant with their own purposefulness that dominates Eakins's art.

His *Crucifixion* is void of any adventitious sentiment. No "spiritual" significance is superimposed on it. No lesson is taught by it. There is no appeal to a sense of drama, no concession to a prurient desire for suffering. The event is set out in its remorseless integrity with no comment by the artist or any visual manipulation toward how it should be seen. It is the event made present. No other representation of the crucifixion in Christian art, except Velázquez's, is so devoid of any theological interpretation. In part for this reason, it is all the more appalling. Theological interpretation provides a distancing; we see the event through the doctrine. There is no doctrine to intrude between the spectator and Eakins's Christ. The painting becomes, then, beyond the intention of the artist, a judgment. The inescapable question is "What think ye of the Christ?"

The paradoxical conclusion is that the painting that might defensibly be called the greatest work of religious art—of Christian, biblical art—ever done in America was done by an agnostic. The paradox is itself biblical, since it is not those who say "Lord, Lord" who merit the kingdom but those who do the will of God even when they do not intend anything by the act beyond its charitable intention. Lincoln himself could, in his integrity, have nothing to do with that strange institution, the nineteenth-century church. Yet no figure in American history has been so iconic to the grace of God, so much a manifestation of power, love, and forgiveness. So Eakins, too, made the Christ present, because he could confront us with the act in all its immediacy, without interpretation.

Light and the Land

There is another major nineteenth-century development that requires careful observation and interpretation, because it is both important and easily misunderstood. I have pointed out how important light was to Eakins; it revealed the life within the integrity of forms. Eakins was principally a painter of indoor scenes, and his landscapes, for all their change in light, have a true intimacy. Their interest is deeply human, the figure *in* the landscape.

This sense of forms in light is met again in the landscape painting of the nineteenth century. This development owes nothing whatsoever to the biblical sensibility, so far as I can tell; it is even nonbiblical or antibiblical in the interpretation of nature that it sets out. Yet it is a centrally important part of the American visual imagination and is therefore an inescapable part of the definition of the American religious imagination.

The American landscape is vast. European disdain for the American obsessions with size is quite beside the point; the land is large and can be dealt with only in large ideas. The land is empty. It is surprisingly empty now, even though the population is more than 220 million; to cross the continent in an airplane is to spend very long periods of time over emptiness. For earlier people, its emptiness was absolute. The native Americans were simply fauna, elements of the land rather than interruptions of it. Both in size and in scale the American land has majesty, an awe-inspiring majesty. It is a dangerous majesty, for it can be as destructive as it is benign. It is fruitful, but it is in part sterile with a deadly sterility. It has, in short, all the attributes that Rudolph Otto has ascribed to the "numinous," that aspect of sacrality or holiness that lies beyond either morality or specificity of creed.

For the biblical sensibility, nature is God's creation and servant. Nature is in no sense sacred in itself nor can God be found in nature, except as he chooses to manifest himself here or there. On the other hand, the great sacral landscapes not only partake of the character of the numinous but also are inhabited by the gods. Even sensibilities alien to the cult can respond to the sacrality of Delphi and can grasp by means of the landscape how such a cult could have arisen at this place. The landscape is impregnated by the myth and generates the myth. The imagination is guided by the ritual that fulfills the myth in the setting of the land. The myth and the ritual establish the gods in the land and control the experience to wholeness.

Nothing of this serves the experience of the American landscape. The religious groups that came into the land had as little sense of sacral landscape as it is possible to have, and the indigenous cults were so alien that they had no role whatsoever to play in the religious sensibility of the settlers. The cultic images defined the nature of the community (the New Jerusalem, etc.), and they often had implications for the use of the land but were of no use in the symbolic intercourse with the land. For that the painters were on their own. They were very nearly on their own in the development of a formal language for landscape. To one degree or another they were aware of the European landscape tradition and tried to use it; the influence of Claude or Poussin or Joshua Reynolds or Gainsborough is clearly seen in the development of the American landscape painting. But these styles were part of a different landscape, a different light, and they were incapable of coping with the distinctively American experience. Consequently, much American landscape painting is pinched, confused, and inadequate.

Slowly there developed a landscape art that was a genuine response to the character of the land itself. The development was often confused and hesitant, confusing size with scale, juxtaposing niggling detail with enormous proportions. But in these difficulties it was no different from the development of any true style, and it did become a true style. Particularly in the early stages of the development, paintings were sometimes associated with a biblical subject. (There are several good examples in Jane Dillenberger and Taylor; see Pl. 18 by Joshua Shaw and Pls. 47–49 by Thomas Cole.) But the biblical subject is quite incidental to the general development and is not present at all in most of them.

What resulted was a genuinely religious art that is genuinely nonbiblical. It is not even a religion of nature, for there is no sense of the divine energies in nature or of spirits that sanctify it. Rather there is a pure sense of sacrality, of sublimity with all the sense of power and mystery that implies (plate 3). This was, as nearly as has ever been achieved, a religion without specificity, a religion identified with the emotions of religion, a religion of pure, unqualified experience.

That is too much. The experience could not be wholly unqualified in the nineteenth century, for it was inalienably linked to the landscape. The problem becomes acute for the understanding of religion only in the twentieth century. Even so, it is not simply the landscape, but the *experience* of the landscape, that is religiously important. The paintings are beautiful objects capable of giving both pleasure and instruction without necessarily implying so large an interpretation as I am giving them. But they are also moments in the formation of a distinctive religious sensibility. This development took two forms, both of major interest in understanding the workings of the American religious imagination, both bearing much the same relation to biblical principles. The more prominent of these includes the landscape paintings that are informed by the desire for sublimity. Sublimity is unquestionably one of the authentic schemata of the numinous, in Rudolph Otto's classic analysis. It is not, however, a particularly biblical principle, and much of the tension in the American religious imagination grows from the disparity between its overt allegiance to a text and its overwhelming emotional allegiance to ideas that effectively go counter to that text. The character of the land enforced a sense of the sublime, and the painters did their very considerable best to translate that sense into the actuality of the painting. As a result, the classic enterprise of Christian art, to bring the biblical principles to presence in the work of art and to interpret the text within the principles of a particular formal language, was reversed; now the Bible was itself interpreted by principles effectively foreign to its own.

In a recent work that is already becoming a classic, Barbara Novak has summed up this movement:

> More orthodox religions, which had always insisted on a separation of God and nature, also capitulated to their union. A "Christianized naturalism" to use Perry Miller's phrase, transcended theological boundaries, so that one could find "sermons in stones and good in every thing". "Nature," wrote Miller, "somehow, by a legerdemain that even so highly literate Christians as the editors of The New York Review could not quite admit to themselves, had effectually taken the place of the Bible. . . ."
>
> . . . Most religious orthodoxies in America obligingly expanded to accommodate a kind of Christianized pantheism. Ideas of God's nature and of God *in* nature became hopelessly entangled, and only the most scrupulous theologians even tried to separate them. If nature was God's Holy Book, it *was* God. (Novak: 3)

This is equally true of that other movement, so productive of some of the loveliest of American paintings, known to modern times as "luminism." Here, too, the sublime is set out in painting but not so much in the mode of grandeur, of size, or of majesty as in the mode of an absolute stillness and quiet, a mood in which the human soul and nature are one. As Novak expresses it:

In the luminist painting, the eradication of stroke nullifies process and assists a confrontation with detail. It also transforms atmospheric "effect" from active painterly bravura into a pure and constant light in which reside the most interesting paradoxes of nineteenth-century American painting. They are paradoxes which, with extra-ordinary subtlety, engage in a dialectic that guides the onlooker toward a lucid transcendentalism. The clarity of this luminist atmosphere is applicable both to air and crystal, to hard and soft, to mirror and void. These reversible dematerializations serve to abolish two egos— first that of the artist, then the spectator's. Absorbed in contemplation of a world without movement, the spectator is brought into a wordless dialogue with nature, which quickly becomes the monologue of transcendental unity. (Novak: 28–29).

Since the emphasis is on experience without mythic, symbolic, or cultic shaping, the principal actor is the individual who has the experience. The American imagination is characteristically the isolated individual contending unaided with the immediacies of experience. This is not biblical, but when the individual imagination is richly informed by a biblical sensibility the results can be notable. Here the test case is one of America's great painters, probably the greatest explicitly religious painter this country has produced— Albert Pinkham Ryder. The problem of understanding Ryder is the problem of this whole essay, for his was the kind of art that could belong nowhere but in this country and his relation to religion is archetypically American.

It may not be quite true—but it is very nearly so—to say that there is no such thing as a truly self-taught artist and that Ryder is no exception. While his training was somewhat eccentric, it was genuine professional training. Even so, to a degree unparalleled in art, almost nothing about his style can be explained by reference to his training or to the tradition. He is certainly not a part of the history of the craft; many of his paintings are near wrecks because he offended so against the principles of the craft, preferring to see the works less as constructions than as embodiments of his vision.

No true artist is indifferent to his materials, and Ryder was a true artist. He lived his life in the slow piling up of the material, seeking the materialization of his vision. But always the vision was primary. His relation to the biblical vision is not exhausted in the subjects, which are not all that frequent in his work. He was as much drawn to mythological as to biblical subjects and meditated on them in the same way. His landscapes and seascapes are very much parts of the same vision. In no sense related to the tradition of visual exegesis of biblical stories is Ryder's art an interpretation of the Bible. It is, rather, a grasping of an essential biblical principle that is not often recognized in Christian devotion. The vagaries of human psychology are such that devotion to anything produces a kind of deadening through familiarity. Devotion to the Bible tends to dilute the raw, elemental power of the Bible. Ryder's biblical devotion was of a kind that shaped his personality as a man and as an artist.

The word "archetypal" comes easily to every pen writing about Ryder. It is a word that has vague and diffuse edges, for even its technical Jungian definition is not very precise. It is entirely appropriate to Ryder in whatever sense the word has. Ryder is not to be considered altogether apart from the landscape artists I have just discussed, for the earth and the sea in his painting are tense with a sense of the numinous. Yet his sense of the numinous is wholly unlike that of the other artists. Theirs both captures and, to a degree, enhances an element in the appearance of things. The light they paint is the light of the American land, and it has precisely that kind of undefined, unspecified religious feeling. While acknowledging the representational accuracy of the work, the religiously sensitive spectator will probably recognize that the significance of the work lies in those feelings which are referred to by that popular word "spiritual." Ryder was as much a true landscape painter as they, although formally speaking he was as uninterested in detail as they were often obsessed with it. His is a different earth, the elemental power of the Atlantic and Hawthorne's doom-haunted land of New England. It is also the earth of the soul, a terrible elemental power of an earth that is immediately under the hand of God.

In the Bible, nature is not the container of spiritual feelings and affections that belong to it by its nature. Nature is testimony to the creativity and the majesty of God. All of Ryder's paintings, when he was in the fullness of his powers, are paintings of that kind of earth.

Sentimental familiarity with the Bible obscures the awfulness of the book. All great mythological books are great because they tell some truths about the human condition without flinching. None is more comprehensive than the Bible or has so great a range. The gentle moments of the Bible are easy to deal with, although the very ease encourages sentimentality rather than an awareness of the strength of biblical gentleness. The terror and the awfulness of the Bible are usually avoided. It is the awfulness of it that Ryder faces in many of his paintings.

The role of subject and intention can be debated in the understanding of the interpretation of art; subjects are an essential clue to the understanding of Ryder's intention. Without the biblical subjects, many of his works, particularly the great sea pieces, would appear to be versions of the nature mysticism that is so much a part of American religious sensibility. The biblical subjects make his intention perfectly clear. Chief among these is his *Jonah* (plate 4).

The *Jonah* is one of the greatest sea paintings. Rarely has any painter so intensely grasped the elemental power of the sea, its surging movement, the sense of its unpaintable depth. This effect is all the more remarkable given Ryder's working method. The characteristic movement of human or natural forms ordinarily can be captured only by rapid, instinctive drawing. If the artist lingers over the image, reworking it, it goes dead and inert. Ryder worked over his paintings, sometimes for years. The result is the greatest possible intensification of the characteristic surging movement, the elemental authority of the sea. In the center of the painting, the boat is impossibly twisted along the lines of force of the rising wave. Nothing so intensifies the sense of the living force of the sea as this distortion of the boat, which serves the further dramatic purpose of unmistakably evoking the shape and therefore the sense of the whale. Below the boat-whale, Jonah is nearly immersed in the water, mouth open and despairing arms reaching upward. In the center of the top of the picture, God appears with arms uplifted, almost mirroring Jonah's gestures, except that one hand (the left!) is vaguely blessing while the other holds the orb of earthly dominion. The Lord God controls the power of the earth and human tragedy. The will of the sea and the will of the human being are subject wholly to the will of God.

It is risky trying to use Ryder's color to interpret his paintings, for the faultiness of his technique has very commonly led to significant changes in his colors. In this case the color appears to be faithful to the theme. The darks dominate as they should for a storm in the depth of the sea. But the surfaces holding the boat and Jonah glow with a golden light emanating directly from God above. Despite the drama of the subject and the presentation, this is not essentially a narrative painting. It is a meditative, devotional work, a profound reflection on the grace of God, which is powerful enough to fill, to dominate, to control the power of the earth. This is wholly a biblical view of nature.

The Biblical Spirit in the Twentieth Century

It remains now to determine—no, simply to examine—whether there is anything distinctively different about the role of the Bible in twentieth-century American painting. The problem is not so simple as it might appear. The critic who thinks the role of religion in general and of the Bible in particular has been small would be correct. But small and unimportant are not synonymous terms. The range of the problem can be seen simply by turning the pages of the Dillenbergers' excellent catalogue, *Perceptions of the Spirit in Twentieth-Century American Art*. A book-length study would be necessary to sort out the various possibilities of interpretation, and even then the conclusions would be uncertain. For the most part they might well be left to the Dillenbergers' judicious comments, which raise good questions without presuming to answer any of them. There are artists who are physically a part of the twentieth century who in innocence and naiveté represent biblical subjects. Accepting the danger of elitist judgments I would suggest that they are not truly part of twentieth-century art in the sense of any constructive definition of a twentieth-century sensibility. These are artists of the second or third rank who use the idiom of twentieth-century art, which was generated for other purposes, for the approximation of biblical subjects.

It is equally true that biblical stories retain a great deal of this mythic power for many very serious modern artists. What this means varies widely according to the specific artist. The most consistent theme in the religious art of the twentieth century is the one we have already met in this sketch and which gave the title to the Dillenbergers' book, the search for the "spiritual." This is often religiously eclectic, often directed toward Oriental mysticisms, often toward a generalized identification with the eternal oneness of the cosmos or the force that suffuses all things. Biblical subjects might be a part of one of these as manifestations of a general religious feeling. Sometimes, particularly among Jewish artists, biblical subjects are part of racial memory and, therefore, ethnic identification (which to no degree suggests that the paintings are less significant as interpretations of the subjects, which are, in fact, Jewish). All these paintings are openings into worlds of private experience; they are not the worlds of a corporate understanding of a common mythological system. This is obviously not the fault of the artist; the Bible is simply no longer the force that shapes the culture. Nor does it detract from the obstructive merits of the situation. Abraham Rattner's *Song of Esther* may not appreciably contribute to my understanding of the story of Esther, but it considerably adds to my grasp of a serious and intelligent man's interaction with his own heritage by means of his art. That is more than just a worthy thing to do; it is a deeply and richly humane thing to do.

This complicates the task of a brief essay, for it really requires an account of the work of each artist separately. Even so, the subject is not quite germane to this essay. There is no artist of consequence in the twentieth century for whom the Bible is decisive. The problem is not so much the impact of the Bible on art as it is on the use made of the Bible in the creation of a number of different individual devotional worlds. In the complexity of the task that is caused by the variety of the subject and the brevity of the essay there is one problem that may be exemplary—the problem of Barnett Newman and Mark Rothko. The more general problem, which is the setting for the specific problem, is that of the religious significance of nonrepresentational art. Our critical equipment is not yet able to cope satisfactorily with the interpretation of art that is not tied to a subject. Style as such we can handle; we are far enough past the academic concern for subject matter to have any problems with that. It is interpretation that gives the difficulty.

This problem is analogous to the problem of religion. What is "religion"? Is there such a thing as "religion" apart from the religions? Or is "religion" a reified construct of the human mind? This problem bears directly on the interpretation of nonrepresentational art. What is being expressed by means of a nonrepresentational painting? Put differently and somewhat more objectively, what is being manifested in it or stated by means of it?

This is adequately handled for some by relying on certain essentially gnostic or Neo-Platonic tendencies in the modern mind: the art work puts the spectator into a direct relation with some form of ultimate reality, the mystic oneness of things, the Ground of Being, the All or the like. Since all these principles are themselves unspecified and quite beyond either specification or proof it does not much matter that what happens in the formal energies of the picture is not very closely specified either.

This is all, however, quite unbiblical, since biblical religion knows nothing of this sort of gnosticism. What kind of art is truly biblical? Is there a nonrepresentational art that is biblical? How do we know? Much that is involved in these questions cannot be answered now, certainly not in the present essay. The best that can be done here is to look briefly at the Newman–Rothko problem as one test case.

Extravagant value judgments are not of much use except as they dramatize a situation. This would be the purpose of asserting that the two greatest religious paintings of the twentieth century are Rothko's Chapel in Houston and Newman's *Stations of the Cross* (plates 5 and 6).

I can discuss the Rothko Chapel in this essay only for the purposes of contrast, since it clearly has nothing to do with biblical influences. It is truly religious, and its religion is singularly difficult to specify. Rothko, however, is of considerable help in this situation, when the terminology of modern art criticism is not. I have, earlier, used the term "nonrepresentational" rather than the more popular term "abstract." This is required by a simple and much ignored fact about art: *all* art is abstract. Yet "nonrepresentational" is almost equally inadequate, for all art represents *something*. The only question is, what does it represent?

Rothko is quite explicit on this point. "I'm interested only in expressing basic human emotions—tragedy, ecstasy, doom, and so on—and the fact that lots of people break down and cry when confronted with my pictures shows that I *communicate* these basic human emotions. . . . The people who weep before my pictures are having the same religious experience I had when I painted them, and if you, as you say, are moved only by their color relationships, then you miss the point" (Carmean and Rathbone: 250). Rothko does not help much with the problem of *how* his paintings are to communicate such ideas, but he has at least and quite unequivocally identified the subject. The communication can only presuppose a direct connection between a certain ordering of colored shapes and corresponding states of the soul so that the one arouses the other. This does not altogether account for the paintings. The ordering of color is such that ecstasy is an appropriate response. Their shaping is imprecise enough to obliterate all sense of the color being attached to objects, even as color "veils." Rather, they are as close as any one has come to presenting color as such. The ordering of colors cannot rightly be called color "harmonies," which would distract attention from the colors themselves to the order of relations between them, and order itself is an object. The arrangement of colors is sufficiently idiosyncratic to create a single unearthly, unobjective note that directs the spirit outside itself.

But there is no escape from the paintings. Rothko himself said of them, with reference to the entrance hall of Michelangelo's Laurentian Library, "He achieved just the kind of feeling I'm after—he makes the viewers feel that they are trapped in a room where all the doors and windows are bricked up so that all they can do is butt their heads forever against the wall" (Carmean and Rathbone: 254). It is significant that Rothko (along with most Michelangelo critics) significantly misreads the entrance hall. The viewers are *not*, in fact, trapped; they ascend the steps into the liberation of the library. But there is no place to go from Rothko's paintings. Is that the tragedy? More should be said about Rothko but it leads away from the subject.

Ostensibly Newman's paintings lead in the same direction. In the apparent simplicity of means, in the complete absence of anything that would traditionally be called a subject, they are rightly associated with Rothko. Nevertheless, just as Rothko pointed the direction in which he wanted the interpretation of his work to go, Newman was even more explicit in public statement and in the titles of his pictures, a large number of which are specifically biblical, *The Word, Adam, Day before One, Abraham*, and above all *The Stations of the Cross*. The subtitle of the series of the last work is "Lema Sabachthani." Newman himself explains:

> Lema Sabachthani—why? Why did you forsake me? Why forsake me? To what purpose? Why?
> This is the Passion. This outcry of Jesus.
> Not the terrible walk up the Via Dolorosa, but the question that has no answer.
> This overwhelming question that does not complain, makes today's talk of alienation, as if alienation were a modern invention, an embarrassment.
> This question that has no answer has been with us so long—since Jesus—since Abraham—since Adam—the original question. Lema? To what purpose—is the unanswerable question of human suffering. Can the Passion be expressed by a series of anecdotes, by fourteen sentimental illustrations? Do not the Stations tell of one event? (Carmean and Rathbone: 202)

Newman was a faithful Jew, deeply knowledgeable of his Jewish heritage, deeply proud of it. In no way was he being disrespectful of his Jewishness nor playing games with a Christian idea when he gave his paintings a Christian title. Jesus was a Jew. It was his passion that, symbolically, most richly reveals the nature and the future of suffering. The paintings do not illustrate the passion; they acquired the name only after several of the paintings had been done, and there is no way to associate any of the paintings with events that are numbered as the "stations of the cross." A sensitive, richly endowed, deeply religious mind could in utmost seriousness relate these paintings to the passion.

An apparently simple formal idea characterizes the paintings; one or more vertical stripes cross a contrasting field. The stripes vary in width.

Some have precise edges, some edges are feathered out. The distance between stripes varies considerably. At times there is ambiguity about whether the painting is dark on light or light on dark. The paintings are not unusually large, and so they do not dominate. They are to be seen as a group, and there is a constant interchange among them. Since the surfaces are delicately handled, it is quite impossible to reproduce them. They are richly harmonic. The appearance of simplicity is quite false. Each painting is complex, and the modulation of the theme multiplies the theme by geometric proportion. The constant reenactment of each painting under the influence of the experience of the others opens the series to infinity.

In no sense do the paintings stop anything; there is no wall to butt heads against. The infinitely delicate modulations carry the eye—and the mind—back and forth, horizontally and vertically. The play of stripes opens the canvas, now as a narrow opening into the infinity beyond, now as an opening through which the beyond spills forward into our own space. The mood is somber, nonsensual, alert. They are, in their own remarkable way, a concentration of all that had been learned in American painting about light. Newman had been known as a powerful colorist (a fourteen-foot wall of color is a powerful experience). In the *Stations* he turned to white, which is the presence of all colors, and black, which is the negation of color. It is the interaction of the two that evokes the sense of light. The surfaces are extraordinarily and delicately luminous. For this reason, every photograph or reproduction is the dimmest possible reflection of the orginal, and the greatest work of religious art of the century seems doomed to remain inaccessible in storerooms.

Rothko's paintings are equally evocative of light, equally dependent on light; the paintings of the Chapel are equally difficult to reproduce, although they do for the dark what Newman did for light. At the same time Rothko presents a colored light that is closer in its effect on the spectator to the luminist painting of the nineteenth century. The paintings are intensely "religious" but religious with the sense of undefined spirituality. This is not the case with Newman.

This cannot be explained by the simple fact that Newman's paintings have a religious title and Rothko's do not. It is an intriguing question whether we could properly decipher Newman's paintings if we did not have the titles. But it is a moot question, for we do have the titles. It is more to the point that there is a decisive act in Newman's paintings and there is not in Rothko's. There are forms of art that are wholly irrelevant to their relation to the spectator. There are those to whom the relation to the spectator is all-important. Rothko's paintings belong to the latter category whereas Newman's are quite different.

Rothko's paintings are absolutely single in their effect, and their effect on the sensibility is a fundamental ingredient of their being. There is no act within the painting since there is only singleness; therefore no act, even a psychic act, is required of the spectator. Since there is an overwhelming effect, the response to the painting is all. The response is an undefined spirituality that is both ecstatic and increasingly somber, tragic with no specification of the tragedy, anguished with no shape or direction to control the anguish.

For all their simplicity, Newman's paintings are built on an act. This is a profoundly biblical principle; in the beginning God *acted*. Among the first of his acts was the division of light from darkness, and both light and dark are good. Newman's paintings are an essay on light and dark. They are not Manichean; light and dark are both good. Light and dark are not opposed to but generate each other. Neither is understandable without the other; it is their *relation* that creates the world and so serves as the primordial image. A single painting could not have done what the series does, for now light dominates, now dark and the changing relation keeps alive the generative interchange between them.

In the realization of this engendering interchange, we ourselves become a part of the act. Where Rothko's paintings are simply (in the sense of purely) a response of a single spiritualized sensibility, Newman's impose an equal obligation on the sensitive intelligence. Rothko's paintings are clearly the products of profound thought, but they do not have to be thought about to be experienced. Newman's require the spectator to think about them. In thought we are more than simple experiences, however spiritual. We have to mobilize our deepest individuality, an individuality that is profoundly biblical. The intelligence is too bound to a richly emotional experience to be pure enlightenment rationality. The experience is too bound to intelligent thought to be gnostic. The paintings, in short, compel a distinctively biblical personality as a condition of their response.

Thus the engendering relation is not simply between the light and the dark in the paintings or the flow of relation from one painting to another. It is also between the spectator and the whole set of the paintings. The paintings are not complete without the spectator, but, equally, they have their own intricate life among themselves without the spectator. They are, therefore, an image of both individuality and community, the community which requires and sustains the individual and the individual who has no purpose apart from the community. This is a critical explanation and justification—in short, an argument. But the paintings are not an argument; they are an experience. The extraordinary luminosity of the surface transposs (that musical term) the argument into a religious experience without dissolving the shape of the argument.

Since the paintings do not dominate the field of vision (as many of Newman's paintings do), they leave us in our own world. Yet they are large enough and strong enough to compel an experience at their own design. They compel meditation, but they also require response. They stand on the boundary of finite and infinite. There is no blurring of the boundary as in modern gnosticism. It is, rather, the meeting of them that concerns the artist—and the man, Jesus; the man, Newman; the man, me—caught at that juncture with the terrible question.

They are profoundly biblical paintings, perhaps the profoundist ever achieved in this country. The Christian may want more; the National Gallery exhibit included, behind a corner, a fifteenth related painting with one red stripe. I am told Newman was not pleased when someone dubbed it "Resurrection." He was too much the Jew for that and his Jewishness should be respected. That is no problem; Christianity ought to be Jewish in its depths and no one should ever think the terrible question will be answered in this life. These paintings have the terror. They also have hope.

Newman's work preserves and continues the American tradition; it does not end or fulfill it. It has the deeply meditated, carefully intended, constructed quality that characterizes the American imagination at its best. Equally it requires a deeply emotional, intuitive participation of both the artist and the spectator, the act and the experience of the individual alone. In its form this does not signify a way out. It is doubtful if Newman himself could have "advanced" beyond the *Stations of the Cross*. The work is what it is. His method, if indeed it can be called that, is quite another matter. There is no deliberation involved in the application of the Bible to the act of painting. Rather the sensibility, the consciousness of the artist, is deeply informed by, given form by, the Bible and the ritual tradition in which it is embedded. The artist then works in terms of his formal sensibility, applying himself to the immediacies of his task.

In this he is more like Ryder than like Copley or Eakins. Between himself and the biblical subject, Copley intruded the screen of a formal language that had no true relation to the subject, thus leaving the spectator essentially isolated from the subject. The transparent honesty of Eakins's style brings the spectator directly up against the subject with no formal or intellectual guidance about what to do with it. Ryder and Newman approached their subjects with sensibilities already shaped by the whole context of the subjects and, therefore, produced richer works.

It is this that is paradigmatic for the work of religious artists. It is also paradigmatic for the work of theologians. With a suddenness startling to those who had been raised on Karl Barth, the "younger theologians" (now no longer young) very nearly departed from the Bible altogether. This can probably be explained in much the same way as the different approaches of the artists and recalls Copley in particular. They had adopted an intellectual style alien to biblical consciousness and then tried to apply it to the Bible. When the results were unfruitful they found fault with the Bible and not with the artificiality of the methods. Their work, as a consequence, lacks the density and weight of Ryder, the delicate and rhythmic sensitivity of Newman.

Theology and art are not so far apart since art is one of the modes of theology. A manner of approach to various problems of experience can be comparable in quite different modes of investigation. There can also be something distinctively rational in an approach; there is an identifiable and worthy American style of thought and work to be found in American painting.

NOTES

/1/   The two Dillenberger volumes provide many illustrations against which these observations can be tested. They are catalogues for two exhibitions that represent landmarks in the understanding of American art. I should be pleased if this essay were understood as a guide through the illustrations in those volumes.

/2/   A colleague who kindly read this essay in manuscript, termed this choice "eccentric." It undoubtedly is in that the painting is not a work of central importance in Copley's work or in the development of American painting. I use it as a symptom only. The more obvious and, historically speaking, more intelligible choices, such as the biblical paintings of Washington Allston, seem to me so tangled up within incompletely digested European elements that they belong more to the evolution of a provincial school of painting than to an account of painting as a genuine biblical hermeneutic.

WORKS CONSULTED

Benét, Stephen Vincent
    1942   *John Brown's Body*. New York: Farrar & Rinehart.

Carmean, E. A., Jr., and Rathbone, Eliza E.
    1978   *The Subjects of the Artist*. Washington: National
                            Gallery of Art.

Dillenberger, Jane, and Taylor, Joshua C.
    1972   *The Hand and the Spirit: Religious Art in America,
                            1700–1900*. Berkeley: University Art Museum.

Dillenberger, Jane, and Dillenberger, John
    1977   *Perceptions of the Spirit in Twentieth-Century
                            American Art*. Indianapolis: Indianapolis Museum of
                            Art.

Novak, Barbara
    1980   *Nature and Culture*. New York: Oxford University
                            Press.

Otto, Rudolph
    1958   *The Idea of the Holy*. Reprint. New York: Oxford
                            University Press.

PLATE 1.   JOHN SINGLETON COPLEY (1738–1815), *THE ASCENSION*.
1775. Oil on canvas. 32 x 29 in. (81.2 x 73.6 cm.). 25.95. (Bequest of
Susan Greene Dexter in Memory of Charles and Martha Babcock
Amory. Courtesy of Museum of Fine Arts, Boston.)

PLATE 2.   THOMAS EAKINS (1844–1916), *THE CRUCIFIXION.* Oil on canvas. 96 x 54 in. 29-184-24. (Courtesy of Philadelphia Museum of Art. Gift of Mrs. Thomas Eakins and Mis' Mary A. Williams.) (opposite page)
PLATE 3.   ALBERT BIERSTADT. *THE SIERRA NEVADA IN CALIFORNIA*, 1868. Oil on canvas mounted on hollow core aluminum panel. 72 x 20 in. (183 x 305 cm.). 1977.101.1. (Courtesy of National Museum of American Art [formerly National Collection of Fine Arts], Smithsonian Institution. Bequest of Helen Huntington Hull.) (above)
PLATE 4.   ALBERT PINKHAM RYDER, *JONAH.* 1885. Oil on canvas. 27¼ x 34⅜ in. 1929.6.98. (Courtesy of National Museum of American Art [formerly National Collection of Fine Arts], Smithsonian Institution. Gift of John Gellatly.) (below)

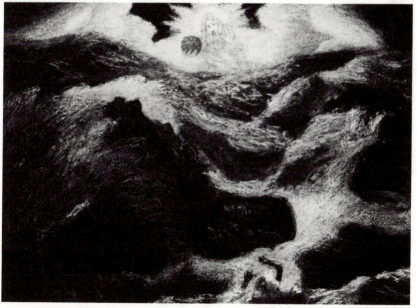

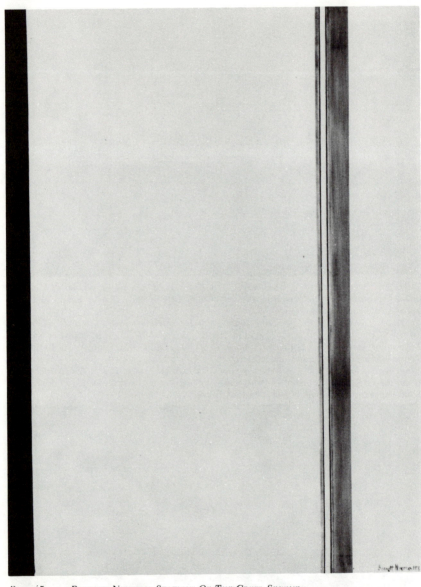

PLATE 5.   BARNETT NEWMAN. *STATIONS OF THE CROSS, SECOND STATION.* 1958. Magna on Canvas. 78 x 60 in. (Courtesy of Annalee Newman.)

PLATE 6.   BARNETT NEWMAN. *STATIONS OF THE CROSS, TWELFTH STATION*. 1965. Acrylic polymer on canvas. 78 x 60 in. (Courtesy of Annalee Newman.)

VIII

The Bible and American Folk Arts

Daniel W. Patterson

The world has so little noted the struggles of folklorists to define their discipline that many readers may think "The Bible and American Folk Arts" a title proposing a dubious paradox. For folklore (in the common view) comprises traditions orally transmitted among the unlettered; the Bible is the central literary text of the culture. Such a conception of folklore would admit only negative examples, lore deviating from the scriptural source. An explanation of current scholarly use of the term is therefore a necessary preliminary to the topic itself.

Like other fields, folklore has been constrained by earlier stages of its own growth. When British folklore studies developed in the nineteenth century, they focused on the archaic. Literary scholars gathered ballads and village customs. Anthropologists described savage customs in far outposts of the empire. In this these writers moved with the intellectual currents of the age: the nationalistic, egalitarian, and antiquarian tendencies within romanticism or the hope that Darwin excited of tracing back from cultural fossils the grand evolution of human society (Dorson, 1968). This bent of British folklore studies influenced the direction taken in the study of American folklore. British ballads surviving in the Appalachians or animal tales of former slaves were the prizes sought by early collectors. They speculated delightedly that children gamboling through "London Bridge" in the dooryard were reenacting ancient human sacrifices (Newell: 204-11).

This preoccupation with lore surviving from the dim past impeded an understanding of the actual scope and meaning of American folklore. Whatever the appropriateness of this search for archaic survivals among a comparatively settled peasantry or in a tribal community, it masked the formative experiences of most of the immigrant American populations. Commoners who tore themselves—or were torn—from traditional Old World villages had here to build a new community. Their dispersal into the American backwoods turned them from specialized artisans into masters of many trades and skills. They mingled with, married, and learned from people of other stocks. They increasingly entered new occupations—seafaring, plantation farming, lumbering, mining, cattle raising, railroad building, manufacturing—that demanded collective labor. They moved into cities. They surpassed their parents in education and began to rise in the social order. These experiences begot bodies of new American folklore.

As Americans passed through these transforming experiences, none of their resources from the Old World proved more useful to them than their religious traditions. None underwent more complex changes. None produced so rich a variety of expressive forms: these span the full range of the verbal, musical, mimetic, graphic, and plastic arts.

This statement presupposes another view of folklore that the reader may wish clarified. Early usage generally limited the *lore* to songs, stories, riddles, proverbs, and other oral genres. Many anthropologists still reserve the term folklore for "oral artistic expression." However, any line drawn between these and other arts transmitted by oral instruction and imitation is only arbitrary. A scholar may choose to discuss the morphology or typology of a single verbal genre, but exploration of its cultural meaning inevitably leads into related nonverbal behavior. Nowadays, folklorists defend their more ambitious explorations by adding to the word folklore a correlative term, calling their field "folklore and folklife."

This broader interpretation is especially relevant to any definition that stresses lore as the product of a *folk*. In British and American scholarship, writers were unwilling to equate the term *folk* with the "national soul," as the Germans did. But the British early used the word to signify a social class, the unlettered rural peasantry. This position got a respectable formulation from the American anthropologist Robert Redfield (chap. 1). His studies in Mexico led him to use the term *folk society* for a small, isolated, relatively immobile, nearly self-sufficient group homogeneous in race and custom, with face-to-face personal relationships, slight division of labor, and simple technology. The dissatisfaction of other anthropologists with so restricted a usage led George Foster to redefine a folk society as a "half-society" in a symbiotic spatial-temporal relationship to the upper classes of a preindustrial urban center.

Most folklorists would grow restive at Foster's qualifying term "pre-industrial." They recognize that even the elite within industrial societies may have active repertories of orally transmitted lore (Dundes: 6–17) and that laboring-class groups within industrial societies—including factory workers—have important bodies of folklore produced directly by the industrial system (Green; Lloyd). Nevertheless, Foster's definition holds a valuable implication that the experience of the folklorist corroborates: that a community may rely chiefly on oral transmission without necessarily being isolated. It may have frequent interaction with the upper classes and with other groups as marginal as itself. It is often not a static society, but one in process of change. Groups that move into the mainstream will for a time carry along folk-cultural baggage. From situation to situation they may operate within contrasting realms, traditional or nontraditional. An individual may simultaneously have membership in groups of contrasting kinds (an extended family, a neighborhood, a church, a union). Within the individual's mind contrasting frames of reference may coexist.

A sense of these complexities underlies Don Yoder's essay "Toward a Definition of Folk Religion" (1974). Although he suggests limiting the term "folk religion" to a form of religion existing "in a complex society in relation to and in tension with the organized religion(s)," he argues that folk religious elements are incorporated within the other forms of religion in his typology: "organized religion" ("the official religious institutions of a culture"), "primitive religion" (the religion of an entire tribe), "popular religion" (religion of "the Norman Vincent Peale level"), and sectarian religion (an "organized and therefore official religion" of a small counterculture group). Yoder recognizes, in other words, not only the "religious dimension of folk-culture" but also the "folk-cultural dimension of religion" (10–11, 14).

For the liberty it allows, I happily accept Yoder's broad formulation. But if it encompasses groups that have, in varying degrees, direct literate knowledge of the biblical text, Yoder's definition of folk religion poses one problem. The "official religion" he posits as a backdrop for folk religion does not exist in the United States. Nevertheless, this problem is useful to my discussion, for it points toward a cleavage that runs through the American religious folk arts, dividing the Anglo-American dissenting traditions from those groups coming from an established state church, whether Lutheran, Roman Catholic, or Russian or Greek Orthodox. The lore of the latter tends, predictably, to fall more into what Yoder calls the "passive/survivalist" category, and that of the Protestants more into the "active/creative" class—and to be more closely tied to the scriptures.

Archaic Survivals

Since the Anglo-American tradition is a product of several rebellions against a state church, virtually nothing survives here from Christian folk art current in England before the Reformation. Perhaps the only such specimens from any artistic genre are "The Cherry-Tree Carol" and "Sir Hugh," both ballads with a limited currency. The "Carol" (Child: No. 54) tells of Joseph's rage on learning from the Virgin Mary's craving for cherries that she is pregnant. "Let the father of the baby gather cherries for thee!" he exclaims, only to hear the unborn Jesus command the tree to bow low that his mother may gather some. The tale gets of course no corroboration from Matthew, Mark, Luke, or John, though it is told in the Pseudo-Matthew's gospel. It circulated widely in Europe, and in England was dramatized in the Coventry Mysteries. "Sir Hugh" (Child: No. 155) is even less scriptural. It derives from a medieval saint's legend about Hugh of Lincoln. American versions close, however, with a biblical twist. Instead of miraculously giving a post-mortem rendition of the hymn "Alma redemptoris mater," as the murdered child does in Chaucer's version of the legend, the ballad character asks to be buried with a Bible at his head and a prayer book at his feet. A Protestant touch, but proper Church of England.

From the German-American Protestant tradition at least one field-worker has reported a biblical glossing of the design and color elements used in another archaic survival, the decoration of Easter eggs (Wood: 12). North Carolina Germans, she heard, formerly prepared the eggs on Good Friday only. They used but two colors: a red dye for the egg shell to symbolize the blood of Christ and beeswax burnt black for the embossed design to symbolize mourning for the crucifixion. The decorators executed the designs with two strokes. One—a dot—they called a "nail hole." The other—a dot with a tail pulled from it—they called a "thorn." From these two strokes they formed the design motifs, some of which also bore names that were biblical allusions, such as "crown of thorns."

Such interpretations are not, however, widespread among contemporary North Carolina egg decorators of German ancestry, whose eggs are generally multicolored and often bear white designs produced by wax-resist techniques. No similar interpretations appear to circulate among other groups, such as the Ukranian-American decorators of *pysanky*. Their much more elaborately decorated eggs bear designs sometimes representational (crosses, stags, and suns), but more commonly geometrical. In her study *An Egg at Easter* Venetia Newhall does report from Europe the use of red as a symbol of the blood of Christ but not the use of black beeswax or names for the strokes or designs formed from them (chap. 9). Most likely, the biblical glossing in North Carolina is a late, Protestant rationalization for continuing a pre-Christian decorative tradition that had attached itself to the church calendar. The meaning of the practice lay in its function: the decorator gave an egg to each close friend or relative as a remembrance.

Local Reinterpretation in Hispanic Arts

In the folk cultures that developed within the state-church context, local reinterpretations tend in the opposite direction, the nonscriptural. Spanish-American folk arts of New Mexico offer the richest illustrations of this. Unlike groups that immigrated in the late nineteenth and the early twentieth century from southern and eastern Europe and were speedily funneled through cities and factories and schools toward the Anglo-American and middle-class mainstreams, the Hispanics of New Mexico had a long period of time in which to develop a distinctive folk-cultural variation of their Roman Catholic heritage. For the two and one-third centuries between 1610 and 1848 they lived within the bounds of their mother culture. But they lay on its periphery, isolated by the rough topography of their land and by widespread illiteracy. Franciscan missionaries established Christian practices in the region. After the bishops began to recall the Franciscans in 1760, the territory often lacked secular priests or was resentful of changes these priests

wished to introduce. The arrival of Anglo-Americans in the nineteenth century both initiated an undermining of Hispanic culture and bred further
conservative resistance to change. In this New Mexican context the religious
folk arts flourished in many forms, especially in drama, painting, sculpture,
and song.

In two monographs Arthur L. Campa surveyed many of the surviving
folk plays (1934a, 1934b). Three of them commemorate events from Old or
New World religious history: *Los Moros y los Cristianos*, which originated
in Spain; *La Aparición*, about Our Lady of Guadalupe; and *Los Comanches*,
a dance drama showing the Comanches' attack upon a Hispanic village and
their subsequent conversion to Christianity. Seven other plays are scripturally derived and originated in the New World. Their unknown authors were
probably members of the clergy, and manuscripts have played a key role in
their preservation and performance. Nevertheless, their authors so successfully aimed them at the populace that folk communities adopted them and
continue to give several of them annual performances. And the plays show
much variation and local adaptation.

The goal of the original authors was to teach biblical stories and official church doctrine to the newly subjugated native Americans. Significantly,
the seven scriptural plays focus on two cardinal points, the Fall and the
Incarnation. Those deriving from the book of Genesis are *Adán y Eva*, de-
picting the first act of disobedience against God, and *Caín y Abel*, the first
crime against a neighbor. Five other plays grow from the story of the nativity. In *San Jóse* the patriarchs choose the future husband of Mary; *Las
Posadas* shows Joseph and Mary searching for lodging in Bethlehem. *Los
Pastores* is about the shepherds' learning of the birth of Christ. *Los Reyes
Magos* deals with the visit of the Magi and with Herod's slaughter of the
innocents. *El Niño Perdido* presents the twelve-year-old Jesus' disputations
with the doctors of Jewish law in the Temple.

The authors of the plays did not feel bound to a literal presentation of
the scriptures. They wanted to draw and hold a peasant audience. *Los
Pastores* omits the angels' song of "On earth peace, good will toward men,"
bringing on instead an assortment of comic shepherds and a blustering devil,
whom the angel Michael finally vanquishes. The authors also incorporated
interesting saints' legends. In *San José* the miraculous blossoming of Joseph's
reed shows that he is the husband divinely intended for Mary. *El Niño
Perdido* stirs the sympathy of the poor by having Dives turn Jesus from his
door. Winning the audience's attention, the authors could also intrude upon
the biblical narrative in order to instruct. In *Adán y Eva* the allegorical
characters Appetite and Sin help to clarify the causes of the Fall. For a
number of reasons, then, the authors deviated from scriptural exactitude,
and the folk performers take full advantage of this artistic license.

The New Mexican Santos

Religious folk painting and sculpture that flourished between the mid-eighteenth and the mid-nineteenth century in New Mexico drifted even farther from biblical authority. One reason for this lay in their function. Occasionally, a retablo showed a scene like "Abraham Visited by the Three Angels" or "The Flight into Egypt" (Boyd: pls. 33 and 34). The paintings were normally, however, not a narrative art but icons serving as a focus for devotions. The second reason is that, like the dramas, they grew from an ecclesiastical tradition broader than the scriptures. The artists depicted figures from the biblical account—Saint Joseph, the Virgin Mary, the infant Jesus, the crucified Christ—but also canonized figures from church history, such as Santiago and San Ignacio. They even showed Acacius and Librata, saints locally popular but rejected by the church as without historical foundation. The identifying symbols in these depictions derived from the iconographic conventions of the church—and hence grew more from Christian legend than from the Bible. Saint Joseph, for example, normally carried his flowering rod.

The frequent depiction of certain saints in Southwestern art discloses the local folk reinterpretation of official Catholicism, and the reasons for their popularity are to be found not in a distinctive reading of the scriptures but in, according to John D. Robb, these saints' "relationship to the vicissitudes of frontier life." He suggests that the "reasons for their popularity become self-evident when the saints' backgrounds are known." Thus San Ramón de Nonato, as the patron of captives, was the one to whom "prisoners of raiding Indians naturally turned" and San Ysidro, the patron of agriculture, was the one "to whom the settlers prayed for protection from locusts and the weather." El Santo Niño de Atocha gained popularity from a belief that it rescued people from "all kinds of dangers" (644).

The Art of the Penitentes

One last saint whose local popularity Robb finds significant is Juan Nepomuceño, a Bohemian priest martyred for refusing to betray the secrets of the confessional. Robb and others see him as "a natural favorite of the secret society of Penitentes." These "Brothers of Our Father Jesus" offer the region's most notable folk expression of Catholicism. At first glance the Penitentes seem to contradict the nonscriptural tendencies in the folk plays and paintings, for the Penitentes' practices did not grow from saints' legends but from the passion of Christ.

Certain elements of the reenactment of the passion gained the Penitentes notoriety in the mid-nineteenth century: their rites of penance such as flagellation and crossbearing. These disturbed Protestant missionaries and church officials alike. However, the devotion of the Penitentes also found artistic expression in forms that increasingly command respect. It produced a repertory of hymns—*alabados*—describing the crucifixion in sometimes powerfully realized scenes:

> Jesus Christ is lost.
> Mary is out looking for him:
> Has there not passed by here
> A shining star?
>
> Lady, he passed by here
> Three hours before dawn.
> He was wearing a white robe
> Which was stained with blood.
>
> He was dragging a cross
> Of very heavy wood;
> He was dragging a rope
> From head to foot.
>
> Let us start our journey
> And go to Calvary.
> He was carrying three nails in his hands
> With which he would be nailed.
>
> Saint John and the Magdalene
> Hold each other by the hand.
> We have walked so long
> They will already have crucified him.
>
> He who sings this *alabado*
> All the Fridays of the year
> Rescues a soul from Purgatory
> And his own from sin. (Robb: 630)

Although many of these *alabados* allude to stations of the cross and other churchly elaborations upon the biblical narrative, Elizabeth Boyd regards the songs as being to a degree heterodox. They stress the "physical sufferings of Christ more than the spiritual mysteries of His life" (450). Artisans influenced by the Brotherhood similarly distinguished themselves by the stark intensity with which their santos presented the sufferings of the crucified Christ. The *santero* carved from wood an elongated, emaciated figure, with wounds gouged into the torso. He painted its scarifications and streaming blood.

These figures the brothers of the order brought forth in Holy Week for use in quasi-dramatic rituals. "In these performances," says George Mills, "it is the 'santo' which moves while the people look on." Often the *santero* provided the carved figure with articulated joints. One statue of Christ regularly displayed at three o'clock on Holy Friday had jaws, set with springs, that opened and shut like those of a man in death agonies (61). The desire of the order "to personally experience the sufferings of the Passion," wrote Elizabeth Boyd, "led to closely realistic repetitions instead of, as had originally been intended, the enactment of a symbolic pageant in its commemoration" (450).

Students of the tradition have suggested reasons for the emergence of the arts and practices of the Penitentes. Alice Corbin Henderson romantically believed the "stark parable of the Crucifixion" to lie close to the soul of a country where the "eternal loneliness" of "this terrible afternoon light on bare mesa and peak" eats into the heart (quoted in Weigle: 1). Boyd, Marta Weigle, and Juan B. Rael saw the Penitente practices as coming directly out of the traditions of Spanish Catholicism as mediated by the Franciscan Order and called forth by historical crises in the local church and culture (Boyd: 440–51; Weigle: 31–47; Rael: 10). George Mills sought a more ethnographic explanation, questioning whether the Penitentes' devotion to "Our *Father* Jesus" might not relate to the macho ideal of males in the culture of Hispanic New Mexico and hence to the dominant role of the father in its family life and of the patron in its village society. Whatever their ultimate motivation or historical roots, Mills also sees the Fraternity and the culture itself as having turned to "drama to keep the faith alive" in times and circumstances when they were "without Bibles or priests" (61). Hispanics in the Southwest drew their understanding of the passion not directly from the Bible but from their memory of official Catholicism. Their *alabados*, their santos, their dramatic tableaux, and their personal crossbearing emphasize the incidents, sufferings, and last words of the passion, as defined by the official liturgy, but selectively emphasized within the local culture.

Illuminated Texts: German Fraktur

Even in "survivalist" art forms of ethnic minorities immigrating from state–church societies, Protestants would take a very different approach to the use of the Bible. The fraktur art—illuminated writings—of the Pennsylvania Germans offers an appropriate comparison. It derives from approximately the same years as the New Mexican santos: its flowering came between the 1780s and the 1830s. It was the product of another minority population continually reinforced by its mother culture, in this case by a stream of immigration between 1683 and 1812. In a population relatively isolated from the surrounding Anglo-American culture by language, kinship, religious affiliation, and occupation, the fraktur makers, like the *santeros* of New Mexico, were able to retain strong ethnic traditions.

But there were also important differences between the contexts within which the New Mexican and the Pennsylvania religious artists produced their work. The *santeros* appear to have been laborers; fraktur artists were frequently rural school masters or even pastors. Except at the Ephrata and Snow Hill Cloisters in Pennsylvania, the artists did not create the fraktur specifically as devotional acts. They normally sold their handiwork to working-class customers. Although occasioned by the world of Protestant piety (the fraktur served as baptismal certificates, house blessings, title pages for religious songbooks, rewards of merit for pupils in parochial schools), these paintings had no function in religious ceremonies.

Moreover, unlike the crucifixes made by the *santero*, the visual designs of the fraktur artists bear a relationship to the Bible both obscure and open to question. Some of the motifs on the fraktur—a "big wonder fish" caught near Geneva, mermaids, parakeets, and American eagles—are clearly not at all biblically inspired. Other fraktur do show scenes from the Bible, such as the temptation of Adam and Eve in the garden, the career of the prodigal son, and the crucifixion. But these are relatively few. In the illustrated catalogue of the Free Library of Philadelphia, the largest collection and presumably a representative one, the biblical scenes comprise only thirteen of the 1,021 plates (Weiser and Heaney). Traditional Christian iconography deriving from the Bible is even rarer in this collection. Seven of the fraktur do show a pelican feeding her young with blood from her own heart, conventionally a symbol, extrapolated from Ps 102:6, of Christ's giving his life for humanity. From an inscription on one of these specimens it appears that the artist did understand the symbol. Beneath the pelican and her brood has been added a small heart and lines urging a reciprocal gift to Christ: "Give Jesus your heart in joy and pain, in life or death; this one thing is necessary."/1/

But what of the more common fraktur motifs, the roses and lilies? John Joseph Stoudt argued that such visual motifs in the fraktur designs derived from the millennial vision of German Pietism, as recorded in biblically inspired hymn verse. In his interpretation the motifs allude to the "lily of the valley" and the "rose of Sharon" (Cant 2:1), symbols of Christ, the church, and the soul (chaps. 2–4). One can demonstrate, however, that such motifs usually serve a purely decorative function. Many of the fraktur bearing scriptural texts—some sixty in the Free Library collection—and a much larger number that hold scripturally influenced hymn verses are decorated with birds and flowers, even though the illuminated passage itself makes no mention of either and contains no allusion to the millennium. It would in fact be impossible to translate most of the passages into visual imagery. Since the recipients of the fraktur were frequently young people, the artists took an instructional tone, choosing passages that urged obedience to God and parent. They could express this theme through depictions of Adam and Eve or the prodigal son, but most often their precepts are notably conceptual. "You children be obedient to your parents in the Lord, for that is right," says one, drawing on Eph 6:1–3. "Commit your ways unto the Lord," says another, a quotation from Ps 37:5, "trust in Him, He will act."

The Verbal Orientation of Protestant Folk Art

The Protestant influence in this art form lies in the avoidance of biblical subjects favored by Roman Catholicism (only Plate 235 in Weiser and Heaney shows the Virgin and Child) and in the emphasis on text, on Bible verses or scripturally inspired hymns. The fraktur accord, then, with Don Yoder's observation that Protestant folk art emphasizes the word (1969: 5).

The visually oriented Roman Catholic folk art developed in an era when illiteracy was common, books rare, and an educated priesthood mediated between the scriptures and the populace; Protestant folk art in centuries when print and literacy were exploding, and common people were beginning to insist upon their own right to read and interpret the scriptures.

A corollary of this is that the principal branches of American Protestant folk art are verbal, not visual or plastic. The exceptions prove the rule. For example, as much as quilting has flourished in pious Protestant households, the form has been notably secular, even among the Amish (Holstein: 77ff.). Probably fewer than 5 percent of the American appliqué and pieced-quilt motifs even bear biblically inspired names like "Star of Bethlehem" or "Rose of Sharon." Album quilts—in which each square can have its own unique design and be highly representational—show Bible scenes only rarely and even then only as incidental designs among many other squares with secular motifs (Safford and Bishop: 204–5, 210). Two remarkable late nineteenth-century specimens by the black Georgian, Harriet Powers, are virtually the only known biblical quilts, and even these mingle depictions of recent remarkable providences and signs and wonders with similar events from the Bible (Fry; Vlach). Gravestone carving, to take a second example, flourished as a traditional craft in Protestant communities, but yielded to commercial popular-culture products early in the nineteenth century. During the folk-culture phase, gravestone cutters nowhere drew deeply on biblical inspiration, confining themselves chiefly to symbols of resurrection. In the South the only common biblical motif is Noah's dove bearing a sprig of promise. In New England the carvers depicted the vine, the tree of life, the trumpet of judgment, the palm of victory, the cock, and the crown of glory. All these are much less common than the death's head and the soul image (Ludwig: 65–232). German carvers were even less scriptural, showing chiefly the soul image, the sun, the swastika, or simply decorative lilies and roses (Barba; Wust; Rauschenberg).

The visual tradition has in fact grown so weak in American Protestant folk culture that when a religious experience stirs a member to create a painting or sculpture, the artist must reinvent a vocabulary of motifs and forms, normally with the help of private dreams and visions (Fuller: 8; Roscoe). This was true already of Shaker artists a century ago, although coteries of them could at least borrow from one another's inspiration (Andrews; Wolfe; Patterson, in press). The present-day black North Carolina folk artist Minnie Evans works alone and shares with the rest of her culture only the biblical source that somewhat distantly influences her visions. Her picture *The Prophets in the Air*, for example, records a dream that she has described:

> I just saw those prophets in the air, and they sang a beautiful song to me. Not that I could understand any of their words, but it was the

most beautifulest song I have ever heard. And I just stood there and smiled and looked up there and they just stayed there a good while, and they were singing and waving and talking or saying something to each other. It looked like there might have been a lot of feathers blowing, blowing you know, turning all over and over to each other.

So after a while they all got together and started off and the last one that stayed, before he went up, dropped his hand down and waved to me. Then he went right on up in the air. But not any words that I understood, you know, what they said or even the song. But the beautiful song they sang. (Starr: 42)

Protestant Spirituals

In the English-language tradition, in particular, the dominant forms of religious folk expression are song and sermon. The American Protestant song tradition stands, however, in a complex relation to both the Bible and folk tradition. It reached its peak in revival, slave, singing-school-tunebook, and sectarian spirituals during the first half of the nineteenth century, but this body of songs was the product of a long series of developments stretching back to the beginnings of the British Reformation, and especially to Genevan influence upon worship practices.

The scriptural premises of this historical development were still much in the consciousness of American singers in the nineteenth century. They saw the act of worshiping in song as a duty taught in the scriptures by both example and precept. The editor of one religious tunebook justified his undertaking by calling on the full range of biblical accounts of sacred song: creation, when "the angelic hosts and seraphim above, like bright morning stars, shining with the most serene brilliancy, sang together" (Job 38:7), the Nativity, when "shining legions of angels" descended "through the portals of the skies" to "sing, while hovering over the Redeemer's humble manger, and around the vigilant Shepherds" (Luke 2:13–14), the Last Supper, when Christ sang a hymn with the disciples "as the last consolation to them" (Mark 14:26), and Judgment, when "eternally after, the choirs of glory will ever worship him with songs of endless praises," singing "Worthy is the Lamb that was slain" (Rev 5:9–12). The precepts were equally numerous in both the Old Testament and the New. "Sing unto the Lord a new song and sing unto the Lord all the earth" he cited from Psalm 33. "Let the word of Christ dwell in you richly in all wisdom," he quoted from Col 3:16, "teaching and admonishing one another in psalms and hymns and spiritual songs, singing with grace in your hearts to the Lord" (Moore: xiv–xv; Caldwell: 4; Walker: [i]).

On this scripturally enjoined duty to worship God in song, nineteenth-century Americans and their colonial and British predecessors based several other views. One was that the song of worship must be congregational. Song in their view was an "ordinance of God's worship in which *all are com-manded to join*" (Caldwell). In the Church of England such a premise might not exclude the professional musician from a place in the service, but radical dissenting branches of British Protestantism disliked having choirs of specialists preempting any part of the congregational role in song (Patterson, 1979: chap. 1). The aesthetic quality of the singing was of less concern to them than that they "sing with the spirit, and . . . with the understanding also" (1 Cor 14:15).

A story that illustrates the view was told by one primitive Baptist elder in Virginia:

> There's a lot of difference in singing. There's pretty singing, and then there's good singing. And good singing is better than pretty sing-ing. I'll give you an illustration. A son had left home, and his father couldn't sing a tune. He could not sing a tune. In a few years, he returned home. And he greeted his mother and said, "Mother, where's Dad?" "Down at the barn, doing his work." And he went down, and when he got in hearing, his daddy was going over the words
>
>> Amazing Grace, how sweet the sound,
>>   That saved a wretch like me;
>> I once was lost, but now am found,
>>   Was blind, but now I see.
>
> And he said he walked around, and as he turned around beside the barn, his daddy had his head over, and he could see the tears dropping, each time he went over those words. Now, he said, it wasn't pretty, but it was the best singing he'd ever heard in his life. (Sutton: 103)

A related view of importance to the Protestant radical was that instru-mental music had no place in worship. This, significantly, they grounded not on the scriptures, where they might have found precedents for worshiping with harps and timbrels and dulcimers, but upon their observation of the base uses to which instruments had been put. They did not wish to worship God with musical instruments that, as one Shaker phrased it, the world had used "to excite lasciviousness, and to invite and stimulate men to destroy each others lives" (Patterson: 30). Underlying this repudiation of instrumen-tal music and choirs lay a wish to guide congregational song in the direction of the stylistic preferences of the Anglo-American traditional singer: unhar-monized, unaccompanied solo or unison singing. A class struggle was being waged on religious and musical grounds.

In the revival and slave spirituals of the early nineteenth century this folk tradition culminated in song that was, by any accepted standard, folk-song. But this development was slow in coming. Although they performed in the traditional British folksong style, early dissenters took Genevan practices as their model. For their song texts they used only metrical versions of the Psalms, and for their melodies either tunes from the Continent or ones com-posed in the British Isles. When the hymn verses of Isaac Watts, John

Wesley, and other devotional authors supplanted psalmody in worship—in America this apparently began during the second half of the eighteenth century, in the aftermath of the Great Awakening—the congregations often sang them to traditional ballad airs. The resulting "folk hymns," as George Pullen Jackson called them, formed the repertory of the Separates, New Lights, Baptists, and other early sects (1943: chaps. 2–3).

The Second Great Awakening at the end of the century and the inter-denominational and Methodist camp meetings and revivals that followed it gave rise to a more purely oral tradition, the "revival spirituals," with repeated lines and choruses that could be caught by ear, often sung to lively traditional dance tunes. Most of this repertory, as well as the folk hymnody, would be lost to us if contemporary musicians had not compiled and published the songs in books for use in northern urban revivals or southern and western rural singing schools. Black singers were participating in most of these musical developments, but they also originated a large body of distinctive spirituals, most of which did not find their way into print until after the Civil War.

All these developments in congregational song got their justification from scriptural authority, but in the first—the "folk-hymn"—phase it is difficult to read a specifically American folk use of the Bible. Each hymn was felt to have a scriptural foundation, which was often cited in an epigraph over the text in eighteenth- and nineteenth-century editions, but the hymns were normally elaborations upon a scriptural allusion. Only three biblical events received extended treatment in the hymns: the birth of Christ, the crucifixion, and the last judgment. The other key subjects were doctrines (grace, imputed righteousness), practices (baptism, the Lord's Supper, washing the saints' feet), Christian exercises (rejoicing, adoration and praise, supplication, admonition, and encouragement), and occasions (weddings, funerals, departures). The hymns then current in America were, moreover, largely of English composition. Lacking knowledge of the relative frequency of their performances, we cannot judge which scriptural passages were most meaningful to the American traditional singers.

Camp Meeting and Revival Spirituals

For the camp meeting and revival spirituals the situation is quite different. These originated in America; oral transmission stamped them with the singers' outlook, and for nearly a century they were recorded in considerable numbers. Biblical scenes and imagery, not allusion, are the fabric of which they are made. In "The Religion of the Spiritual Choruses" Dickson D. Bruce, Jr., argues that the imagery is predominantly derived from the Old Testament. The singers were "on their way to Canaan" or "bound for the promised land." They headed "away over Jordan" and "had but one more river to cross." But he recognizes that their use of this imagery was essentially millenarian. It was the book of Revelation that informed their cry:

> Farewell, my friends, I must be gone;
>   I have no home nor stay with you;
>   I soon shall shine like the morning star,
>   In the new Jerusalem. (McCurry: 138)

On occasion the songs exhort the sinner and the faltering saint with explicit echoes of Rev 6:12–17:

> Oh, sinners do get ready,
> Oh, sinners do get ready,
> Oh, sinners do get ready,
> For the times are a-drewing near.

> Oh, there'll be signs and wonders,
> Yes, there'll be signs and wonders,
> Oh, there'll be signs and wonders,
> When this world is to an end.

> Oh, the sun she will be darkened,
> Yes, the sun she will be darkened,
> Oh, the sun she will be darkened,
> When this world is to an end.

> Oh, the moon she will be a-bleeding,
> Yes, the moon she will be bleeding,
> Oh, the moon she will be bleeding,
> When this world is to an end. (Fleishhauer and Jabbour)

But painting the terrors of judgment was the role of the preacher in the early nineteenth-century revivals. The saints generally supported conversions by sweetly singing the joys of their own blessed assurance, an alternative the sinner could make his own.

In the "Canaan language" of these songs Dickson Bruce finds a "radical world rejection" that he believes to have been born of the disappointment the plain folk felt in being unable to penetrate the closed political and social structure of the ante-bellum South. "However much they wanted to break into the Southern system," he writes, "there were few openings, and most people who were not born in the planter elite never entered it" (123). There are several reasons for caution in accepting this theory, not the least of which is the fact that the "Canaan language" had widespread use outside the range of the slave economy. Many of the Southerners among whom the songs circulated were in fact those least aware of and least attracted to the plantation ideal: the Scotch-Irish and German settlers of the Carolina piedmont, upland Georgia, the Appalachians, and the Tennessee and Kentucky frontier. For such people as these, the camp meetings seem instead a response to the chaotic social conditions of the newly settled backwoods (Johnson: chap. 1). But the meaning may be even broader. One can find the same Canaan imagery in northern revival songs, which are often traditional variants of the same spirituals the southern books printed (Jackson, 1943: chap. 11). One finds it also in the German-language spirituals of the "bush-meeting Dutch" of Pennsylvania

(Yoder, 1961: 344–48). The songs would seem to corroborate Donald Mathews's hypothesis that the Second Great Awakening served as a "nationalizing force" that "enveloped the entire country" and created "a common world of experience," not through a strong national organization but through "strong local churches that shared common values and norms" (42–43).

But unless one can assume a widespread craving among Americans for national unity, Mathews's hypothesis describes a consequence rather than a cause. The imagery of the songs may, however, reflect a different social origin. Their texts are filled with verbs of motion. The singers are "marching," "journeying," "traveling on." They can "tarry but a night." On their journey they call themselves pilgrims and strangers who "camp a while in the wilderness." They long for a world where "there's no more stormy clouds arising" and "sorrows have an end." What the songs tell of is departure, separation from kin and friends, travel and toil. They speak not of social exclusion but of a decision to depart. The singers' vision of their destination, moreover, is of a Canaan synonymous with reunion. They say they are "going home" and call on fathers and mothers, sisters and brothers, to join them within the walls of Zion. I suggest that so far as a social condition can explain these songs, the background is the great migrations taking place in the North, the Midwest, and the South between the mid-eighteenth and the mid-nineteenth century.

These were, however, not merely spatial resettlements. The history of one southern singing family illustrates a full range of geographic, ethnic, denominational, occupational, and social migrations. The founder of the line, Martin Hauser from Alsace, came to Pennsylvania as a Lutheran in 1727. With most of his family he converted to the Moravian faith during the Indian troubles in North Carolina in the 1750s. By 1800 two of his grandsons, Martin and Samuel Hauser, were Methodist preachers there and active in the revival. Samuel reportedly composed two of the most popular of the camp meeting spirituals, "Shout Old Satan's Kingdom Down" and "Old Ship of Zion"—one of them about the destruction of an old order and the other about passage to a new. About 1807 Samuel moved to Kentucky and joined the Shakers, for whom he composed many new spirituals. His nephew William Hauser, whose mother was the daughter of a Quaker from Maryland and one of whose sons would later convert to Mormonism, became a singing master in the 1830s and moved to Georgia. There in 1848 he edited *The Hesperian Harp*, a shape-note tunebook holding many spirituals Hauser learned from oral tradition. This was the music he loved best, the camp meeting songs of crowds of "happy christian white folks and negroes" who became "filled with the Holy Ghost" and dropped "the trammels of form." But Hauser also had an eagerness for self-improvement and social advancement which led him to make mail-order purchases of an encyclopedia of music and the scores of two oratorios and six Italian operas. Although raised a farm boy with little schooling, he had studied medicine with a country doctor and in 1859 was offered a teaching post at a medical college in Savannah, in the heartland of the southern plantation society. He himself became a slave holder and passionately defended the southern cause. After the Civil War, he expanded his sympathies toward the northern middle class. In publishing a tunebook aptly named *The Olive Leaf* he drew on aid from musicians outside the South, including one who had served in the army with which General Sherman conquered Savannah. The trajectory of the Hauser family's career leads, then, from the traditional society of ethnic sectarians and yeoman farmers, through evangelical revivalism, into distinctively American forms of religion and, in William Hauser's case, to a place in, first, the southern establishment and then in the general American middle class. The family history corroborates the implication of the texts of the camp meeting songs: that they grew out of, and facilitated, rapid social change (Patterson, 1980).

Black Spirituals

The slave spirituals offer a contrasting example. The condition of the singers was of course the opposite of that of the whites. They were trapped within a closed system. In consequence, when they drew upon the same repertory of images for their spirituals, they used the biblical sources very differently. Like whites, the blacks used "Canaan language," but they extended its range forward to the conquest of Canaan and backward to the exodus from Egyptian bondage. They sang of Joshua fighting the battle of Jericho and bringing the walls tumbling down. They had numerous songs— ones with few parallels in the white repertory—about the children of Israel led safely through the Red Sea by Moses:

1

Gwine to write to Massa Jesus,
To send some valiant soldier,
To turn back Pharoah's army, Hallelu!
To turn back Pharoah's army, Hallelujah!
To turn back Pharoah's army, Hallelu!
To turn back Pharoah's army, Hallelujah!
To turn back Pharoah's army, Hallelu!

o   o   o

4

When the children were in bondage
They cried unto the Lord,
He turned back Pharaoh's army, etc.

5

When Moses smote the water,
The children all passed over,
And turned back Pharaoh's army, etc.

6

> When Pharaoh crossed the water,
> The waters came together,
> And drowned ole Pharaoh's army, etc. (Marsh: 132)

While to both whites and blacks the children of Israel symbolized the community of the saints, a spiritual family, to the blacks the Israelites were more particularly the chosen people rescued from oppressors. The Old Testament offered black slaves a theory of history that explained their sufferings. It gave them a determination to fight on and a hope that God would once again intervene to save his chosen. "Didn't my Lord deliver Daniel?" they sang, "and why not a every man?"

Their situation gave black singers a distinct perspective on many other biblical accounts. Seizing upon one spiritual that the Adventists sang (Anon., 1843: 41–42), which surveyed religious history from the fall through the nativity, crucifixion, and resurrection to the last judgment, blacks stripped it back to its opening, elaborated upon the scene, and cast it into an African responsorial song form:

(leader)		(group)	
	Adam in the garden		Pinning up leaves
	Adam in the garden		Pinning up leaves
	God called Adam		Pinning up leaves
	God called Adam		Pinning up leaves
	Adam wouldn't answer		Pinning up leaves
	Adam wouldn't answer		Pinning up leaves
	Adam!		Pinning up leaves
	Adam!		Pinning up leaves
	Where art thou?		Pinning up leaves
	Where art thou?		Pinning up leaves
	God, I'm ashamed		Pinning up leaves
	God, I'm ashamed		Pinning up leaves

(Lomax, 1961)

In this song the black singers turned their attention less to "the fruit of that forbidden tree, and all our woe, with loss of Eden" than to the comedy of the detection of a disobedient servant. Their response to the crucifixion would similarly be to feel the parallel between their own situation and that of Christ, who when whipped "never said a mumbling word." One twentieth-century black woman, after singing a song on the nativity, retold the story of the search for room at the Bethlehem inn with an equally immediate sense of its relevance to black experience. While the bell boy, the porter, the matron, and the waitress of the hotel watch helplessly, the manager turns Joseph and Mary away, with a "harsh, mean look" on his face, saying, "No. No room here." And the baby Jesus, comments the singer, "had to be born in that stable on that nasty old hay trodded in by cows. . . . He had a hard time coming into this world—and that's the reason I love him, 'cause *we* have a hard time" (Vera Hall Ward in Courlander: Side 1; Lomax, 1959: 116–17). The slave songs "state as clearly as anything can," writes Lawrence Levine, "the manner in which the sacred world of the slaves was able to fuse the precedents of the past, the conditions of the present, and the promise of the future into one connected reality" (51). The achievement was not limited to the ante-bellum years. This use of the Bible still underlies Afro-American religious song (Heilbut: 20–28). In the 1960s it would make these songs one of the most powerful weapons of the civil rights movement.

Shaker Spirituals

For an equally distinctive reading of the Bible in white folksong, one must turn to one of the more extreme sects, such as Shakerism. Its song repertory overlapped scarcely at all with the spirituals of other groups and spanned many more genres than other groups had. Each Shaker song form had its own relation to the scriptures. The lengthy folk-hymn texts of the decade following 1805 used a typological reading of the Bible to expound the Shaker doctrine of the second coming of Christ in the person of Ann Lee. The homophonic anthems the Shakers created in the same years had texts pieced together from Isaiah, Matthew, or Revelation. It was, however, in their one-stanza songs, produced in very great numbers for the period of nearly a century, that they made their most characteristic use of the Bible. Some of these one-stanza spirituals were marching songs, a genre in which they often sang of "advancing to Canaan's happy shore" (Patterson, 1979: 308). But Shakerism was a postmillennial faith, and many of its songs are of travelers already arrived in the New Jerusalem:

> Here we walk in the verdant grove
> Where lillies fair are growing
> Here in love and sweet repose
> And gentle rivers flowing. (374)

These rivers are not Jordan, the symbol of death through which the Christian had to pass to reach the Promised Land, but the waters of life flowing from the throne of God. A similar reinterpretation of biblical imagery shows in many other Shaker songs. The valley is not the valley of the shadow of death but the vale of humility. The dove is neither Noah's dove nor the Holy Spirit, but an emblem of the humble soul. The lamb is not the Lamb of God, but a humble follower of the Good Shepherd.

As many of these reinterpretations imply, Shaker millennialism left room for aspiring to a continuous spiritual growth. Drawing on John 15:1–8, in which Christ declares himself the true vine, his followers the branches, and his Father the husbandman, the Shakers would sing:

> I am the true vine which my Father hath set
>   In his lovely kingdom fair
> Every branch found in me which bringeth forth fruit
>   He purgeth it with care.
> But the vine that is barren he will reject
>   And from him he will cast away
> Withered branches he'll shake off and cast in the fire
>   That in me there be found no decay. (412–14)

Or, identifying Shakerism with the body of Christ, they would sing:

> O we have found a lovely vine in Zion's valley blooming
> Whose blossoms shoot, and promise fruit that's beautiful and
>   cheering
> Whose verdant branches spread so wide it shades the meek and lowly
> Its dazzling light does shine so bright it truly fills the valley. (205)

In addition to taking imagery and themes for their songs from the scriptures the Shakers also drew upon the Bible to explain and defend some of their more unusual musical practices. From the earliest times they had erupted into bodily manifestations during worship services, and this sometimes took the form of holy dances, performed to wordless mouth music sung by some leather-lunged member. In the 1790s a Shaker leader raised this into a congregational exercise, making it "emblematical of the *one spirit* by which the people of God are led" (Youngs: 584–88). The practice was not founded on biblical injunctions, but the Shakers found nineteen precedents in the scriptures with which to defend their dancing. A second unusual song type developed from their interest in 1 Pet 3:18–20 and 4:6, passages which they interpreted as describing Christ's preaching to the dead. In the 1840s the Shakers themselves often witnessed to the dead, particularly to "native" or Indian spirits who came seeking the gospel. Through "instruments," members whom the spirits possessed, these natives in return sang songs to the Shakers in pidgin English or in "native tongues." Believers learned, recorded, and often sang these songs. A third unusual song type—the "solemn song" of the 1780s and 1790s—was performed in unknown tongues, memorized, and sung by the entire congregation. Believers held these songs to be the "new song" of the virgin followers of the Lamb, that none could understand but the 144,000 who had been redeemed from the flesh (Rev 14:3).

Apocalyptic Visions

Their attraction to the book of Revelation shows also in another expression of Shaker inspiration, the apocalyptic vision. Oral accounts of visions must have been commonly exchanged in the Shaker villages, but in the 1840s and 1850s members also sometimes recorded scenes from them in drawings and frequently set down the entire vision in writing. These prose accounts echo biblical diction and syntax, and their most common narrative subject is a journey to heaven, where the landscape and beings derive largely from the scriptures. The climax of one such vision combines, for example, the wheat field of John 4:35 with the reaping angels of Rev 14:14–18. The visionist beheld a "richly loaded field of wheat, bending under its immense weight of golden clusters." On each side, she said,

> stood an Angel with a sickle in his hand; and at this moment there appeared to me the spirit of the prophet Isaiah, and he said, "Child, what seest thou?" I answered a golden harvest and bright Angels with sickles in their hands. And he said, this is given you as a sign. . . .
>
> Shortly after I saw an Angel riding upon a white horse hastening towards us. His path was narrow and grown over with very beautiful white flowers. As he approached us I saw that he was decorated with gold and jewelry from the crown on his head to his feet; and a flag waving in his hand wheron was written in large letters of gold LIBERTY. He rode to the field where the Angels stood, and commanded them to commence reaping, which they readily obeyed. (Barber: 109–10).

Such visions normally carried instruction. They also validated Shakerism through revelations of future judgments upon the world and a promise of blessings, which the visionist was to deliver to the community of Believers.

Conversion Narratives

Particularly in black tradition, such apocalyptic visions are often subsumed within another verbal genre, the conversion narrative, which similarly blends motifs from a variety of scriptural passages, but is more pointedly personal in application. The narrator of one account, who had always felt herself a child of God but passed through a severe crisis, said that God struck her dead. She fell to the floor powerless to move or speak. In this state she saw hell and the devil and found herself "crawling along a high brick wall" through the "dark, roaring pit." She looked to the east, where she saw Jesus. As he had called Peter to walk to him upon the waters, so he called to her, "Arise and follow me." He was standing, she said, "in snow—the prettiest, whitest snow I have ever seen. I said, 'Lord, I can't go, for that snow·is too deep and cold.' He commanded me the third time before I would go. I stepped out in it and it didn't seem a bit cold, nor did my feet sink into it." Christ led her to glory, where everything seemed "made of white stones and pearls." There she saw the "Lamb's book of life," and her own name was written in it. A voice then spoke to her and said, "Whosoever my son sets free is free indeed. I give you a through ticket from hell to heaven. Go into yonder world and be not afraid, neither be dismayed, for you are an elect child and ready for the fold." This was a comforting message for one who earlier had lamented in prayer, "Lord, it looks like you come to everybody's house but mine. . . . I have lived as it is becoming a poor widow woman to live and yet, Lord, it looks like I have a harder time than anybody" (Clifton H. Johnson: 58–59).

Sermons

Like the apocalyptic vision, the conversion narrative itself was often employed within yet another verbal genre, one of much greater importance in the American religious folk arts and more directly and consciously related to the scriptures, the sermon. The precondition for the folk sermon was the plain oratory that the Puritans had demanded, sermons intelligible to those without education. To this the Great Awakening had added an evangelical concern and a delivery described by its enemies as "a strange, unnatural singing tone," that tended mightily to raise the "affections" (Goen: 179). In this same era must have developed too the key trait of the folk sermon, its "spirit directed" improvisational performance. This tradition survives strongly in black churches of many denominations, even those of the urban middle class. It can be found in white congregations that have remained autonomous and local in orientation, especially among the primitive, old regular, and various independent Baptists, and in a multitude of churches within the Holiness and Pentecostal camps.

In *The Art of the American Folk Preacher* Bruce Rosenberg began the scholarly study of the folk sermon. The preachers deliver their words, he found, in highly stylized rhythmic and tonal patterns. They employ five kinds of formulaic phrases and draw upon a shared repertory of conventional "themes," which Rosenberg defines as "series of related ideas, images, or actions, expressed by the relatively stable sequence of formulas." Some of these themes are nonscriptural ("The Deck of Cards," "The Postage Stamp"), but more of them derive from the Bible itself ("The Eagle Stirreth Up Its Nest," "Dry Bones in the Valley").

Rosenberg's study stops short of exploring the ethnic, denominational, or regional variations in the folk sermon. But the function, the content, the verbal formulas, and the chanting styles vary with at least race and doctrine. The Calvinist sermon of the primitive Baptist is for the feeding of the flock. It employs detailed exegesis but may grow lyrical and symbolic. By contrast, the evangelical sermon aims at snaring the sinner's attention and converting him. In the hands of a preacher like the Methodist circuit rider Peter Cartwright, it could be humorous, terrifying, or thrilling (Finley: 323–25). To achieve these objects it typically makes much greater use of narratives. These may be examples drawn from common lore or from personal experience, or they may be vivid retellings of biblical stories, as in the Easter sermon that the Reverend Sin-Killer Griffin preached in 1934 to black inmates of a Texas prison:

> I seen while He was hanging, the mountain began to tremble on
>   which Jesus was hanging on.
> The blood was dropping on the mountain, holy blood, dropping on
>   the mountain,
> And it corrupted the mountain.

I seen about that time, while the blood was dropping down, one—
    drop—after—another,
I seen the sun that Jesus made in Creation,
The sun, my dear friends, and it recognized Jesus hanging on the cross.
Just as soon as the sun recognized its Maker, why, it clothed itself in
    sack clothing and went down—
(singing) *Oh-h-h-h, went down in mourning.*
"Look at my Maker dying on the cross."
And when the sun went down, we seen the moon—that was its
    Maker too—
(singing) *Oh-h-h-h, he made the moo-o-on,*
My dear friends, yes, both time and seasons—
We seen, my dear friends, when the moon recognized Jesus dying on
    the cross,
I seen the moon, yes, took with a judgment hemorrhage
And bled away—good God looked down.
(singing) *Oh-h-h-h, the dying thief on the cross*
Saw the moon going down in blood.
I seen, my dear friends, about that time they looked at that, and
    when the moon went down, it done bled away.
I seen the little stars, great God, that was there, they remembered
    Jesus when He struck on the anvil of time
And the little stars began to show their beautiful ray of light,
And the stars recognized their Maker dying on the cross—each little
    star leaped out of its silver orbit, come to make the funeral
    torches of a dark benighted world.
It got so dark until the men who was putting Jesus to death, they said
    they could feel the darkness with their fingers.
Great God Almighty, they were close to one another, and it was so
    dark they could feel one another,
They could hear one another talk, but they couldn't see each other.
I heard one of the centurions say, (singing) *"Sholy, sholy—*
This must be the Son of God."

In the preaching of men like Sin-Killer Griffin there is a paradox. The
Bible is the text from which they preach, and they accept it as the revealed
word of God. Yet they also believe themselves to be God's representatives.
Like the Old Testament prophet and the New Testament apostle, these
preachers have been called, often even with signs and visions that mirror
biblical precedents. One, for example, "dreamed he was under a white cloud
and a white hand and arm put through and the neck of a phial protruded
out of the palm of the hand and anointed him to go and preach." After two
more visions (all three corroborated by his wife's simultaneously dreaming
the same thing), he felt "confirmed of the heavenly calling" and "sprang out
of bed and exclaimed, 'Lord, I'll go'" (Pittman: 287). But such a preacher
further regards his very words as divinely inspired. He marvels at the
uncommon powers of thought and speech that awaken within him at the
pulpit. Like the disciples gathered on the day of Pentecost, he finds his
tongue seized by a higher power. "I believe preaching's done," he says, "by
the Holy Ghost sent down from Heaven . . . , which power I don't, ability I

don't have to reach up and bring down at my own time, at my own desires"
(Evans). The Bible and inspiration, then, supplement each other, giving the
preacher's words great weight.

The preacher's word draws power also from a third source, its fidelity to
the hearers' view of life. Like most members of folk communities, they live
painfully vulnerable to disaster, which can come at them from both the natural
world (through a crop failure, a crippling injury on the job, the untimely death
of a spouse or child) and from human acts (cheating at the plantation
commissary, laying them off at the mine, or stealing the attentions of a lover).
The folklore of the Old World responds to such threats with a belief that the
knowing or gifted can partly foresee the coming of trouble by means of signs
and second sight and can even manipulate events and people with amulets,
precautionary magical rites, or the aid of a sorcerer. Donald E. Byrne suggests
that in the eyes of the American folk community biblical supernaturalism
validates and is validated by these ancient assumptions (174). In the Bible they
can also see, however, assurance of a benign order beneath the unpredictable
accidents of life and also find reason for trusting that divine intervention may
directly relieve apparently hopeless distress. The traditional preacher finds a
responsive audience, then, for the repertory of providential judgments and
deliverances (Byrne).

Many of the American religious folk arts rest on similar assumptions.
The Hispanic villager in New Mexico prays to the santo for relief from
drought and even scolds or locks in a chest the santo who fails to give the
aid requested (Mills: 59). But whereas in Hispanic Catholic culture the
beliefs and the attendant folk arts serve to reinforce the received customs
and religion, in the Protestant dissenting tradition they foster change.

The Protestant Folk Arts and Cultural Change

Byrne offers one explanation for this. Exploring frontier Methodist tales
of the early nineteenth century, he sees a correlation between their emphasis
on remarkable providences that contravene the customary order and the fact
that the settlers had "fled the stifling social and economic order of the East"
(174). But similar tales flourished earlier among the Shakers and later among
the Mormons, and circulate today among Pentecostals and charismatics—a
diversity of groups in varying circumstances. So far as tales of remarkable
providences relate to social change, they must flourish not merely in populations dispersing westward into the frontier but also among those moving
outward from ethnic enclaves, townward from rural communities, and upward from the lower classes.

Tales of remarkable providences, moreover, are not the only religious
evidence that these populations held an expectation of a dramatic change in
their circumstances. Widespread in their theologies was a belief in sudden
conversions, like that of Saul on the Damascus road. A typical instance is

that of one young man who in 1867 was "riding along horseback thinking that some day he would be a rich man, and at a very old age would get religion," when suddenly "a very dark object appeared coming directly at him, with a glittering sharp point in front of it, and like lightning it thrust through him and a voice said, 'Already too late.'" Deeply convicted of sin, he "lamented his condition" for five years until given a second vision in which he heard "the sweetest sound of music and looking up saw a white cord letting down from heaven and a bud on the end just ready to open," which entered his bosom. At the close of the vision he "felt free from sin and that he would never have any more sorrow" (Pittman: 287).

The pattern is of radical changes not only in the converts' feelings but also in their values. This same young convert, for example, in his vision "saw the world a black ball and God fanned it out of existence with one fan of his hand." In the Protestant dissenting tradition millennial longings for a new heaven and new earth often accompany such a repudiation of the world. The converts may seek to reform themselves or to change the world itself. Some, notably the Shakers, let the Spirit guide them to a reconstruction of virtually all material, social, and religious arrangements. In forms of artistic expression—song, dance, painting, wood-working—they also sought to "make all things new."

The Importance of the Bible as a Source for the American Folk Arts

In *American Folklore*—a dated book, but still the only major effort to survey the entire scope of American lore—Richard M. Dorson allotted only 7 percent of his space to religious traditions, virtually all of that to colonial tales of remarkable providences, Hispanic mystery plays, or Mormon Nephite legends. The Bible, however, has played too complex a role in American culture to have so small a presence in the American folk arts. It influenced them directly as a subject for folk discourse, song, and painting, and it indirectly provided conceptual and institutional frames within which the folk arts flourished. Some folk communities used biblical authority to legitimate old customs and to defend themselves against change and loss of identity. Their arts are expressive of these ends. Other groups have used the Bible to justify and even to incite rebellion against existing social and religious structures. Their arts are especially innovative and deeply rooted in scriptural texts.

For such reasons the religious lore has been better able than secular forms continually to renew itself. Sea shanteys died when sails gave way to steam and capstans to motor-driven winches; the black gospel quartet absorbs the latest electronic developments—singing with microphones, electric guitars, amplifiers, mixers, monitors, and speakers—and puts them all in the service of the local community and of a repertory and song style rooted in oral tradition. The drive-in movie, the TV show, and the pop music album usurp the place of extended tale-swapping in the home, but the religious service each Sunday remains a vigorous communal performance and the evangelical sermon a major story-telling session. Industrialization and the development of merchandizing networks have virtually killed all American folk handicrafts but quilting. Yet, although bereft of traditional visual models, members of folk communities are frequently impelled by overwhelming religious experiences to invent new artistic vocabularies, often out of their biblically inspired visions.

The seriousness with which American folk communities often regard the Bible has also given high status to the religious folk arts. For those who enter the religious fold, the sermon is not entertainment, as tales are, but a needful feeding of the flock or an instrument for salvation. For them, sacred song has such overwhelming power that they normally put aside their secular repertory and lay down the fiddle or the guitar as a trivial toy or an actual evil (Bastin). In the folk community, to join the brotherhood of the Penitentes or to graduate from fiddling or playing the blues to singing in a church often signals that the member has accepted a mature social role.

It follows then that the biblically based American folk cultures would have been extraordinarily creative. The sheer volume of the output in the religious genres dwarfs anything in the secular repertory. Native Anglo-American ballads, according to G. Malcolm Laws, total fewer than five hundred songs. The surviving Shaker spirituals alone number between eight and ten thousand, and black spirituals are literally uncountable. Clearly the religious impulse unlocked creative energies that would otherwise have lain dormant. "And what makes it more striking," wrote one Shaker leader, "it is those who had never learned to sing at all—they could scarcely follow after those who were singers; Now they will sing as beautiful as I ever heard anyone; yea beautiful Anthems & Songs, all given when they are under the beautiful operations of the power of God" (Patterson, 1979: 457). In short, the American folk religious communities have abundantly demonstrated, as another Shaker pointed out, that there are "many able faculties among the people, capable of producing beautiful & appropriate compositions" (Cook: 38).

NOTE

/1/   Frederick S. Weiser and Howell J. Heaney, *The Pennsylvania German Fraktur of the Free Library of Philadelphia: An Illustrated Catologue*, vol. 1 (Breinigsville: The Pennsylvania German Society and The Free Library of Philadelphia, 1976), plate 150.

WORKS CONSULTED

Ames, Kenneth A.
1977   *Beyond Necessity: Art in the Folk Tradition.* Winter-
                        thur, DE: The Henry Francis du Pont Winterthur
                        Museum.

Andrews, Edward D.
1969   *Visions of the Heavenly Sphere: A Study of Shaker
                        Religious Art.* Charlottesville: University of Virginia
                        Press for The Henry Francis du Pont Winterthur
                        Museum.

Anonymous
1843   *Second Advent Hymns Designed to be Used in Prayer
                        and Campmeetings.* Rev. and enlarged. Exeter, NH:
                        A. R. Brown.

Barba, Preston A.
1953   *Pennsylvania   German   Tombstones.*   Pennsylvania
                        German Folklore Society, Vol. 18. Allentown, PA:
                        Pennsylvania German Folklore Society.

Barber, Miranda
1851   [Commonplace Book], Western Reserve Historical
                        Society, Shaker Manuscript, Pike No. VIII:C–1.

Bastin, Bruce
1973   "The Devil's goin' to get you." *North Carolina Folklore
                        Journal* 21: 189–94.

Botkin, B. A.
1943   *Negro Religious Songs and Services.* 33⅓ rpm phono-
                        disc. AAFS L10. Washington, DC: The Library of
                        Congress.

Boyd, Elizabeth
1974   *Popular Arts of Spanish New Mexico.* Santa Fe:
                        Museum of New Mexico Press.

Bruce, Dickson D., Jr.
1974   *And They All Sang Hallelujah: Plain-Folk Camp-
                        Meeting Religion, 1800–1845.* Knoxville, TN: University
                        of Tennessee Press.

Byrne, Donald E., Jr.
1975   *No Foot of Land: Folklore of American Methodist
                        Itinerants.* Metuchen, NJ: Scarecrow Press.

Caldwell, William
1837   *Union Harmony; or Family Musician.* Maryville, TN:
                        F. A. Parham.

Campa, Arthur L.
1934a   "Spanish Religious Folktheatre in the Spanish Southwest
                        (First Cycle)." *University of New Mexico Bulletin,
                        Language Series* 5 (Feb.): 5–69.

1934b   "Spanish Religious Folktheatre in the Southwest (Second Cycle)." *University of New Mexico Bulletin, Language Series* 5 (June): 5–156.

Child, Francis J.
1962   *The English and Scottish Popular Ballads.* 5 vols. Facsimile reprint. New York: Cooper Square Publishers.

Cook, Harold E.
1973   *Shaker Music, A Manifestation of American Folk Culture.* Lewisburg, NJ: Bucknell University Press.

Courlander, Harold
1956   *Negro Folk Music of Alabama.* Vol. 5: "Spirituals." 33⅓ rpm phonodisc. Folkways FE4473. New York: Folkways Records.

Dorson, Richard M.
1959   *American Folklore.* Chicago: University of Chicago Press.
1968   *The British Folklorists: A History.* Chicago: University of Chicago Press.

Dundes, Alan
1980   "Who are the folk?" In *Interpreting Folklore.* Bloomington, IN: Indiana University Press.

Evans, Walter
1970   Sermon preached at Little River Primitive Baptist Church, Sparta, NC, 18 July 1970. Tape recording in the Folk Music Archives, University of North Carolina at Chapel Hill.

Finley, James B.
1853   *Autobiography of Rev. James B. Finley; or, Pioneer Life in the West.* Edited by W. P. Strickland. Cincinnati: By the author.

Fleishhauer, Carl, and Jabbour, Alan
1973   *The Hammons Family: A Study of a West Virginia Family's Traditions.* 33⅓ rpm phonodiscs. AFS L65–L66. Washington, DC: Library of Congress.

Foster, George M.
1953   "What is folk culture?" *American Anthropologist* 55: 159–73.

Fry, Gladys-Marie
1976   "Harriet Powers: Portrait of a black quilter." In *Missing Pieces: Georgia Folk Art 1770–1976.* Edited by Anna Wadsworth. Atlanta: Georgia Council for the Arts and Humanities.

Fuller, Edmund L.
1973   *Visions in Stone: The Sculpture of William Edmondson.* Pittsburgh: University of Pittsburgh.

Goen, C. C.
1962   *Revivalism and Separatism in New England, 1740–1800.* New Haven: Yale University Press.

Green, Archie
1972
"Folksong and folk society." In *Only a Miner: Studies in Recorded Coal-Mining Songs*. Urbana: University of Illinois Press.

Hatcher, William E.
1908
John Jasper, the Unmatched Negro Philosopher and Preacher. New York: F. H. Revell.

Heilbut, Tony
1971
The Gospel Sound: Good News and Bad Times. New York: Simon and Schuster.

Holstein, Jonathan
1973
The Pieced Quilt: An American Design Tradition. New York: Galahad Books.

Jackson, George P.
1943
White and Negro Spirituals: Their Life Span and Kinship. Locust Valley, NY: J. J. Augustin.

Johnson, Charles A.
1955
The Frontier Camp-Meeting: Religion's Harvest Time. Dallas: Southern Methodist University Press.

Johnson, Clifton H.
1969
God Struck Me Dead: Religious Conversion Experiences and Autobiographies of Ex-Slaves. Philadelphia: Pilgrim Press.

Laws, G. Malcolm, Jr.
1964
Native American Balladry: A Descriptive Study and a Bibliographical Syllabus. Rev. ed. Philadelphia: The American Folklore Society.

Lee, Hector H.
1949
The Three Nephites: The Substance and Significance of the Legend in Folklore. Albuquerque, NM: University of New Mexico Press.

Levine, Lawrence W.
1977
Black Culture and Black Consciousness: Afro-American Folk Thought from Slavery to Freedom. New York: Oxford University Press.

Lloyd, A. L.
1967
"The industrial songs." In *Folk Song in England*. New York: International Publishers.

Lomax, Alan
1959
The Rainbow Sign: A Southern Documentary. New York: Duell, Sloan and Pierce.
1961
Southern Journey: A Collection of Field Recordings from the South. Vol. 2: "Georgia Sea Islands." 33⅓ rpm phonodisc. Prestige 25002. Bergenfield, NJ: Prestige Records.
1968
Folk Song Style and Culture. New Brunswick, NJ: Transaction Books.

Lomax, John A., and Lomax, Alan
1941   *Our Singing Country: A Second Volume of American Ballads and Folk Songs.* New York: Macmillan.

Ludwig, Allan I.
1966   *Graven Images: New England Stonecarving and its Symbols, 1650–1815.* Middletown, CT: Wesleyan University Press.

McCurry, John G.
1973   *The Social Harp.* Facsimile reprint of 1855 edition. Edited by Daniel W. Patterson and John F. Garst. Athens: University of Georgia Press.

Marsh, J. B. T.
n.d.   *The Story of the Jubilee Singers; with Their Songs.* Rev. ed., 75th thousand. Boston: Houghton, Mifflin.

Mathews, Donald
1969   "The Second Great Awakening as an Organizing Process, 1780–1830." *American Quarterly* 21: 23–43.

Mills, George T.
1967   *The People of the Saints.* Colorado Springs: The Taylor Museum.

Moore, William
1825   *The Columbian Harmony.* Cincinnati, OH: Morgan, Lodge, and Fisher.

Newall, Venetia
1971   *An Egg at Easter: A Folklore Study.* London: Routledge and Kegan Paul.

Newell, William W.
1963   *Games and Songs of American Children, with a New Introduction and Index by Carl Withers.* 1903. Reprint. New York: Dover Publications.

Oliver, Paul
1965   *Conversations with the Blues.* New York: Horizon.

Patterson, Daniel W.
1979   *The Shaker Spiritual.* Princeton: Princeton University Press.
1980   "The Shape-Note Tunebook as Emblem of Social Change: A Study of William Hauser's *Hesperian Harp* and *The Olive Leaf*." Paper presented at the Annual Meeting of the Society for Ethnomusicology, November 1980.
in press   "Gift Drawing and Gift Song: A Study of Two Forms of Shaker Inspiration."

Pittman, R. H.
1909   *Biographical History of Primitive or Old School Baptist Ministers of the United States.* Anderson, IN: Herald Publishing Company.

Rael, Joan B.
    1951   *The New Mexican* Alabado. Stanford University
                           Publications, University Series in Language and Litera-
                           ture, Vol. 9, No. 3. Stanford: Stanford University Press.

Rauschenberg, Bradford L.
    1977   "A study of Baroque- and Gothic-style gravestones in
                           Davidson County, North Carolina." *Journal of Early
                           Southern Decorative Arts* 3 (Nov.): 24–50.

Redfield, Robert
    1930   *Tepoztlán, a Mexican Village: A Study of Folk Life.*
                           Chicago: University of Chicago Press.

Robb, John D.
    1980   *Hispanic Folk Music of New Mexico and the South-
                           west: A Self-Portrait of a People.* Norman, OK:
                           University of Oklahoma Press.

Roberts, Allen D.
    1979   "Where are the all-seeing eyes: The origin, use and
                           decline of early Mormon symbolism." *Sunstone* 4 (May-
                           June): 22–37.

Roscoe, Lynda
    1974   "James Hampton's Throne." In *Naives and Visionaries.*
                           Minneapolis: Walker Art Center.

Rosenberg, Bruce A.
    1970   *The Art of the American Folk Preacher.* New York:
                           Oxford University Press.

Safford, Carleton L., and Bishop, Robert
    1974   *America's Quilts and Coverlets.* New York: Weather-
                           vane Books.

Starr, Nina H.
    1969   "The lost world of Minnie Evans." *The Bennington
                           Review* 3 (Summer): 40–58.

Stoudt, John J.
    1966   *Pennsylvania German Folk Art: An Interpretation.*
                           Pennsylvania Folklore Society, Vol. 28. Allentown, PA:
                           Schlechter's.

Sutton, Joel B.
    1977   "In the good old way: Primitive Baptist traditions." In
                           Long Journey Home: Folklore in the South. Edited by
                           Allen E. Tullos. Special double issue of *Southern
                           Exposure* 5 (Summer and Fall).

Vlach, John M.
    1978   *The Afro-American Tradition in Decorative Arts.*
                           Cleveland: Cleveland Museum of Art.
    1981   "Quaker tradition and the paintings of Edward Hicks: A
                           strategy for the study of folk art." *Journal of American
                           Folklore* 94: 145–65.

Walker, William
1854   *The Southern Harmony, and Musical Companion.* Rev. ed. Philadelphia: E. W. Miller.

Weigle, Marta
1976   *Brothers of Light, Brothers of Blood: The Penitentes of the Southwest.* Albuquerque: University of New Mexico Press.

Weiser, Frederick S., and Heaney, Howell J.
1976   *The Pennsylvania German Fraktur of the Free Library of Philadelphia: An Illustrated Catalogue.* 2 vols. Breiningsville: The Pennsylvania German Society and The Free Library of Pennsylvania.

Wolfe, Ruth
1980   "Hannah Cohoon, 1788–1864." In *American Folk Painters of Three Centuries.* Edited by Jean Lipman and Tom Armstrong. New York: Hudson Hills Press in Association with the Whitney Museum of American Art.

Wood, Monnie S.
1975   "The beauty of an egg." Manuscript in The Southern Folklore Collection, Library of the University of North Carolina at Chapel Hill.

Wust, Klaus
1970   *Folk Art in Stone: Southwest Virginia.* Edinburg, VA: Shenandoah History Publishers.

Yoder, Don
1961   *Pennsylvania Spirituals.* Lancaster, PA: Pennsylvania Folklore Society.
1969   *Pennsylvania German Fraktur and Color Symbolism.* Lancaster, PA: Landis Valley Associates.
1974   "Toward a definition of folk religion." *Western Folklore* 33: 2–15.

Youngs, Benjamin S.
1856   *Testimony of Christ's Second Appearing.* 4th ed. Albany, NY: United Society, Called Shakers.

IX

The Biblical Basis of the American Myth

Sacvan Bercovitch

The major legacy of Puritan New England is not religious, or moral, or institutional. The Puritans are not particularly responsible for the Calvinist strain in the United States, or for any attributes in particular of the "American character" (whatever that is), or for any particular civic forms or structures. The Puritans did not invent guilt, or the Protestant work ethic, or individualism, or contractual society. All of these were part of the New England way, and together they give substance to our sense of "Puritan influence." But the distinctive contribution lies in the realm of rhetoric. The Puritans provided the scriptural basis for what we have come to call the myth of America. In this sense their influence appears most clearly in the extraordinary persistence of a rhetoric grounded in the Bible, and in the way that Americans keep returning to that rhetoric, especially in times of crisis, as a source of cohesion and continuity. This speaks to only one aspect of the culture, but a very significant one, with far-ranging implications. Just where the significance lies—what those implications entail—is the theme of this essay.

Perhaps the most direct way to state my theme is by reference to a familiar biblical text: *In the beginning was the word, and the word was with the New England way, and the word became "America."* And let me open the text by citing two very different views of America, neither of these Puritan, and both written some thirty years after the Revolution. My first example comes from Washington Irving, surveying the new republic in the guise of a visiting Muslim:

> I find that the people of this country are strangely at a loss to determine the nature of their government. Some have insisted that it savors of an aristocracy; others maintain that it is a pure democracy; and a third set of theorists declare that it is nothing more nor less than a mobocracy. [Yet] the simple truth of the matter is, that their government is a pure unadulterated *logocracy*, or government of words. In a logocracy, thou well knowest, every offensive or defensive measure is enforced by wordy battle and paper war; he who has the longest tongue is sure to gain the victory. [Then], without mercy or remorse, [he will] put men, women, and children to the point of the— pen! [Or he will send] them a long message, i.e., a

huge mass of words, all meaning nothing; because it only tells them
what they perfectly know already; [whereupon they will be] thrown
into a ferment, and have a long talk. Nations have each a separate
characteristic trait, by which they may be distinguished from each
other. [For example,] the Italians fiddle upon everything; the French
dance upon everything; and the windy subjects of the American
logocracy talk upon everything (135–44 [ellipses deleted]).

I take my second example from a letter by John Adams, one of the windiest
subjects of the time: "We have no Americans in America. The Federalists
have been no more American than the anti-Federalists" (letter to Benjamin
Stoddert: 582).

No Americans in America. The contrast with Irving makes for an interesting "inside commentary" on the way a myth may be said to exist. For
Irving, America is a people held together by the power of words. For
Adams, the name exists, but not the people—only the word "America" in a
vacuum, like the spirit of rhetoric brooding over a primal chaos. Taken
together, as a bi-valent cultural symbol, these two images suggest something
of the New World experience in extremis. I refer here not only to the Revolutionary era but also to the prototypical experience of the first European
colonists. In their case, of course, the image of an "America without Americans" meant a society still to be created, an "open," "savage" country awaiting the advent of civilization. For most emigrants, the native culture was
there to be displaced. For some, the act of displacement became a fact of
language and perception, the first principle of a New World metaphysics.
They simply saw no native culture out there at all, just a blank continental
slate. Either way, the New World was a mixed blessing, threat and opportunity entwined.

The threat lay in the potential for violence in this untamed land, the
specter of lawlessness, degeneracy, and social disintegration. The advantages
centered on prospects for improvement. By its very openness, the New World
invited colonists to undo the constrictions of the past. The absence of Old
World tradition elicited schemes for social perfection—the Arcadian dreams
of Maryland and Virginia, the theocratic utopias of New France and New
Spain. These schemes were fired by visions of fresh opportunity; they also
expressed the sense of danger I mentioned, by their emphasis on order and
compliance. The result was a marked ambivalence toward authority. To
varying degrees this sort of ambivalence characterizes all European–American
communities through the nineteenth century, but it was especially pronounced
in the new republic. From the start the United States was not only a culture
infused with late Renaissance visions of the good life but also a nation founded
on revolution, nourished by emigration, and dedicated to progress.

This is one important reason for the influence of the New England Puritans. They were the revolutionary-idealist emigrants par excellence. In religious terms, they were radical dissenters: nonconformists by profession, and by

temperament militant individualists. In secular and civic terms, they represented the forces of modernization that were to shape the American culture. They were the Massachusetts Bay Company, Incorporated—essentially a contractual society, a voluntary association of investors, lawyers, merchants, and artisans eager for profit and committed to a code of enterprise, mobility, and progress. And they justified their code and contract by the highest standard, the Holy Word itself. This points to a second, more important reason for their influence. The Puritans were inveterate believers in words. They were extreme Protestants in many ways, but especially in their insistence on the principle of *sola scriptura*. Their obsession with scripture may be traced throughout that astonishing verbal outpouring, published and unpublished, which distinguishes seventeenth-century Massachusetts from other colonies. It is not too much to say that the Puritans replaced the traditional rituals of the church (Anglican as well as Catholic) with the rituals of the word: the texts of scripture, interpreted ad tedium in sermons and treatises, privately applied in diaries, memoirs, and journals, publicly affirmed in histories, almanacs, poems, and biographies, and re-presented day by day in the lives of visible saints.

In those obsessive verbal rituals the Puritans sought and found the answer to the problem of authority in a strange New World. Their solution was as simple as it was sweeping. They sanctified their society by the Bible's figures and types. That is, they vindicated the political and economic structures of the Massachusetts Bay Company, Incorporated, by the rule of scripture, *as* scripture brought to life. Consider John Winthrop's famous definition of the colony as a "city upon a hill." The direct reference is to the fifth chapter of Matthew, which speaks of the individual believer, the pilgrimage (by grace) of the redeemed soul. Winthrop retains this meaning, but he enlarges its application to include a grand prophetic design. *His* "city upon a hill" is also a community, a company in covenant, summoned by God to a historic mission. What he means in this sense is that the colony at large is a *figura* in sacred time. The wayfaring saint, at every stage in his journey, foreshadows the saint in glory he is to be. New England, as a city upon a hill, looks forward to the New Jerusalem that is to descend upon Mount Zion. In Winthrop's discourse, these two levels of meaning, personal and historical, are more than analogous or parallel. They are reciprocal, intertwined—the verbal paradigm of a community of saints, "knit together by the bonds of love, as one man in Christ," and by "special commission" engaged upon an errand to the end of time (Winthrop: 76–93).

The verbal paradigm was above all a form of socialization. As New Englanders (and later, Americans) used the phrase, the "city upon a hill" became a ritual summons, a call for order in a community committed to progress, mobility, and free enterprise. Directly or indirectly, these were the functions it served. First, the "city upon a hill" identified personal goals with those of the community; it fused the concepts of spiritual and social fulfillment, private and corporate progress. Second, as a model of identity, the "city upon a hill" worked to erode past allegiances, genealogical and national. The emigrants, it implied, were not Europeans in a foreign country, but a New Israel in New Canaan. Third, as a social ideal, the "city upon a hill" displaced the Old World hierarchy of aristocracy and crown with a new model of authority—a company in covenant, the forms of the modern corporation sanctified by Bible prophecy. Finally, the "city upon a hill" centered the prophecy on the meaning of the locale. To found an outpost of New Jerusalem was by definition to launch an errand into the wilderness. And although at first that wilderness was confined to territories surrounding Massachusetts Bay, the concept itself had far wider, continental implications. In this sense, as in the others, the Puritan migration began a long errand into rhetoric, from the New England Way to the myth of America.

A long errand, and (as the word "America" implies) one that started well before the founding of New England. Let me take a moment, in the interest of accuracy, to account for origins. In the beginning, only the Indians were Americans. Of course, "Indians" is not quite accurate. That name too derives from myth—the dream of a passage to India, a fiction imposed on geography which inspired a fateful series of explorations and provided the framework for what the Mexican historian Edmundo O'Gorman has termed "the invention of America." So we might revise our text to accommodate that fiction: *In the beginning was the word "Indian," and the word was with the inhabitants of the continent, and the word was the inhabitants of the continent.* Again, this is not quite accurate. As it happened the Indians were somewhere else, in a country the English later named India. But this discrepancy was easily resolved by the qualifying fiction "America." The inhabitants of the New World were *American* Indians. No matter that it was not Amerigo Vespucci who "discovered" the New World. That is just a fact, and what counts in this case is invention, the *symbolic* act of discovery. In fact, the New World of America was neither new nor a world nor America. Symbolically, the continent did not exist until it was invented by Europeans. And that symbolic act was cognitive and ideological: it gave conceptual unity not only to the unknown terrain but to the people who lived there. The word "American Indian" compressed a multiplicity of customs, traditions, languages, and religions into a single comprehensive meaning. It explained away the otherness of the native inhabitants by translating them all into a symbol (including the bi-polar values inherent in the symbol: savage/innocent, devil/child of nature, etc.).

Still, a problem remained. The American Indians owned the continent, and the inventors, the symbol-makers, wanted possession. Their solution here was historical: they simply asserted the rights of a superior culture—Christianity over paganism, the white race over the dark, enlightened over primitive societies. By any name, the assertion itself reminds us that for the first explorers and colonists, "America" was a secular concept, a symbol in and of this world. They invented it for geographical and social purposes.

However fanciful it was in fact, however sinister in implication, "America" was meant to describe a continent, as Europe was, only uncivilized, with inhabitants such as one might expect to find, more or less, in any primitive society. This was the view of most Europeans (Spanish, Portugese, French, Dutch), and it involved them perforce in a conflict of cultures. Their very rationale for conquest was a form of comparative anthropology. It called attention to differences in ways of life, divergent notions of religion, politics, and the law. The very term of their self-justification conveyed the conditions under which certain groups of emigrants came to dominate or decimate certain kinds of indigenous peoples. We might call the pattern they followed of invention, symbolic naming, and historical conflict the Europeanizing or creolization of America.

The New England emigrants had a better idea. They discovered America in the Bible. The Puritans were concerned with exegesis, not invention. America was a prophecy in their eyes. Their interpretation centered on sacred, not secular history. They sought not the right symbols but the true texts; and they found the texts they sought in biblical passages which earlier Protestants had identified as signifying the "latter-day church of God": apocalyptic verses about the ends of the earth; the sun that would rise from the West; the migration of a "holy remnant" to a New Zion (which would then be made to blossom like the rose); the outcast woman in the wilderness who would bear the "man-child" Messiah; the revelation of a new heaven and a new earth; the "foresaken," "desolate," and "hidden" daughter of Zion who would arise, when the trumpets sounded from the earth's last imagined corner, and shine forth *pulchèrima inter mulieres*, as the last and loveliest of Christ's brides. To an indifferent or incredulous world the Puritans announced: "AMERICA is legible in these Promises" (quoted in Miller: 187–88; biblical references are to passages in Psalm 18; Luke 12; Jeremiah 3, 58; Hosea 2–6; Canticles 6; Isaiah 60, 61, 65, 66; Revelation 12, 20, 21). And for those who objected in principle to this sort of (mis)reading they had a ready reply. Scripture was full of "dark meanings," waiting to be discovered in due time. There, the New World lay concealed in image and metaphor, until the great latter-day events: first the Reformation, then the voyage of Columbus, then the printing press, which made the Bible available to all believers, then the rise of Protestant England, and finally God's covenant with His New-English Israel in the New World. For them He had reserved the keys of discovery to the meaning of America.

It amounted to an imperialism of the word unrivaled in modern times. The Puritans came to America not to usurp but to reclaim, not to displace an alien culture but to repossess what was already theirs by promise. And the promise entailed a full-scale myth, with a beginning, a middle, and an end. On one side was the Bible; on the other, the millennium; and at the center, a saintly remnant on a special mission, for America first and then the world. Significantly, it was the New England Puritans who first used the word "American" to describe the country's white Protestant emigrants. The first epic of the American myth is Cotton Mather's *Magnalia Christi Americana*; it has its sequel in Timothy Dwight's epic of the Revolution, *The Conquest of Canaan*, featuring George Washington as the American Joshua. These facts are symptomatic. The word "America" gave other settlers, from Canada to Brazil, a sense of unity, a means of control, and a rationale for conquest. So it was also in the case of the Puritans, but they discovered something more in it—a new, American identity that obviated the common-sense limits of history. They took possession by designating America as text and then interpreting the text as themselves. This was their legacy: a New World whose newness is moral or spiritual and therefore beyond mere geographical definition; a community defined by its sacred origin and telos and therefore impervious to cultural relativism; a corporate symbol, "America," whose meaning transcends territorial limits, so that it could be extended, in a sort of movable feast, from New England to the thirteen states of '76 to any place (including Alaska and Hawaii) that could be invested with the sacral qualities of the myth—any place, that is, of which it could be said: "this land was placed here by some divine plan. It was placed here to be found by a special kind of people, a new breed of humans called an American . . . [destined] to begin the world over again . . . [and to] build a land here that will be for all mankind a shining city on a hill" (Reagan: B7).

These words come from Ronald Reagan's televised election debate with Jimmy Carter, and we need only change "found" to "discovered" to see the continuity I have suggested. For Reagan was not just echoing stock phrases; he was drawing upon a basic mode of national self-definition. To be an American is to discover oneself by prophecy. It is to reformulate one's identity with a "divine plan," where the form is the word of promise, and reformulation, the ritual process by which the text comes to life, logos becomes logocracy. So considered, the long foreground to Reagan's speech lies in a procession of sacred texts that continually rediscover the meaning of America: Winthrop's *Arbella* address of 1630, the ritual "model" of the New England way; the Declaration of Independence, through which a group of disparate colonies were united, justified by "self-evident truths," and consecrated under God, all by verbal fiat; the mid-nineteenth-century July Fourth orations, which discovered a "manifest destiny" in the westward movement and then interpreted manifest destiny as the unfolding of a prophetic script.

I do not mean by this to claim that the culture was homogeneous, much less monolithic. It was always a diffuse, regional, multiethnic, emigrant culture, tending toward fragmentation, precariously held together by the loosest of social bonds, the ideological tenets of free enterprise—and therefore urgently in need of a myth of consensus. Nor am I forgetting the many changes in rhetoric along the way. On the contrary: nothing more clearly shows the sustained power of the myth than its capacity to accommmodate new forms. By the mid-nineteenth century, for example, nature was supplanting scripture as the source of prophecy; but the effect was to *reinforce* familiar patterns. Scripture and Nature were seen as complementary. They were the Old and New Testaments, as it were, of the American way. The Bible had foretold America; the New World landscape radiated the types of things to come. It was a second Genesis and Apocalypse combined, a new cosmic author-ity for the nation of the future. This was the principle of landscape painting throughout the period. The enormous canvasses of the romantics and luminists comprise nothing less than a national iconography: crosses in the western sky, forests and plains graced with baptismal founts, pioneers directing caravans through mountain passes like Moses pointing the way to Canaan. As Frederic Church said of his most popular work, he wanted Niagara to speak through him, so that viewers could hear for themselves its prophecy of the American Jerusalem (Wilmerding; Huntington: 1, 9, 44, 61, 104, 122).

The same sort of vision informs classic American literature. Whitman's discovery that "the United States themselves are essentially the greatest poem" (Whitman: 453), Thoreau's discovery at Walden of the "only true America" (Thoreau: 279), Emerson's discovery in nature of "America's errand of genius and love" (Emerson: 537–38)—these acts of exegesis have a different premise from that of European contemporaries. There, nature was viewed as a state distinct from society. It signaled for poets the possibility of a higher state of consciousness, as in Blake's "America." For political thinkers it meant the "primitive state" as opposed to civilized "refinement," as in Locke's famous remark: "in the beginning all the world was America" (Locke: 319). The American version reads: "In the beginning was the word, 'America,' and its sacred meaning was made manifest in the virgin land and the Garden of the West, or (mutatis mutandis) in eidólons of the leaf of grass, the hieroglyphics of the white whale, the national promise ambiguously inscribed in the morning star above Walden Pond and the scarlet letter in the sky." These symbols are very different from one another, but all express the same process of discovery. All of them transform history into hermeneutics. All read into "America" the "last, best hope of mankind," where the ambiguity of "last" means either (and *only*) redemption or cataclysm. And all of these symbols, to one degree or another, reflect the dual function of the myth, its relation both to the real conditions of social growth and to the *equally real* need on the part of Americans for something which those conditions did not themselves provide: a sense of spiritual purpose, some supraempirical sanction for the dominant ideology of a new community in a new land.

From the start, the rhetoric derived its authority from both these functions, social and spiritual. The result by 1800 was the logocracy that Washington Irving described, with its tireless polemics and proclamations, its "long messages (i.e., huge masses of words) all meaning nothing" because they only told what everybody knew perfectly well already. Consider the "wordy battles" between revisionists and fundamentalists over the "true meaning" of the Constitution; or the "paper wars" between right- and left-wing historians about the *real* tradition of the founding fathers; or the invective hurled back and forth, across three centuries, between progressivists and conservationists, each side firmly entrenched in its own version of the nation's "natural" promise. Or consider, finally, the alternative claims upon the promise by the self-reliant individual and the self-proclaimed nation of individualism. In that conflict lies a central cultural contradiction: the threat to society inherent in the very ideals of self-interest through which society justifies itself. The "resolution," predictably, has been the ritual word "American," with its symbolic double claim to power and the spirit, national progress and personal fulfillment. Hence the contrasting types of the American hero: Franklin's Ben versus Henry David's Thoreau; Horatio Alger's Ragged Dick versus Mark Twain's Huck Finn; Gatsby the social climber versus Gatsby the failed dreamer. At first glance, the contrasts suggest something like cultural schizophrenia: a constant criticism of American society through a series of "true Americans," each one an epigone of free enterprise. But this is the sort of criticism that social rituals thrive on—dissent from within; a mode of affirmation by negation that is perhaps best understood through the concept of co-optation.

The more serious threat, I believe, lies in a weakness inherent in the very origin and structure of the myth: *In the beginning was the word "America," and the word was in the Bible, and the word was made flesh in the Americans, this new breed of humans, destined to build a shining city on a hill*. Unavoidably, the central term is the Bible, not "America." For though the Puritans and their heirs surely arrogated the Bible to themselves, still they were bound by its mythic patterns, Judaic and Christian. The two patterns have often been conflated, but in fact there is a fundamental difference between them. The myth of Christ is a completed personal drama; for all its abiding general applications, it is essentially spiritual, individual, and retrospective. The Judaic myth is an incomplete national (or tribal) drama. For all the examples it offers of heroic lives, essentially it is a story in process—communal, historical, prospective.

The American myth builds on both these patterns. From Mather's *Magnalia* through George Bancroft's epic *History of the United States*, the continuing national drama is presented through a series of imitations of Christ (Washington as New World savior, Lincoln as martyred leader) and a complementary parade of success stories, all cast more or less in the mold of Ben Franklin, model "of a *rising* nation" (Vaughan: 185). The rhetoric implies that America's future, and by extension the fate of humanity, hinges on the efforts of the individual representative American. And the social effects have been plain enough: a pervasive anxiety about "making it" (along with a pervasive tendency to violence about *not* making it), a constant emphasis on the need to "do it yourself" (and to "do it now"), countless pieties (and handbooks) concerning the duties, pleasures, and benefits of "self-realization." Again, it amounts to a triumph of rhetoric as ritual; but here the logic of the rhetoric is less secure. The future itself, to repeat, depends on a procession of representative Americans—in any given generation, a community of individuals who will fulfill the myth, and a succession of such communities from one generation to the next, even unto the end of the world. But what if the individuals do not want the myth, or the successive generations, or the world?

I am not referring to the failure of the dream. The response to that vision of catastrophe is all too familar: those endless cautionary lamentations about the ever-imminent "fall of America" (Ginsberg), the doomsday chorus of American literature, stretching from the Puritan Jeremiahs through (say) George Lippard and Henry Adams to West, Mailer, and Pynchon, which has always served in its grim way to *confirm* the belief in "some divine plan." No, the threat I refer to involves something rhetorically less dramatic but far more consequential in the realm of common sense. It may be identified by a simple fact: America is not the Bible.

For the simple fact, as it happens, makes for a crucial distinction between the myth of America and that of either Judaism or Christianity. Significantly, it is an a priori of the biblical myths that you cannot ask, What if the Jews refuse to return to Zion? What if there are no Christians left to celebrate the Second Coming? The Judaic myth, I just said, differs from the Christian in that it is national and processual. But the Judaic myth, too, is fully inscribed in the Bible. Finally, it depends not on works in time but on restoration by miracle; and the miracle is guaranteed—already accomplished, as it were—rhetorically secure in scripture, like the miracles of Christ, past and to come.

By contrast, the American myth, which has profited so much from historical accident, is peculiarly vulnerable to history. Surely that is one reason why Americans have always had recourse to the doomsday threat as a means of social revitalization. Surely, too, that is why they have always needed to blast about their openness to the future; to assure themselves (in Reagan's words) about their "destiny" to "begin the world over again"; to write what Melville called a New World "Bible of the Free," which would "gospelize the world anew" (Melville, 1970:150; Pierre, 1971:273); to paint into their landscapes another Book of Revelation; or better yet, literally to find a Book of Revelation, as Joseph Smith did—a brand-new Bible for Americans, by an American, and about America—in the caves of upstate New York. This long effort to create scripture ex nihilo is not at odds with but complementary to the chorus of apocalyptic lament. Both modes are inherent in the myth of America, as alternate strategies of a rhetoric designed to transcend history— or in practical terms, to preclude historical alternatives to the American way. By and large, both these strategies have succeeded. But behind both, I am suggesting, lies a sense of foreboding, an intimation (rarely articulated and perhaps only dimly conscious) that it is history which gives symbols an earthly substance and a name, and history done which "rules the life and death of mythical languages" (Barthes: 110). In this view, the real threat is not that there may be (in John Adams's doomsday phrase) no Americans in America, but that there may be no America for Americans. What happens when history severs the symbol from the nation, the logos from the logocracy? It is a prospect that returns us full circle to the Puritan discovery three centuries ago: *I have been to the Bible and America does not exist.* What happens when history separates "America," divine plan and all, from the United States?

Nothing much. Only relativism; the day-by-day grind, the facts of fragmentation; a certain modesty about the "boundaries of national allegiance"; a more mundane distinction between the Old World and the New, as denoting geographical division rather than the progress of humanity; a more traditional concept of "frontiers," as signifying secular barriers, rather than a heaven-sent summons to expand; a sense of the difference between liberal ideals and transcendental truth, and along with this, perhaps, a genuine debate about ideological alternatives, none of them secure, instead of the redundant intracultural dialogues that have confined American political and intellectual life and warped the growth of American studies. It is a consummation devoutly to be wished.

It would also be the beginning of a new set of problems. The most immediate of these lies in another simple fact, the truism implicit in the astonishing persistence of Puritan rhetoric from Winthrop to Reagan. I mean the human need for absolutes, the persisting demand even (or especially) in our bleak modern world, for symbols and ideals. What authority can replace the rhetoric of America in the United States? Granted that "America," as the Puritans discovered it, was a myth designed for a certain social system. Granted, too, what Marxists tell us, that the system is in transition. Still, a remarkable fact of modern history has been the failure of alternative systems, including the Marxist, either to provide an adequate myth or to prove that communities can cohere without one. And until one or the other happens, "America" will probably endure by default, if only as an archaic dream of discovery, a relic of bourgeois biblicism in our demystified New World of semiotics, computer science, and sociobiology.

WORKS CONSULTED

Adams, John
 1856   *Works IX.* Edited by C. F. Adams. Boston: Little, Brown, and Co.

Barthes, Roland
 1972   *Mythologies.* Translated by A. Lavers. New York: Hill and Wang.

Emerson, Ralph Waldo
1903–4   *Works XI.* Edited by E. W. Emerson. Boston: Houghton
                Mifflin Company.

Ginsberg, Allen
1972   *The Fall of America.* San Francisco: City Lights.

Huntington, David
1966   *The Landscapes of Frederic Edwin Church: Vision of an
                American Era.* New York: George Braziller.

Irving, Washington
1860   *Salmagundi,* No. VII (April 4, 1807) in *Works XXII.*
                Edited by E. A. Duyckinck. New York: G. P. Putnam.

Locke, John
1960   *Second Treatise of Civil Government.* In *Two Treatises
                of Government.* Edited by P. Laslett. Cambridge:
                Cambridge University Press.

Melville, Herman
1970   *White-Jacket, or the World in a Man-of-War.* Edited
                by H. Hayford, H. Parker, and G. T. Tanselle.
                Evanston, IL: Northwestern University Press.
1971   *Pierre, or the Ambiguities.* Edited by H. Hayford,
                H. Parker, and G. T. Tanselle. Evanston, IL: Northwest-
                ern University Press.

Miller, Perry
1961   *The New England Mind: From Colony to Province.*
                Boston: Beacon Press.

O'Gorman, Edmundo
1961   *The Invention of America.* Bloomington, IN: Indiana
                University Press.

Reagan, Ronald
1980   "Closing Statement." *The New York Times,* Sept. 22,
                1980, B7.

Thoreau, Henry David
1950   *Walden.* Edited by B. Atkinson. New York: Modern
                Library.

Vaughan, Benjamin
1981   Letter to Franklin (Jan. 31, 1783). In *The Autobiogra-
                phy of Benjamin Franklin.* Edited by L. Lemay and
                P. M. Zall. Knoxville, TN: University of Tennessee Press.

Whitman, Walt
1949   "Preface" (1855) to *Leaves of Grass.* In *Walt Whitman.*
                Edited by S. Bradley. New York and Toronto: Rinehart
                and Company.

Wilmerding, John, ed.
1980   *American Light: The Luminist Movement, 1850–1875.*
                Washington, DC: National Gallery of Art.

Winthrop, John
1965   "A Model of Christian Charity." In *Puritan Political
                Ideas, 1558–1794.* Edited by E. S. Morgan. Indianapolis:
                Bobbs-Merrill.

GENERAL INDEX

INDEX OF SCRIPTURE REFERENCES